MESSAGE ON THE WIND

A Spiritual Odyssey
on the Northern Plains

MESSAGE ON THE WIND

A Spiritual Odyssey on the Northern Plains

Essays from Beyond the Grid

by Clay S. Jenkinson

The Marmarth Press
May 2002

Published in 2002 by Marmarth Press
A Division of Empire for Liberty LLC
6015 S. Virginia Street, Suite #458, Reno, Nevada 89502

Marmarth Press is a trademark of Empire for Liberty LLC

Distributed by Empire Catalog
A Division of Empire for Liberty LLC

Printed in Canada

10 9 8 7 6 5 4 3 2 1

First Printing

International Standard Book Number: 1-930806-12-4
   Message on the Wind:
   A Spiritual Odyssey on the Northern Plains

Library of Congress Catalog Card Number: 2001092454

The paper in this book meets the requirements of ANSI/NISO
Z39.48-1992 (Permanence of Paper).

∞

Oh, we would ride and we would listen
And hear the message on the wind.
The grass in morning dew would glisten
Until the sun would dry and bend
The grass to ground and air to skying.
We'd know by bird or insect flying
Or by their mood or by their song
If time and moon were right or wrong
For fitting works and rounds to weather.
The critter coats and leaves of trees
Might flash some signal with a breeze —
Or wind and sun on flow'r or feather.
We knew our way from dawn to dawn,
And far beyond, and far beyond.

From *Anthem*
Buck Ramsey (1938-98)

Dedication

Leo^2

For my mother Mil Jenkinson
who gave me life
and liberty
and still urges the pursuit of happiness.

For my daughter Catherine Missouri who is life itself.

Acknowledgements

THIS IS A BOOK OF HUMANITIES ESSAYS. Everything I have written sits atop the pyramid of literature that I first began to encounter as a late-blooming reader in the 1970s and which has been the center of my life ever since. I have, in this book, quoted scores of sentences from Shakespeare, Homer, Thoreau, Milton, and many other texts. In a sense, all humanities texts are commentaries on everything the author has ever read, and everything those authors have read. One does not need to be a postmodernist to realize that originality is an exceedingly problematic term.

Most of the people I want to thank are characters in this book. A few others who are spoken of in coded language know who they are. Without Mike Jacobs, great-souled Gerhardt Ludwig, Timothy Billings, Mike Waldera, Anne Rawlinson, my mother, my father, and Jim Fuglie, and above all Patti Perry, there could have been no book.

The most important person absent from these pages is Everett C. Albers, the director of the North Dakota Humanities Council. In many ways this is a book about mentors and mentoring. Nobody has done more to shape my adult consciousness, my career, or my vision of the place of culture in a complete life than Ev. I know this book could not have been written had Ev Albers not reached out to invite me into his world of ideas when I was a callow sophomore in college. *Message on the Wind* is a collection of humanities essays. Whatever is valuable in them is a byproduct of the work of the National Endowment for the Humanities and the North Dakota Humanities Council. Ev Albers is as gifted a man as the National Endowment for the Humanities has discovered. The Great Plains tent Chautauqua makes a number of appearances in this book. Emerson said an institution is the lengthened shadow of one man. The modern Chautauqua movement is the lengthened shadow of Everett C. Albers.

This book was inspired by Robin P. of Virginia, who asked the question about spirit of place that led to everything else.

My dear friends Annie Hall (AKA Lovie Howell), Monique Laxalt, Stephanie Kruse, Cindy Lewis, Sherie Woods, Hal Bidlack, and Sheri Bartlett Browne read the manuscript and improved it in important ways. So did Anne Campbell, Kate Magruder, Tracy Panzarella, and my superb travel partner Michele Basta. Laura Trounson helped with research.

Janie Guill made it all happen.

Anne Rawlinson is not only one of the primary characters in this book, but she performed a thousand small but important research and editing tasks to make it possible, and she read all the drafts with her usual grace, intelligence, and good sense. She laughed early at transcriptions of Timothy Billings' conversation and gave me confidence to continue.

Strangely enough, the person whom most I wish to impress is my sister Leslie Jenkinson Ringen.

Patti, this is your book.

Reno, Nevada
November 2001

In the dry places, men begin to dream. Where the rivers
run sand, there is something in man that begins to flow.

Wright Morris
The Works of Love

Preface

A YEAR OR TWO AGO I took a film crew to the Cross Ranch on the west bank of the Missouri River north of Bismarck, North Dakota. I was the only North Dakotan. All the others were from Miami or Raleigh or Chicago. None of them had ever been to the Great Plains before. We set up quickly and got the footage we needed. It was mid-August. We'd been watching a storm front move towards us from the west all afternoon. Now it was getting close to dusk. We could not afford to miss our shoot. Everyone was in a hurry to get back into the crew vehicles and drive on to Williston, where there would be motels, and dinner, and drink.

Cross Ranch is a state park on one of the last relatively free-flowing segments of the Missouri River. It contains the most magnificent cottonwood trees in North Dakota. So it is an image of what North Dakota was before we did to it what we have done to it.

The storm struck like clockwork as we were putting the last of the equipment into the truck. We'd been listening to the quickening of the thunder for more than an hour, and watching heat lightning high in the sky and, occasionally, a terrible steak of lightning that burst from the heaven to the earth. First there was sudden wind, and the great giant cottonwoods bent over like reeds along a prairie creek. Then came a few scattered drops of hot rain, dust-spattering rain, and thunder and lightning like no member of our crew, perhaps including me, had ever witnessed:

thrashing, scouring, clashing, streaking, urgent, crashing, orgiastic, pounding, anarchic, punishing, apocalyptic, zigzagging, cross-hatched, grotesque, pandemonic lightning. And then, briefly, heavy rain, or rather sheets of water pretending to be rain. A slow lowering of the wattage of the lightning storm. A few gusts of rain and a few last lovely gusts of wind. The smell of ozone. And finally charcoal dusk lit up from time to time like a firefly by squibs of heat lightning.

At the height of the storm, when death by lightning was a serious possibility, everyone scrambled for the vans, except the videographer from Chicago. He was a gentle, thoughtful, bookish man, who liked to talk about ideas in the intervals between our professional labors. We stood side by side admiring the pyrotechnics of the storm, and between explosions of thunder I explained to him why it was inevitable that the Lakota (Sioux) worshiped sky gods and thunder beings. He asked if it was unsafe for us to stand out in the middle of the storm.

"Yes," I said. He said, "good."

As the storm began to ebb, he said, "If you were teaching a course on American pantheism or on the Transcendentalists, all you would have to do is bring your students out into a storm like this. It's astonishing that Christianity has survived in America. If there is a God, it's out here in nature. There was god in this storm. There is god in these amazing trees. If what we just witnessed wasn't the direct voice of God, I don't know what it would take. Who would ever believe that the best place to encounter godhead and things of the spirit is in the pew of a drab Congregational or Baptist church? The roof alone is like an umbrella designed to keep off the Holy Spirit. Why import a near-eastern tribal god to a landscape every inch of which is alive with sacred energies?"

After a pause, he said, "Nobody who opened his soul to this storm could be a Christian—or an atheist."

Maybe so.

This book is a love song to that lonely country where we stood through that storm. I call it the landscape of the improbable. The promise of America is that we will create a society equal to the magnificence of the continent on which we have planted it. It is not quite too late. The promise has not been completely broken, not yet. I remember how inspired I felt the first time I heard Wallace Stegner's phrase, "a society to match the landscape."

At a time when rural America has fewer advocates than at any previous era in our history, I wish to argue that our national renewal must come from the empty quarter, the backwater villages and the unvisited buttes of the American West. As a nation, we are being destroyed by mobility, abstraction from nature, alienation from the macrobiotics of the food chain and the food supply, and addiction to homogenized comforts that deracinate us from the life of the spirit. This is a book about spirit of place. Perhaps spirit of place is available anywhere, but I can declare with certainty that it percolates through the biosphere of the Great Plains.

This book is also an elegy for North Dakota, where I was born, raised, and eventually naturalized. North Dakota is dying—or rather rural North Dakota is dying, and what is distinctive in the North Dakota character is dying. When I was growing up almost every North Dakotan lived on a farm, or had relatives or family friends who lived on a farm, and every North Dakotan, therefore, spent some portion of every year in nature. No longer. Today most North Dakotans are no more rooted in nature and agriculture than their counterparts in Toledo or Nashville. My great mentor Mike Jacobs, who inhabits every page of this book, told me recently that the Jeffersonian agrarian dream is dying on the Great Plains during this decade.

It is not and it cannot come to good.

Like all expatriate Dakotans I sometimes shed hot tears over my loss and I ache every day to be walking the windswept ridges of the trans-Missouri country. The only advantage of being away is that it whets the memory. These essays are about a place, the most improbable place in America. If there is a person at the center of them, it is a person situated in a landscape, which alone makes him worthy of notice. I feel uncomfortable writing in these essays about my own life. The plain truth is that I am a person of insufficient importance and achievement to be worthy of autobiography or spiritual memoir. If I play a role in these essays, particularly in the last of them, my only justification is that I believe my experience is representative, not unique, and I believe strongly that these essays explore questions of place, gender, wilderness, spirituality, and race relations that the Great Plains—and the nation—need to resolve.

I have no confidence that I have any answers, but I know well that I am on to some of the right questions. In some of these essays, particularly the first of them, I am quite critical of the society we have erected on the Great Plains. The fact is that I respect, admire, and envy the people who are living their lives out there. Hardly a week goes by when I don't scheme of ways to return to my homeland. Mostly my life is a congeries of doubts, but I know with iron certainty that I will never be happy or complete until I plant a homestead in the sacred corridor. The society of the Great Plains contains all the strengths and weaknesses of American civilization—the weaknesses, in fact, are a little less pronounced, and the strengths, I believe, are significantly more evident than elsewhere. And I never permit myself to forget—for an instant—that the people of the Great Plains are producing our food supply—farming, as the Farmers Union likes to put it, is everybody's bread and butter. Nor do I ever forget that I am, like Paul, the chief of sinners. If it is true that I admire the landscape more than the people who live on it, it is because the landscape is one of the world's greatest geographical treasures, and it has almost never been accorded the respect it deserves.

This is a book about friendship.

When I began these essays, I did not intend to write about gender. But the essays in many ways wrote me, and gender relations, and the social construction of gender, have emerged as a major theme. I do passionately believe that until we find a way to re-construct American maleness with greater attention to the poetry of the soul, we can never graduate—as a nation—from the triumphalist, testosteronic, mythological, and violent stage of American history. That we need to graduate to a higher standard of male character is everywhere in evidence: in our popular culture, in our sport, in our lovemaking, across our environment, in our foreign policy, in our economy, in our hero-cults. And indeed in the mirror I gaze into from time to time.

Standing somewhere else Samuel Clemens said, "All the me in me is in Hannibal, Missouri." Maybe that was the finest thing he ever said. Well, I'm no Mark Twain, but it's true that all the me in me is walking out along the Little Missouri River in southwestern North Dakota, miles from nowhere, in the heart of the heart of the country, among the bones of plenty, and far beyond the bedroom wall.

These essays are all about spirit of place, about the way landscape shapes character and character informs landscape. I remember the germ of them all, tossed off by a conference speaker in Riverton, Wyoming, years ago, who closed his remarks by quoting Wright Morris' *Works of Love*: "In the dry places, men begin to dream. Where the rivers run sand, there is something in man that begins to flow." I've been haunted by those words ever since, though I promise I'm not setting myself up as a desert father.

I have throughout tried to write in the paratactic style of the Homeric epics. The Great Plains are an epic landscape. The spiritual journey I have tried to describe is both a physical odyssey and an unfinished psychomachia. I have written these essays with the fantasy of their being read aloud by rhapsodes to small groups huddled around cottonwood campfires. Each essay invokes an episode of Homer's *Odyssey*. I hope these allusions are not as artificial as they might at first seem. My spiritual odyssey has been filled with monsters, mighty temptations, single combats, hospitality rites, goddesses in disguise, and even a descent into hell. Those who know Homer will find this book more interesting, perhaps. Those who do not will take it on its own terms. (There is a key to the Homeric references at the end of the book.)

These essays are written for my beloved daughter, Little Mo, and for those who still like to light out for the territory ahead of the rest. My dream is that these words will put North Dakota on the map without taking it out of the margins.

In the words of Chaucer, "Go little book, go little my tragedie."

Clay Straus Jenkinson
November 2001

Table of Contents

In this Happy Hunting Ground they have danced the buffalo back
They have prayed the Eagle home and the Salmon back from the sea —
These Powers of peoples together have given new life to the sun!
And this is the second home we long for: before the sound
Of clocks
         before the smell
                 of oil
                        or of gunpowder. . .

Thomas McGrath
Letter to an Imaginary Friend, Part Four

Invocation

Sing In Me Muse . . .

C OYOTES ARE CROONING at the vault of the sky. Stars spangle. I lie on my back in a splendid sleeping bag in some improbable backwater of the American West. The river slips past my feet on its way to the gulf. The winds nudge the cottonwood leaves above, whispering, whining, lazily stirring the planet. The air is dense with loneliness and mystery.

A satellite races busy across the sky, annoyingly attractive, a crude false star filled with diodes, the Alpha Centauri of sitcoms and people reaching out to touch someone halfway across the planet. Or perhaps it is a military reconnaissance satellite plotting destruction for Baghdad. I try to fix my gaze on the true stars, but the glistering satellite fixes my attention. And though its purposes are either banal or violent, I am lost in wonder at humanity, creator of prosthetic stars, and televideo black holes, man the launcher.

I am perfectly alone in the wilderness. Only coyotes and antelope and ants know of my presence, and they must be as alarmed by my supine intrusion into their territory as I am by their vague rustlings. But surely I am not the only backpacker resisting for a moment the technological tug of the satellite above me. As I settle in for the night, I have a vision of thousands of wilderness sojourners scattered across the immensity of the American continent, loners lying on their backs fathoming the stars and thrusting their souls upward, couples interlaced of leg, probing with half-attentive fingers the secrets of the other, small parties of friends talking the issues in low tones, configured like the spokes of a wagon wheel around a dying fire, drifting in and out of the conversation of wonderment.

I think: what if there were a satellite photograph that could pinpoint all the flickering campfires of the continent on this autumn night, in this single instant of time? A handsome poster to be displayed on the walls of the adventurous and the discontent, a portrait of the remnant Thoreauvians, of the unredeemed children of the wilderness. Such a photograph would be as fine a tribute to idea of America as one could imagine, a serene rival to the famous image of the blue watery earth taken by Apollo astronauts. When John Locke wrote, "In the beginning, all the world was America," he meant that the whole earth was unsettled once, and a handful of macrobiotic people were diffused over its vastness, and most of it was unchanged since the creation. That was America in 1680. Even now, three hundred years later, as the twenty-first century begins, America is a nation that has not utterly severed its umbilical to the wild. On any given day, scores of quiet adventurers are still willing to chap their lips and miss a hot shower to seek out the primal experience of the brave new world. Those few who live—or venture—off the grid are our medicine men, who "keep alive that sacred fire which otherwise might disappear from the earth."

Canis Americanus shrieks into the vastness of space. I try to hold open my eyes against the gravity of fatigue. And so to sleep somewhere in America.

Whatever pushes the grass through the bloodstained soil of the plains, be my Muse.

Whoever inspires the call of the coyote, speak too through me.

Let me learn to voice the voice of the plains.

Teach me to hear the message on the wind.

The Sacred Corridor

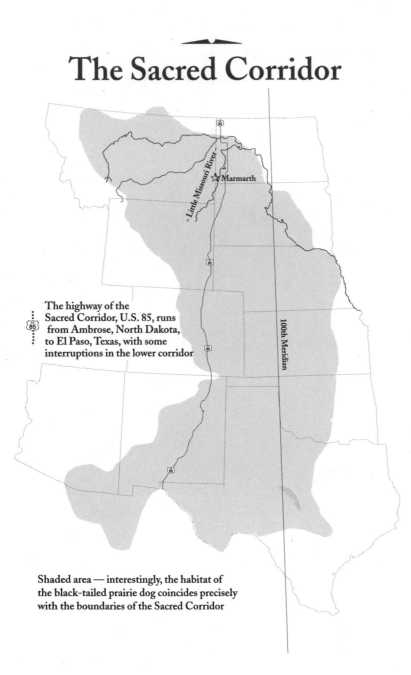

The highway of the
Sacred Corridor, U.S. 85, runs
from Ambrose, North Dakota,
to El Paso, Texas, with some
interruptions in the lower corridor

Little Missouri River

☆ Marmarth

100th Meridian

Shaded area — interestingly, the habitat of
the black-tailed prairie dog coincides precisely
with the boundaries of the Sacred Corridor

Grailing in the Sacred Corridor

Scylla and Charybdis

I CALL IT THE SACRED CORRIDOR. That's a poetic name for a district that most people would do anything to avoid, a corridor travelers pass through as quickly as possible, with their souls and windows closed, and describe later as the flattest, dreariest, most isolated country they have ever seen. It used to amuse me to see my former wife get indignant when people would say, "Kansas, man, that's flat country," and she would insist that it's anything but flat. She was right. They were right too. Where you stand depends upon where you sit—or perhaps where you grew up. I grew up on the Great Plains—and that has made all the difference.

The sacred corridor is the western Great Plains: the western half of North Dakota, South Dakota, Nebraska, Kansas, Oklahoma, and Texas, and the eastern half of Colorado, Wyoming, and Montana. It is "sacred" because even now it's the homeland of those ingenious sky god peoples, the Sioux (properly Lakota), the Cheyenne, the Crow, the Arapahoe, the Blackfeet, the Assiniboine, the Mandan, the Hidatsa, and the Arikara. It's the home of many of America's largest Indian reservations. It's dotted with places sacred to native peoples, like Bear Butte, the Black Hills, Devils Tower, Killdeer Mountain, and the Medicine Rock. It's sacred too because it is the landscape of American tragedy: Sand Creek, Wounded Knee, the Bozeman Trail, the Powder River War, the Rosebud, the Little Big Horn, the Washita, the assassinations of Sitting Bull and Crazy Horse, and Custer's fatal 1874 trespass of the Black Hills. It's sacred because it is one of the least-densely populated regions of North America, and the landscape of the region, therefore, although it has been assaulted by the full strength of the industrial revolution for one hundred years, is still largely untouched by the hand of Euro-American man.

Although the topography of the sacred corridor varies more than most people think, there is a certain sameness to the pattern. Endless treeless plains, not flat, but not exactly curvaceous either, are broken up mostly by river systems that create a linguini strand (it's spinach linguini) of cottonwood and willow that meanders within a fettuccini ribbon of breaks that in turn glides through a ribbed lasagna noodle of low pine-covered ridges. Out in this country you tend to drive from ridge to ridge. Sometimes it takes hours, and, at the top of the next ridge, it looks pretty much the same. Stiff lasagna noodles in all directions.

It's grassland. Ireland-green for a few glorious weeks, then brown, gray, russet, tawny, golden, and mauve for the rest of the year. An infinity of grass in every direction. And wind. The wind blows like a sonofabitch.

The sacred corridor includes Canada, up to the lakes and the tundra, but the bulk of it consists of the shortgrass strip of the treeless plains from the top of North Dakota all the way down to the Texas-Oklahoma border, and maybe even a bit beyond. Thomas Jefferson purchased almost all of it for three cents per acre in 1803. It was one of the greatest moments in diplomatic history, a one night stand between the cynical warlord Napoleon and the feline idealist Jefferson. It was the making moment of the American experiment, in part because it doubled the size of the United States with a single stroke of the Sage of Monticello's elegant pen, in part because even the strict constructionist Jefferson realized that the Constitution would have to be construed elastically from time to time. Jefferson, shelving his quasi-pacifism for a moment, could not avoid calling his acquisition an "empire for liberty." What Jefferson had in mind was a continent diffused with mild-mannered, liberty-obsessive, Greek-reading, and self-sufficient family farmers.

Jefferson bought the American interior and then sent his protégé Meriwether Lewis out to reconnoiter. The Lewis and Clark Expedition was America's first space program, a combination of science, epic, and shrewd geopolitics. Somehow the Third President found it possible to micromanage the Voyage of Discovery from his fortress of solitude at Monticello, even though he ostensibly placed the command in the hands of the mercurial Lewis and his even-tempered pal William Clark. Lewis and Clark never ventured far from the fettuccini of the Missouri River. It was, to be sure, the greatest strand of fettuccini in North America. But when Lewis saw the lay of the land beyond the margins of the river, he chose to call it the "great plains" of America. That name stuck. Lewis and Clark found the plains rugged, treeless, windswept, alkaline, intemperate, and above all arid but, as usual, the cheerful, notional President did not let disagreeable facts get in the way of a favorite idea. "My father," said Martha Randolph, "never gave up a friend or an opinion." Agrarianism is the core of Thomas Jefferson's vision of an American republic: "Those who labor in the earth," he wrote, "are the chosen people of God." In the soul of the magnificent utopian fictionist Thomas Jefferson, myth trumps fact as scissors cut paper. Meriwether Lewis came back from his encounter with the American sublime and killed himself. No one is quite sure why. It cannot have been easy to be Thomas Jefferson's protégé.

Almost all of the sacred corridor lies west of John Wesley Powell's 100th Meridian (which runs roughly from Bismarck,

North Dakota, through Pierre, South Dakota, North Platte, Nebraska, along the western edge of non-panhandle Oklahoma, through San Angelo, Texas and beyond, pole to pole). The West begins at the 100th Meridian because beyond that imaginary Enlightenment line there isn't enough rain to support crops, and— it turns out—rain does not follow the plow. Powell, who was America's first water czar, addressed the North Dakota Constitutional Convention on August 5, 1889, and begged the Founding Fathers to think seriously about water *before* they laid out the infrastructure of the state. Eastern North Dakota, he said, always gets enough rain, central North Dakota sometimes, western North Dakota never. The Civil War hero and explorer argued that western states should not attempt to impose the habits and institutions of Jeffersonian pastoralism on a landscape that cannot support them. Powell called for scientifically-based environmental realism and urged the abandonment of the Jeffersonian rectangular survey grid system in favor of what he liked to call "watershed commonwealths." North Dakota, and a few days later Montana, refused to listen.

On its west end the sacred corridor stops somewhere short of the Rocky Mountains. If you can see something that looks like a foothill, you're probably still in the corridor. If you can see a genuine mountain range, you're about to stray beyond the precinct. I recently examined a map that delineated the habitat of the prairie dog. It was the most precise map of the sacred corridor that I have ever encountered.

The land I am describing, the western Great Plains, embraces the central sections of the great ladder of rivers that are the western tributaries of what Meriwether Lewis called the "mighty and heretofore deemed endless Missouri": the Smoky Hill and Republican in western Kansas and Nebraska, the heartbreaking Platte with its maze of interlocking threads and sand bars, and the Niobrara; the Cheyenne, White, Belle Fourche, and Grand of South Dakota; the Tongue, the Powder, the Bighorn (and its infamous little cousin) which flow up through Wyoming to meet the mythic Yellowstone in Montana; in North Dakota the Cannonball, the Heart, the Knife, and the river I claim as my totem, the Little Missouri, which begins near Devils Tower in northeastern Wyoming and discharges its sluggish sedimentary load in west-central North Dakota. Above all the sacred corridor means the Powder and the Platte. When Crazy Horse was asked where he wanted to locate the reservation that was promised him in return for a cessation of hostilities, he chose the Powder River country (but we killed him first). I have dreams of hiking each of those great unspectacular rivers, source to mouth. But I have many dreams.

II

I LOVE TO DRIVE ACROSS EMPTY SPACES. Unless I'm in a hurry or the weather is especially dangerous, I avoid the freeways. By definition almost all freeways follow the path of least resistance through the least impressive landscapes of the country.[†] When I'm hurtling along the interstates' wide concrete surfaces in a cross-country stupor, I find myself eating at McDonalds and Pizza Hut, listening to the wrong kind of radio when I ought to be meditating my dreams and miseries, and being sucked into the morass of American homogeny. I feel shallow on the interstates, virtuous on the backwater blacktops, William Least Heat Moon's blue highways. Few experiences in life are more completely satisfying than knowing you are going to spend the entire day driving the West, but in no particular hurry, knowing there will

---

[†]There are exceptions, particularly Interstate 70 through Glenwood Canyon in Colorado, one of the most beautiful highways, indeed one of the most beautiful engineering projects, on earth.

be time to stop here and there to walk the hills, and having no idea what modest motel will serve as your host for the night. These days they all leave the light on for you.

When the heat breaks and the light softens in the late afternoon, and you've paid your respects to the rush-hour minutes of plains villages you've bisected, and you're beginning to keep alert for reckless deer, a road intoxication sets in that makes you feel like a prosthetic centaur. It's a kind of hyperalert numbness, the wages of many hours of hard driving in the empty quarter. The body has been shut down by daylong sedentariness, and the mind has been blown to cumulousness by excessive visual stimulation. A landscape that took Lewis and Clark three backbreaking months to traverse, you have just whipped over in a handful of hours. The mind, close to tilt, has decided merely to splay across the landscape. In that moment, the divide between man and machine relaxes somehow and a kind of sensuous harmony awakens, envelops your car like an aura, and you feel—among other things—that you could drive forever. The pedal meets the metal meets the pavement in an endless, slightly numbed drift across the vast outback of America. There is nothing quite like it. It makes you want to make love. You begin to notice things in the landscape that failed to register all day long. In empty places you wake up.

I never drink and drive, but I seldom drive a long distance without reading a book.[†] In the empty quarter, where the roads are straight and unembarrassed with traffic, this is not quite as reckless as it might seem. My mother not so politely disagrees, and when I spent a weekend once crafting a steering wheel book cradle out of wire clothes hangers and Radio Shack heat-shrinkable tubing, she gave vent to a rare—and blistering—form of maternal peevishness. She very nearly aborted an elaborate

---

[†]Warning: Do not try this at home. Reading and driving is stupid, illegal, and irresponsible. If you are tempted to read and drive, please get professional help immediately.

family car swap when I delighted in the fact that my new vehicle would be equipped with a perfectly focused map light on the driver's side. (Night car reading, I admit, is an acquired skill). When I walk into the old family home after a long day's drive, she invariably asks, "You weren't reading on the road today, were you," followed, without any pause, by, "On second thought, don't tell me. I don't want to know." It is true that from time to time I have narrowly missed an orange construction zone barrel or two, and I've done my share of frightening the bejesus out of oncoming traffic, but this does not seem to me too high a price for the satisfaction I have felt in finishing off a novel while crossing Nebraska, or anticipating a night at Devils Tower by reading in Robert Utley's *Last Days of the Sioux Nation*. I never read when I have passengers (this seems to unnerve them), though if I can get away with it, if they are dozing, for example, I sometimes glance at a book that rests next to my right hip. But furtiveness removes most of the pleasure of the sport.

I am not alone. My former mate used to read and drive, as did her father. In fact, when I meet someone new from the Great Plains, I sometimes take the risk of hinting very subtly about this illicit practice, as one might raise the issue of recreational drugs in the carefullest and most deniable possible way. A relatively large percentage of plains people (of those, that is, who read) will admit to this dread pathology on condition of anonymity. I like to think there is a worldwide underground club of road readers, perhaps with a secret sign or a trick handshake, and that it would be possible to spot them—fellow travelers—on the road the way vacationing children look for two-toned, four-door cars with license plates from Connecticut.

Give me a good book and the open road. And thou.

III

THIS IS THE KIND OF LANDSCAPE you can get out and walk on almost anywhere. Just pull over to the place where the shoulder meets the borrow ditch and get out and saunter. Walk to the ridge. Walk back. Watch out for prickly pears, for men who have convinced themselves that they have property rights to the wind, and for rattlesnakes—in about that order. Only once in a couple of decades of free walking have I had to face an angry property owner. He was, it is true, very angry. But once he realized that I was just an idiot—and not a rustler or an escaped convict—he shut the lights off in his pickup, lowered his shotgun to the ground, kicked up a little dirt, gave me a lecture on John Locke, and roared off in his half-ton. Except for the fact of his gun, I might have given *him* a little lecture in the manner of Chief Seattle—how can you sell your mother?—but I have learned this much from life, that there are times when it is useful to beat down the whippersnapper impulse.

On another occasion I was walking across an endless plain on mingled public and private property, on land too cheap to meter. I saw an old pickup trailing me for a couple of miles. I felt considerable apprehension, but there was nowhere to hide on that vast stage, and cowering amid the sagebrush seemed unmanly. Eventually the rancher pulled up beside me, rolled down his window, looked at my frail body and the ninety pound backpack that belittled me, paused the pause of the western cornpone, and said, "Now I've seen everything." And drove away.

My roadside hikes are always spontaneous: something in the distance I want to investigate, a sudden inrush of disquietude about my sedentary life, a thunderstorm I want to understand, a certain slant of afternoon light, an unmarked historic place I have been reading about. I am seldom away from the car for more than two hours, seldom less than one. And every time, I have to fight the same impulse: to take the keys out of my pocket, close my eyes, and hurl them with all my might into the chasm of space. I have never actually done this, but there have been times, particularly alongside rivers, when the urge has been almost unbearable. Perhaps the only thing that stops me is the vision—comic except to me—of my spending the rest of my week on hands and knees combing the yucca and cactus flats for those same keys.

When I get back to the car I always wonder, for an instant, if it will start. It always does. Thank you Isaac Newton. Thank you Henry Ford. Thank you Thomas Edison. Thank you Dan Porter Honda. The reliability of automobiles at the end of the century has degraded the adventure of travel. The best way to see the Great Plains is in a vehicle that might just break down in the middle of nowhere. Knowing that the alternator and the radiator are at issue concentrates the mind wonderfully. I have known the exhilaration of a dying clutch. But when the industrial paradigm was still asserting itself (1920-1975), and a car could come undone in any number of ways, and the probabilities were that it *would* do so from time to time, and a long automobile excursion was a kind of gamble, a flirtation with discomfort and—at the far end of conceivability—with death, road trips had deeper significance. It's hard to know whether vehicle reliability or air conditioning has done more damage to life on the road.

In John Steinbeck's America the yeomanry were always squatting by the side of the road fixing flats and forming revolutionary cadres. More recently we have hermetically sealed the sedan—and the soul. Closed cars weaken experience and reinforce the runaway American class system. When I'm feeling strong I open the windows and ingest the wind. All my favorite experiences in the American West have involved an admixture of chaos and raw nature. In recent years, I have, while driving, found myself reading, taking notes, making calls, changing clothes, listening to books-on-tape, recording commentaries and dictating correspondence, performing craftwork, even sending and receiving faxes at 75 mph in my gleaming road office, no more part of the experience of the West than Paul Harvey, who is inventing ironies on my car radio as I move from point A to point B, asleep in every essential way, as always. The center cannot hold.

A flat tire reminds you that you have entrusted your life to a machine.

IV

THE TOWNS OF THE SACRED CORRIDOR all have a generic Quonset feel to them. The light poles are decorated with sun-faded chamber of commerce (excuse me, Chamber of Commerce) guidons, proclaiming some dying, dead-end, minimalist town to be the Queen City of the Prairies, A Town for All Seasons, the Sugar Beet Capital of the World, the Gateway to the West, Beef Country, the Heart of the Country. There's a WPA swimming pool or town hall dilapidating off main street, and a cutsie emporium called Chez Barb or a combination barber shop and donut house called Locks and Bagels. Hair stylists seem to be the most creative nomenclaturists in these villages: Kurl Up and Dye! Usually you can find a fleet farm supply house out on the edge of town, and a Dairy King, Dairy Princess, or King Cone (franchises are expensive). The motels were built back when motoring through America on the blacktop highways was exotic. It's sad to see them now that the sterile chain sleeperies have shouldered them into ma and pa oblivion. I'd stay in them if they were not so wretchedly uncomfortable. They are named E-Z Inn, or Ho-Hum, or the Sunset, names that no longer inspire confidence. Their swimming pools, if they have them, seem bacterial. They feature direct dial phones, cable TV, kitchenettes, deep valley beds, and orange shag carpet. And oak-framed prints of the slumped-over vanishing Indian.

The municipal library is open Tuesday mornings. A grant has just been submitted to a state bureau to make it possible to keep it open for two additional hours on Thursday evenings. The library is anemic, void of anything worth reading, but the video store down the street rocks, though void of anything worth seeing. Somewhere in the center of town there is a gleaming new quick shop (with some appalling name like Kum & Go, or EZ In & Out), which serves as the town center, and is to a forlorn village what a shopping mall is to a city, and the agora to the graceful Athenians. People gather there, especially adolescents. The old men congregate to gossip and shake their heads at the administration. The farm implement dealership on the edge of town has bright green or red behemoths lined up in tight formation, worth more than all the commercial buildings in the community. Lately their profits are mainly from spare parts. During the holiday season one of the big tractors sports twinkle lights round its gigantic tires, and people traveling through think, "Isn't that clever," and stop to try to take a picture to show how quaint the outback folk are. There is on the edge of town a car wash where young men gleam their pickups for sexual conquest. The Ford dealership has about ten stocky American cars and a computerized diagnostic machine that the assistant mechanic went off to Tampa to train for. Every town has its taxidermist, where jackalopes abound.

On the edge of such villages you see the wind-battered handmade 4-H signs: "Busy Bees 4-H Welcomes You," "Butte County Beavers At Work Here!" (you know that one has been the subject of endless pubescent jokes). As often as not there is a locally-painted sign, on plywood, depicting in miniature—though not by much—the very town you are about to enter, but with some elk or antelopes airbrushed in to remind you that you are in the Wild West. In some towns a brick building has been decorated with unconvincing trompe l'oeil—the subject is almost invariably a steam locomotive, a grain elevator, or Wild Bill Hickock doing something irresponsible.

The dentist's and the lawyer's and the doctor's houses are out on the edge of town, set ostentatiously back from the highway, stretch ranch houses with expensive wooden fences and big dogs that cost money. I came up over a hill once just after one of those dogs had been hit by a car. It lay preternaturally still on the line where the road meets the shoulder. Perhaps it was still alive, but there could be no doubt that it was mortally wounded. And coming up the drive in a half run were a lean professional man's wife, dressed in catalogue wear, and her seven or eight year old daughter. They were hand in hand, half running, and both of them were crying uncontrollably like the Kent State woman with the Delacroix[†] face—the famous woman of the 1970 photograph. Her name was Mary Ann Vecchio and some news magazine tracked her down a few years ago. Her life had been a hard one. In fact, she had just been drifting through Kent, Ohio, when all the trouble happened and she had gotten caught up in it, and rendered immortal by one of the greatest photographs of the twentieth century.

But these two, mother and daughter, were not just passing through. They lived here on the edge of town, proud of their status as the most prominent family in the district, and they lived more elegantly than the others, and often sent their children off to private academies far away, and the wife was known to be active in the state arts council. But now their beloved dog was dead on the asphalt, its torso still warm and yielding to the touch. I shot

---

[†]French painter Eugene Delacroix (1798-1863) epitomizes romanticism. He is best know for his 1830 painting *Liberty Leading the People*. Student riots erupted at Kent State University in Kent, Ohio, on May 1, 1970, to protest U.S. President Richard Nixon's extension of the Vietnam War into Cambodia. Four students were killed by the Ohio National Guard on May 4, 1970.

through this proscenium at 60 miles per hour, and though I slowed, I could not bear to stop. It all seemed like slow motion. In my memory, mother and daughter will always be half-running up that drive, the daughter will always be a child of seven, the mother always tall and lean and well dressed and heartbroken more for her daughter than herself, and that English setter will always be motionless on the margin of the road. It reminds me of Keats' great paean to frozen time, the *Ode on a Grecian Urn*:

Fair youth, beneath the trees, thou canst not leave
Thy song, nor ever can those trees be bare;
Bold lover, never, never canst thou kiss,
Though winning near the goal—yet, do not grieve;
She cannot fade, though thou hast not thy bliss,
For ever wilt thou love, and she be fair!

They will always go back into the house to call husband and father and he will always be initially annoyed to be interrupted at work and then contrite and sympathetic and he will always say, "Pumpkin, we'll get another dog just like it." It's heartbreaking.

Drive through such villages in the fall and you'll see fifty boys, most of the high school males, out scrimmaging on the football field in bleached white uniforms, frail boys in big helmets, with coaches raging up and down the line like Agamemnon. They teach social studies by day with breathtaking mediocrity and smugness, make their classes watch Encyclopedia Britannica films while they make a few calls to cleat suppliers, drink at the Elks Club on Friday nights and tell (again) the story of the time they almost met Joe Namath at a Chrysler party at Superbowl VIII. On the edge of the same field perky, big-haired, semi-virgin cheerleaders make up in enthusiasm and gossip what they lack in gymnastic adroitness, and they all dream of going to Homecoming with Craig (the Bomber) Schroeder, who quarterbacks the team and is said to move fast with the women he takes to the local one-screen theater.

It is Main Street and Lake Woebegon and it is Winesburg, Ohio, and Spoon River—all of them sucked dry of moisture and culture, which is the child of moisture. These are sad places, mostly, and seedy, in palpable decline, and yet as redemptive as they are sad, and as you drive through them five miles faster than the speed limit permits, you feel a kind of pang of nostalgia for their *To Kill a Mockingbird* simplicities. This, you think, is America! And then you pass on. Decent, dying, disconsolate plains towns.

It would be foolhardy to idealize this land as Jefferson's rural Eden, where mild men work their fields by day and read Homer in the original Greek at night, while the women nurture orderly gardens, bake bread, nurse their children, and teach them to read. There is, in the sacred corridor, alcoholism, wife-beating, child-abuse, rape, teenage pregnancy, drug-addiction, incest, HIV, ignorance, tax-evasion, pettiness, homophobia and every other form of bigotry, plus provincialism and a streak of militia-maniacal hatred of government, susceptibility to pathetic conspiracy theories (from Jewish internationalism to the Chicago Board of Trade), and a gun obsession the size of Montana. It is, in short, a place like other places. *Et in Arcadia eqo.*

And yet when a crusty, not-much-liked farmer gets a liver transplant and it looks as if he will not be able to put up his wheat crop, it really is the case that over the ridge one Saturday morning come rolling rolling rolling a score of combines and grain trucks, and wives and girlfriends with fried chicken and corn bread and flat cakes covered with a half-inch of frosting blazing with No. 3 Red Dye, and iced tea steeped on the back porch in a yellow gallon jar purchased at the Gambles or Gimbles store in the next town. The whole 1200-acre crop is harvested in a single day, and the men get off their rigs from time to time to wipe their brows with their red handkerchiefs and not say much and sip hot bitter black coffee from a thermos mug—somehow, in this crisis, the whole morass of life is redeemed in a way that it could not be in Seattle or Kansas City. The scale and the decentralization and the naiveté of these communities give this district a form of grace. I have seen this moment. It is not merely a scene from the movie *Witness*[†]. On the whole these are the most admirable people on the continent, especially in crisis, and their decency makes up for a world of lesser deficiencies. They are an endangered species.

V

MY PARENTS LIVED NEAR THE TOP of the sacred corridor in Dickinson, North Dakota, the self-styled Queen City of the Prairies (more recently, "The Western Edge"), but their orientation was east to west not north to south. My father, uneasy in this place, subscribed to the *Minneapolis Tribune* for its urbanity and faraway Delphic pronouncements. He spent his life looking east. He never realized that the north-south axis is more interesting.

At the top of the country, near the Canadian border, there is the confluence of the Missouri and the Yellowstone Rivers, in the mid-nineteenth century one of the most important commercial and strategic places in North America, now a pathetic Lions club picnic site twenty-some miles west of Williston, North Dakota. So much has changed in transportion, in the economy, in the way we think about and harness the continent that those few who visit the place today are seldom impressed by the confluence of two of the world's great rivers.

But Meriwether Lewis and William Clark knew enough to be impressed. Lewis reports on April 26, 1805, that he was so "much pleased at having arrived at this long wished for spot," that he

---

[†]Australian director Peter Weir takes a big-city cop (Harrison Ford) on a journey to Pennsylvania's Amish community in the 1985 movie featuring rural scenes patterned after the Dutch painter Vermeer (1632-1675).

"ordered a dram to be issued to each person; this soon produced the fiddle, and they spent the evening with much hilarity, singing & dancing, and [the men] seemed as perfectly to forget their past toils, as they appeared regardless of those to come." Lewis, it turns out, could not finally live without a dram. On the same day, Clark suggested that the confluence of the Yellowstone and the Missouri "affords a butifull commanding situation for a fort." And the forts came. The great Sitting Bull surrendered here at the U.S. Army's Fort Buford in the year 1881. A replica of the commercial Fort Union has been constructed recently on the north bank of the Missouri, a tasteless memorial to racism, imperialism, militarism, epidemia, and the systematic bilking and demoralizing of Native American peoples. Buffs flock to it. It is a beautiful white building with a black karma.

Lewis and Clark saw the future of America at the confluence of the Yellowstone and Missouri Rivers. They saw far, but they could not envision a time when America would abandon its rivers. They lived on the other side of the internal combustion engine.

Below the confluence of the Missouri and the Yellowstone is the north unit of Theodore Roosevelt National Park, home of the "grand canyon" of the Little Missouri River. The claim is not as ludicrous as it sounds. It would not be a national park in a better state, but it is, by North Dakota standards, sublime. For a long time it was a National *Memorial* Park. Then it graduated. There are two types of people in this world: those who admire the Little Missouri River when it is spectacular, as here, and those who love it better when it is not. I love it best when its sublimity is a counter-intuitive koan. When I see a park service sign with a binocular or camera icon, I turn away in disgust. I do not wish to be Pavlov's tourist. I do not seek mediated experience. Nor do I like to be alerted to the sublime.

Below the national park lie bighorn sheep badlands, the marvelously absurd village of Grassy Butte, "where history still stands" (but needs a hip replacement), endless red-scoria-road oil country, and, on the Little Missouri River, Theodore Roosevelt's isolated Elkhorn Ranch site, by now just a fenced-in patch of deep grass and cottonwoods, a breathtaking view of the river bluffs, and perhaps a square nail if you are really lucky with the toe of your boot. I bumped into the biggest coyote of my life there, one September afternoon, after a miniaturized local thunder storm. The lightning exploded out of the sky and the coyote exploded out of the tall wet grass ten feet in front of me, a silver streak like pure Medicine. I did not sleep that night.

Below that are the dry "badlandsy" badlands of the Little Missouri valley, which embrace the south unit of Theodore Roosevelt National Park. Roosevelt had a ranch here too, and the famous French aristocrat Antoine Amédée Maraie Vincent Amat Manca de Vallombrosa, the Marquis de Morès, built a plank wood chateau overlooking the river and a village nearby that he named for his American wife Medora von Hoffman. North Dakota, the most democratic place in America, sucks up to aristocracy at every turn. Roosevelt and the Marquis de Morès are our royalty. Medora, a village of a hundred or so people, is the least offensive national park border town in America, perhaps because the park is so out of the way, so little visited, so low rent by the standards of American tourism. It is also the beneficiary of the inherent modesty of the North Dakota people.

South of that, but still in North Dakota, is the forlorn butte country of the Little Missouri River with scattered clouds and hardscrabble summer fallowed wheat fields carved into the flat places. Almost no one lives here. This is the empty quarter—not that the rest of it is exactly full. Buttes are flat, grass-topped mesas, typically crew-cut, that rise above the plains, and remind us that the whole country was once higher, before the wind and the rivers carried most of the earth south and east, into the sedimentary rivers and down to the wine-dark sea. By virtue of little quirks of soil composition and perhaps the feng shui of the plains, the buttes are all that remain of the previous elevation of the country, like the high water marks on bridges. Climb a butte into the past. I have a list somewhere of all the buttes in North Dakota—they are legion—and my dream is to spend a night on each of them before I die. But I have many dreams.

In the heart of this district lies Marmarth, the little ghost town on the defunct Milwaukee Road rail line that plays such a significant role in this book. Talk about spirit of place: bury my heart not at Wounded Knee or the cemetery at Fergus Falls, Minnesota, or in the Old Quadrangle at Hertford College, Oxford, but in the barrens north of Marmarth. I sang the praises of that forlorn village so often that two of my favorite people, a California academic couple, decided to investigate one year on their way to Montana. They drove through Marmarth east to west and then north to south trying to figure out just what it was that so appealed to me. They walked around and took a few photographs. They sat down for a jumbo beef burger at Mert's Café. They spoke to nobody. Then they went to the tiny 20x20 green Quonset post office to send me a card proving that they had taken up my challenge. As the part-time postal clerk was fitting them out with a stamp, the phone rang. She answered it. There was a pause. She glanced up furtively. And said, "Yeah, they're here. No, no, they're fine." Marmarth is tiny. Marmarth is marginal. Marmarth is sometimes xenophobic. Marmarth could not be Marmarth if it were sited in Wisconsin, or California, or even eastern North Dakota. Marmarth is what it is because it is miles from nowhere, in a region declining as fast as corn wilts in the fields. Marmarth is just off the grid. Marmarth depends on improbability. So does everything significant in existence.

So much for North Dakota. Like the rest of the Great Plains, it's a lot of country all spread out. The North Dakota-South Dakota border is nothing but a pointless Jeffersonian grid line, what the Sioux might have called a Medicine Line, on the great subtly-curved continuum of the earth; but, even so, in the homestead era, Congress appropriated $25,000 to survey the border and plant seven-foot quartzite markers three and one-half feet into the ground precisely every half-mile along the 360-mile border. Unless you know the work of the historian Gordon Iseminger,[†] you can live your whole life without ever knowing of the existence of these markers, erected shortly after statehood in 1889. Now *that* was a make-work project. If there could be said to be even the slightest justification for demarcating the indistinguishable Dakotas in this way, there would be border stones between Maryland and Virginia, or California and Arizona, where borders count, where there are issues to consider. North and South Dakota are the same place with different names. When I was a boy, I spent a weekend camped next to the marker that pinpoints the North Dakota-South Dakota-Montana border. We threw up a Montgomery Wards tent and a giant long-wire antenna and broadcast amateur radio signals to a hungry world. Ham operators, at least, found the border stones and our simultaneous encampment in three states fascinating. My friend Philip Howard accidentally burned down the tent. We shivered through the nights in pre-high-tech sleeping bags. A few weeks later, the people we had communicated with by radio received QSL (amateur radio acknowledgement) cards specially printed to commemorate our pointless feat. Between flashes of technological infatuation, I remember feeling for the first time awe towards the landscape of the Great Plains. I was sixteen.

As with the famous *New Yorker* map of America, my cartographical mastery begins to diminish somewhat beyond the North Dakota line.

[†]*The Quartzite Border: Surveying and Marking the North Dakota-South Dakota Boundary, 1891-1892*, 1988.

Northern South Dakota is butte country—it embraces, in fact, some of the most beautiful and desolate buttes in the world. I have photographed them all, and hiked many of them. One begins to notice more pine trees dotting the ridges now, particularly on the northern face. The romance of pine country is immense, especially for a grass-fed North Dakotan. Just off U.S. 85 north of Sturgis,[†] South Dakota, is a place modestly denominated the "Center of the World." It is a monument so out of the way that as you stand there, in some ways more on top of the world than you would be at McKinley's or Whitney's summit, and gaze out on endless gray land of the most marginal sort, you cannot decide whether there has to be a God or there cannot possibly be a God. The local Lions or Kiwanis maintain the Center of the World after a fashion. That is, they have a work day twice a year and see to it that the oil barrel trash bin is painted and that the outhouse is survivable and snake-free. By the time you venture out of your car to stretch and take a look around, you feel more alone than you have ever felt. This is the middle of nowhere. You have to climb a rather steep set of terraces to reach the actual butte ridge, and all the way up you are thinking, "I believe I can already be said to have got the point here. Am I to understand that the landscape will look *more* godforsaken and desolate once I reach the summit?" or, "If my car doesn't start this is going to be the longest day of my life." But climb you do. And it *is* more stark from the top, if only for the violence of the wind that blasts it like a heath.

I made love there once, to an amazing plains woman, in the middle of winter, on top of the "Center of the World." Where else make love? It was the coldest day in human history, so you know it was early in the relationship. We were all goose down and parkas, blankets and blind gropings just to discover where some flesh lay. Nobody interrupted us, of course, but we did not

---

[†]The home of the annual motorcycle riot.

linger much before or after. I never go past that spot now without stopping to climb the hillock, searching for our spot, hoping that the grass is especially lush there where we lay, or scoured away forever by the sky gods, and remembering the contours of that winsome day, and wondering if it really ever happened, and thanking my god that I live in a place that is so perfectly absurd.

If the term "spirit of place" means anything, it must have something to do with the fundamental influences in one's life, one's character, one's soul. We all know where we were when John F. Kennedy was killed (Cub Scouts), when the Challenger blew up (a student union), when the World Trade Center's twin towers came down (Phoenix), but these were accidental burns on the hard drives of our beings. The great desideratum of life is to have loved first or deepest in a place that contributes to the soul of that experience, a place that is not merely accidental.

In the ideal existence, the essential moments of life are rooted in a meaningful landscape and they are inconceivable elsewhere.

One wants to have formed one's value system not just in a place, but partly because of it. One wants to have engaged in sexual play in a landscape that is so essential that it is virtually a character in the drama. One wants one's religion to be centered not merely in a text, a doctrine, a creed, or a chapel, but in locale, a sacred precinct, a circle of land and sky, a place where the wind bloweth where it listeth. One wants one's firstborn beloved child to have been born not merely in a hospital in Reno or an air force base near Munich or Stuttgart, but in the place that matters most of all the places that mean something in one's life. One wants a true, deep, rooted home, a refuge to return to to seek clarity and unconditional love. One wants landscape in one's soul, and one's soul to dwell in a landscape somewhere.

Where would you go if you were diagnosed with cancer or the AIDS virus, if your whole world collapsed around you and only one point on the planet could help to heal? Where would you take the significant other who was hopelessly, boundlessly, endlessly, head-over-heels in love with you and she or he asked, take me to the place that means more to you than any other place in the cosmos? There, if anywhere, you will find spirit of place.

VI

WHETHER THE BLACK HILLS OF SOUTH DAKOTA ARE SACRED is a strangely contested issue, thanks in part to the new western historical skepticism of Donald Worster[†], who has argued that Sioux assertions of holiness are recent forms of legal and political argumentation rather than a genuine spiritual tradition—as defined, apparently, by the French theorist Mircea Eliade. Besides, Worster argues, the Sioux are as nouveau on the northern plains as the Declaration of Independence, about as recent, in fact, as Lewis and Clark, having been eased out of their Minnesota and Wisconsin lake cabins by the muzzles of Chippewa guns. Leaving Worster's scholastic concerns aside, it seems to be beyond dispute that the Black Hills are *not* sacred to Wasichu, the white man, who has turned one of the loveliest places on earth, certainly the loveliest place on the Great Plains, into an extraction machine. Sioux tradition and testimony would seem to me to count for more than a French intellectual's taxonomy of the sacred. Recent immigrant or not, the Sioux holy man Black Elk received his great vision at Harney Peak, the tallest peak (the Sioux "center of the world") in the Black Hills. And the Black Hills are sacred to me, if by sacred one means that they deserve to be visited thoughtfully, on foot, in hushed tones, and with all of one's sensitivities on special alert. If you can play miniature golf, you are not in a sacred place.

[†] *Under Western Skies: Nature and History in the American West*, 1994.

Let me add, as intemperately as I can, that I resent the very presence of white homesteaders and entrepreneurs in the Black Hills. I believe that the existing non-Indian inhabitants should be allowed to remain where they squat until they die and then all their holdings should be placed in trust for the Sioux, the Cheyenne, the National Park Service, and Wakan Tonka (the Great Spirit), that meanwhile the Sioux and Cheyenne should be paid, in gold dust, the $400 or so million they are owed for the theft of the Black Hills in 1876, that all the Wasichu (white man's) names (from Harney and Terry Peaks to Custer State Park) should be erased and replaced by native nomenclature, that Mount Rushmore should be defaced and the misguided Crazy Horse Monument abandoned, that the entire tourism industry of the region should be taxed at 25 percent for Native American cultural renaissance programs and Indian health care initiatives, and that timber, gravel, gold, and water extraction should be terminated immediately. Beyond that, I have no strong opinions about the future of the Black Hills.

Bear Butte, a lonely volcanic spur northeast of the Black Hills, is unquestionably sacred. The state of South Dakota says it's so. It may be the most sacred place on the Great Plains and, so far as I know, even Professor Worster does not deny it its status as an ecumenical prayer and meditation site. I never fail to stop to pray at Bear Butte, no matter how great my hurry. The butte always delivers. My life has been made immeasurably more meaningful for my pilgrimages to its crest.[†] It sits beside the road that takes me from the Black Hills to my boyhood home in North Dakota. It was also, it turns out, my road to Damascus.

Not so far to the west of Bear Butte, I spent the greatest night of my life, alone, except for the gods, in the heart of the heart of the sacred corridor. It was north of the village of Camp Crook,

---

†Bear Butte is the subject of the last essay in this book.

South Dakota. The term "middle of nowhere" is inadequate to register the utter remoteness, the complete insignificance, the absolute desolation of the place. I was two weeks into a two-month walk along the Little Missouri River and I was beginning to get my groove back. My body at last was no longer calling (that is, whimpering) attention to itself. My soul was alive again. As I attended to the rhythm of my body and the river and the plains and the sky, I had begun to dream again. After a twenty-mile day on the grassy spine of the North American continent, I stopped for the night on a ridge a mile or two from the banks of the Little Missouri River. I cooked my dinner in silence. Thunderstorms were getting into formation far off to the west. The clouds were magnificent: charcoal, pink, rose, black, gray. Coyotes nipped at my heels. Then, at the moment when I least expected it, the sacred reached out and throttled me for a half-dozen hours.

To describe precisely what happened would be to blaspheme the experience. It lifted me to heights of awareness that knocked on the doors of mysticism, and it eventually harrowed me with a vision of death for which nothing in my experience—in books, in travels, in human relationships—had ever prepared me. Until you have met death you cannot know the Great Plains. On that night, the vast gulf between I and thou, between me and the rest of creation, collapsed briefly into Unity. I lost myself and found myself in the most improbable place in America. By the time the night was done and the crescent moon had set, I felt that I had, like Jacob, wrestled with the Angel of God. It was the closest I have ever come to being fully awake. My campsite of that night is a secret place to which I have never taken anyone, nor wished to. I go there from time to time and ache for all that I have lost.

I do not believe that moment could have come to me in the splendid lake districts of Minnesota or England. I do not believe I could have felt what I felt, seen what I saw, or dreamed what I dreamed, in the Bitterroot Mountains or the Baghdad Hilton or even Tibet. There are some things that are unique to the sacred corridor. I aspire to be one of them.

VII

THE BADLANDS OF SOUTH DAKOTA ARE TRULY BAD. These are the baddest badlands in the country. They are bad enough to be a national park. By comparison, the badlands of North Dakota seem miniature and muted, almost sweet. North Dakota's badlands needed the makeweight of Theodore Roosevelt to achieve recreational status. Alone they were just not bad enough. All badlands operate by the same principle—the erosive power of wind and water have desolated a landscape until it achieves an eerie kind of beauty. In the North Dakota badlands you can graze a few cattle. In the South Dakota badlands, you couldn't graze a grasshopper. It seems fitting that the Native American Ghost Dance religion found its purest expression on Cuny Table, which is a lonely tongue of good grassy land extending itself, like a proscenium arch, right out over the badlands of South Dakota. The Ghost Dance was a desperate minuet performed by a desperate people in a desperate place. When a people reaches the lowest trough of desperation, they begin spontaneously to dance.[†] And it ended in the assassination of Sitting Bull, and the massacre at Wounded Knee (December 29, 1890).

I lay my naked form down on the forgotten grasses of Cuny Table once in the midst of a beautiful harmless thunderstorm and felt the throb of the Ghost Dance in every pore of my being. How can any baby boomer white bread consumer ever begin to imagine the *dans macabre* of the Sioux? No rational being can want to have been a part of the Ghost Dance phenomenon of

---

[†]In the Middle Ages, when the Black Plague (1347-1352) carried off one in three Europeans, a spontaneous dance of death, the *dans macabre*, sprang up all over Europe. In Uganda in the last decades of the twentieth century, when the gun-toting goons of Idi Amin attacked tribesmen equipped only with sticks and stones, another *dans macabre* occurred, much to the astonishment of the international media.

1889-90, but who does not wish to have participated in something, somewhere, at some point in life, so close to the marrow of existence? It is so pathetic to be a mere bourgeois.

On the northern edge of Alliance, Nebraska, where an itinerant Methodist preacher taught me the difference between Red Cloud and Crazy Horse, between accommodationists and absolutists, and thus changed my life, there is a mystic structure (I had almost said sculpture) of uncertain origin called Carhenge. Several dozen large junked cars (all four-door sedans) have been planted on end in an ingenious circle perhaps two hundred feet in diameter, the cars buried in the earth, though not always in a perfectly perpendicular fashion, some pairs topped with a car shell in the traditional horizontal position (like the Greek letter π). The cars have all been painted a dull white. A few of the cars are randomly disbursed over the site, perhaps having fallen from their previous status as capstones. Carhenge is, in short, a ruin. In walking through the entirely unsupervised site (alas, there is no brochure, no register, no staff, no interpretive sign), one has the feeling that there was definite purpose in the construction of the sculpture, if only it could be recovered at this remove. Learned opinions vary. Some say it is a monument to the American God (it is true that no Hondas, no Mazdas, no BMWs have ever been found on site), others that it must have served at some point as a celestial measuring device, perhaps an immense agricultural calendar, still others that it was built to circumvent Lady Bird Johnson's 1965 highway beautification legislation. All that is definitely known is this: visitation increases dramatically at the equinoxes and the solstices, and bed sheets mysteriously disappear from the hotels of Alliance.

Note: there is said to be a stone replica of Carhenge on the Salisbury plain in England. Imitation, indeed, is the truest form of flattery.

Nebraska is where they killed Crazy Horse in 1877. Chadron—the nearest population center—is as close to the definitive Great Plains town as exists. It's all dust and windsweep. The Oregon and Mormon trails bore me (I despise all forms of white triumphalism), and the alchemical conversion of the sacred waters of the Platte River into corn for livestock for hamburgers for prostate cancer for Viagra offends me to the core. I do love to squat with my back to my car fender, binoculars in hand, and observe the delicate Sandhill cranes at Easter time along the Platte's braided meanders. One of my closest friends from Oxford University grew up on Buffalo Bill Drive in North Platte. I love to think of some sedentary "clerk of Oxenford" typing his home address into the university's records, lifting her ink-stained, nail-bitten Brit fingers from the keyboard for a few minutes to daydream America ("Buffalo Bill's defunct," said e. e. cummings, "who used to ride a watersmooth-silver stallion and break onetwothreefourfive pigeons just like that Jesus he was a handsome man and what I want to know is how do you like your blueeyed boy Mister Death"), before moving on from Doug Faulkner of Nebraska to Nigel Folkgrove of Notting Hill. One night in the common room at Hertford College, Oxford, primed with fine sherry, Douglas taught me all the capitals of all the nations of Africa, and spelled Ouagadougou too. He also made wild claims for the pan steak at the Plainsman restaurant in Thedford, Nebraska.

The finest place in Nebraska is the Dismal River in the Sand Hills. The Sand Hills remind us that the sacred corridor is desert country periodically covered (in the wet cycles) by a veneer of grass. Scratch this fragile integument with the bronze edge of drought and suddenly it is sand dunes in every direction. Even so, the Dismal River runs clear among the oceanic swells of the Sand Hills even in times of prolonged drought. The name is apparently a piece of irony, like Greenland. I have canoed the

Dismal. Long ago, I narrowly missed the chance to canoe it with Debra Winger's boyfriend. Now, every time I pass through, I stop at a forgotten rest area on the banks of the Dismal north of North Platte. It is delightful to stand on its margins on starry December nights when the wind chill is about forty below zero, listening to the subterranean gurgling of the river flowing beneath the ice crust. There is a little homestead nearby that puts up Christmas lights every year. I have always wanted to stop by for coffee and a chat, to find out what they think of things, but I am not the kind of person who stops by strangers' homesteads for coffee and a chat. It was in the Sand Hills that I discovered the work of the Nebraska writer Mari Sandoz. *Old Jules* (the biography of her appalling father) is crusty and delightful enough, but her biography *Crazy Horse* is indispensably interesting and—that rarest of things—authentic. Sandoz knew Indians. She interviewed men and women who had spent their lives with Crazy Horse. She championed the cause of the Sioux and Cheyenne without slipping into romanticism. Her *Cheyenne Autumn*, much of which unfolds in the Sand Hills, is the best badly written book about the American West. Of course like everyone else I have done my time atop Scottsbluff, one of the most prominent features of the central plains.

Nebraska is where they killed Crazy Horse. More recently, they've named a highway for a college football coach. Could there be a greater soullessness than that?

Kansas is less rugged than its cousins to the north. It is also infinitely less interesting because virtually all of its native peoples were pushed or rubbed out early in Kansas history. North Dakota, Nebraska, and especially South Dakota are Indian country. Kansas is sunflower country. Kansas, moreover, has pretensions that its northern neighbors would never indulge: great universities, an Edward Hopperesque great American city, soybeans. Kansas takes itself too seriously to be a true plains state. It hankers after midwesternness and respectability. A plains state without Indians is a dull blade. The presence—even the marginal presence—of Indians gives the rest of the Great Plains a compelling edginess. The other plains states are forced to deal with Indians and Indian issues. This gives them some interesting mirrors.

My former in-laws owned a big industrial farm towards the bottom of the corridor—on the same parallel as Denver, more or less. My father-in-law had been a pioneer irrigator in the district and a model farmer, but he had been nipped by the Carter inflation years and the farm had never fully recovered. At its zenith, the farm had been a mighty impressive operation, with nine miles of aluminum underground pipe and wells tapped into the Ogallala Aquifer (an underground pool of fossil water the size of Lake Huron) that gave you a Henry Fonda smile.

I used to perform some unspectacular fieldwork for my in-laws on occasion, when they were seriously labor-starved, on giant cab-sealed tractors, grinding the soil from section line to section line, day after day, 15 feet above the ground. It is a strange and troubling feeling for a soft outsider to bestride the colossus of a four-wheel drive tractor and roar around tilling the earth. It would be a bit like permitting a kite enthusiast to pilot a Boeing 747 or a wheel barrowist to grade a road with a Caterpillar. These tilling machines are gigantic and enormously powerful, and operating one—it turns out—is not at all like driving a Honda Civic on well-marked roads. I had many Chaplinesque scrapes on the big John Deere rigs, most of which would have been hilarious had I not been toying with more than a hundred thousand dollars of metal.

My father-in-law used to drive out to check on me a few times every day, bring me coffee and words of encouragement, and pull me off the tractor to talk about current events. He was a remarkably curious and thoughtful man and, like so many in the empty quarter, lonely as hell for real conversation. He'd say, as he walked away,

"Watch the cultivator blight," or "Be careful with the iron weed," by which he meant, "If you don't line up the cultivator in the field any better than that, you'll destroy more corn stalks than you save." Thereafter, I'd concentrate with all my might to drive straight while howling at the whoppers of Rush Limbaugh. But you drive better when you simply relax into the groove.

Sometimes I'd go with my father-in-law to work on a wellhead. But the sound of two Chrysler V-8 engines running at top end with rust-perforated mufflers, sucking the fossil waters of the Ogallala Aquifer up to irrigate corn and sunflower seeds, was so great that we could only communicate by signs. It was not exactly Jefferson's pastoral Eden as we screamed monosyllables at close range under the vast plains sky, our hands begrimed with oil, but it was not Alexander Hamilton's commercial paradise either, for it cost more to raise the crop than the crop sold for, and the national government grudgingly made up some of the difference with a Byzantine system of deficiency payments and guaranteed loans. Even so, we loved the farm and all it symbolized. In spite of the paradox that we were growing food at the apex of a gigantic petrochemical pyramid, food that was not really valuable enough to pay the cost of growing it, at least within the confines of the existing world distribution grid, on land that should never have been plowed in the first place, and that the social cost of this system of food production was isolation, a weak cultural infrastructure, provincialism, and unending economic anxiety, we all—even I the gentile—took pride in what we were doing and we felt like "this American, this new man," described by Jefferson's French pal J. Hector Saint Crèvecoeur in 1782. Just how a man driving a tractor whose tire he could not change if his life depended upon it can feel marvelously independent is not clear, but that is the unmistakable mythology of the place. And I swallowed the whole hog.

I do not know much about Oklahoma. I have camped under stunning cottonwoods in the Cimarron National Grasslands. The word "Cimarron" is one of the most beautiful and evocative of plains words. It seems to mean "wild," or "untamed," and it may have something to do with runaway slaves who hid out in the hills. I've been as far south as the Washita Hills, which are often called the southern terminus of the Great Plains. I wanted to see the Washita battle site, where George Armstrong Custer made his name as an Indian fighter in 1868. Still choking on his Civil War ration of testosterone, he wiped out a peaceful village of already co-opted Cheyenne Indians at dawn on November 29, 1868, permitted the butchery of defenseless women and children, abandoned one of his own detachments to certain death, slaughtered a whole Cheyenne horse herd (more than 800 pintos were shot at close range), looted and then burned the village (destroying seven hundred pounds of tobacco, more than a thousand buffalo robes, immense quantities of meat), and (probably) took a Cheyenne mistress named Mo-nah-se-tah. Meanwhile, he penned lyric (and interminable) letters to his wife Elizabeth, full of the rum-rim-ruff of his colossal ego. For all of this carnage and carnality he was lionized as a patriot, a great man and a fabulous Indian fighter. I spent a couple of days once nosing around the battle sites trying to get a feel for the spirit of the place, but Oklahoma did not speak to me. It always feels like a Will Rogers monologue on red soil.

Texas could claim to be a plains state if it didn't claim everything else under the sun. I leave it to its own vast dream of grandeur.

VIII

I'VE SPENT YEARS DRIVING THE SACRED CORRIDOR ALONE. I've only known one other person who appreciated the corridor as much as I do and we no longer mingle our souls. There's no fun in driving that country with someone who is not enamored of it, because you're always either apologizing for the desolation or promising that something just around the bend is spectacular, and then finding out that it is spectacular only to you. I love to amble along the narrow asphalt roads, stopping at will to stretch, pee, run, nap, take photographs, write a journal entry, read a few pages, listen for coyotes, gaze at the stars, or lie on my back on the warm earth. I stop in all the towns at whatever passes for the bookstore, hoping for a find, sometimes settling for a heat-curled, cover-bleached Bison Book, a badly written and badly conceived study of something that might have been interesting, like the forts of the Upper Missouri or the tales of a Texas cowhand.

I've driven most of the paved roads in the corridor, and plenty of gravel ones, and occasionally I mess around on the four-wheel drive trails if they are dry. I hike and chant and pray in odd places—they are sacred to me because I have read the literature of the plains closely and I know some of what happened here, especially during the five decades of the Indian wars. For many years I have had the habit of sitting afternoons—at the thunderstorm hour—on a pine ridge somewhere where no one could find me if I perished, smoking my Sioux Indian eagle's claw pipe carefully filled with kinnickinnick, praying for a burning bush of some recognizable sort, getting as much of my near-naked body in contact with the grass and the earth as possible, trying to work my body into a spirit antenna. It always fails, this quest, though I have lived through stupendous lightning storms and nearly-terminal blizzards, and when my soul-quest fails I have never concluded that the cosmos is inert, only that I am a toxic man with a bent antenna. As I look from the ridge I am sitting on to the other ridges in the district, and see lonely gravel roads meandering across the middle distance, I invariably say, out loud, "I will visit you one day soon, yon hills, and see what you are about." And sometimes I do. I would like to be known as the man who knows the territory and its history and all of its crevices better than any man alive. But I have known a few such men and they are all lore-obssessives.

And as I pass the gorgeous hidden places of the plains, I plan decentralized careers in high-tech, environmentally-pure, elegant but modest Palladian houses I will build in the draw near the chalk bluffs, and use the worldwide web and the fax machine to make a good living far from the madding crowd. Today it is the Wildcat Hills of the panhandle of Nebraska. Next time it is the Cave Hills west of Buffalo, South Dakota, a bend along the Dismal River in the Sand Hills of Nebraska, or a niche in Bullion or Sentinel Butte in my home state. I think of how expensive the driveway is going to be, and difficult to maintain, and whether I'll need a pickup with a snowplow on the front, and how deep the well will have to be and whether the water will be any good when they finally get to a pool worth tapping. When I was growing up the toilets of most of the country houses were iron-stained from the heavy concentration of minerals in the aquifer. So I am planning to drill deep. Nobody visits twice if your water is no good. And I wonder if there is any woman who would agree to live with me in such a place and not secretly curse the day she met me. I plan goat herds and chevre cheese production and an Appaloosa horse for my daughter and a sweat lodge and a woodworking shop, and a John Neihardt sacred-hoop garden, and a 1957 International Harvester tractor with which to till my ten-acre garden, a modest industrial Candide. And I wonder if the community will accept me and even boast a little, "Oh, he's that reading guy who came out here to live because he loves the country, and he's said to be writing a novel about this part of the world," or maybe it will be one of those Carol Kennicott stories of rejection and misunderstanding and a mutual reinforcement of insecurities. I have many dreams.

IX

IN THE SACRED CORRIDOR A CAR RADIO IS A FORM OF FRIENDSHIP.
By day you can hear a handful of 50,000-watt blowtorch stations
with cornpone talk shows and moment-by-moment unfoldings
of the Chicago futures markets. I find myself glued to the swap
lines, where you learn what's for sale in the heart of the heart of
the country (everything but love and patriotism), and you can
call to request anything, from a used crib to tickets to the Lacey
Dalton concert at the Custer County fair. The announcer for these
shows is always clever—playfully hinting that he could go postal
at any time—but patient with folks who have never called a radio
station before, and downright tender with senior citizens who
wish to sell grandfather clocks and acetylene torch welders.

You can hear religious radio everywhere. You can be saved by
any doctrine save Papism. I have even heard, with lurid fascination,
a sparsely-syndicated program called *Jews for Jesus*. The West has
never really recovered from the silencing of Herb Jebko's late night
lonely hearts chat show, *Night Cap*, on KSL Salt Lake (1160 AM),
where you got five minutes to tell your tale of wonder or woe
before a warning sound, "Tinker Bell," announced that your wistful
musings must end. Nor have things been quite right since the
assassination of KOA Denver's incredibly clever bombasticator
Alan Berg by Aryan extremists on June 18, 1984. Music stations
out here are either top forty or straight country, and the DJs make
public appearances from time to time at the remodeled Napa Auto
Parts store on the edge of town and "interview" the owners while
offering free coffee and a hotdog to anyone who wants to "come
on down." Hint: they seldom look like they sound.

On Saturday mornings you will find "Coach's Corner" on a half
dozen stations no matter where you happen to be, and all the
coaches are the same effusion of the Little Prince with a lethal
urge to violence. They all formulate judicious excuses for the

Kostilacky boy's failure to rebound at the semifinals on Friday (after all, the coach and Gordon Kostilacky golf together), and the coach invariably explains why his decision to start his own son at quarterback was perfectly disconnected to their consanguinity; in fact, he had not intended to start his boy, but the other fathers had come up to him at the Lodge and said it would be wrong to let his own squeamishness get in the way of the team's prospects. And so on.

The local weekly newspapers have smug insider editorial notes by editor Melvin "Jigs" Slawson speaking in the royal we, hinting at scandals he cannot divulge and intimating reforms he has no courage to demand in plain English, plus perky canning columns by the county home economist, just graduated from the state land grant university and eager to be useful. In a typical cooperative extension column you might learn how to keep your pickles from getting soggy, and get a tip about how to remove cranberry stains or chewing gum from the carpet. The sports section, which is the heart of the paper, features large grainy black and white photographs of the last nine-man football game, where the Trojans acquitted themselves quite well against the boys from that big consolidated from mid-state, and it's unfair, really, that schools of such different size should be grouped in the same conference. In the want ads you can find a ranch hand job that pays $15,500 plus a gas allowance and a singlewide on the spread.

The citizens of these villages are hard-working and law-abiding. They pay their taxes in full and on time. They fight our wars without protest. Selective service registration among eighteen-year-olds approaches 100 percent. They return wallets with the cash intact to their owners. They neighbor. They vote. They are pious, patriotic, and unpretentious. They are enormously resourceful—stunning in a crisis. They perform essential services for American civilization at the raw end of the spectrum. They drill for oil, eviscerate coal, raise herds, and transport goods. Above all they grow our food for us. They dress sensibly, eschew ostentation, use resources responsibly, and resist fads (though the recent rage for cappuccino is alarming). The center of their lives is family. They'd rather do it than talk about it. They don't call attention to themselves. They resist the national obsession with tan, trim, toned bodies. They go about their business quietly and with great practical skill. They detest the welfare state (except in agriculture). If the whole nation consisted of such people, there would be few prisons.

At night the lords of the sacred corridor are all in their houses watching TV, the great homogenizing template of American life. Once I spent a week in Colby, Kansas. I was strolling around a tan-brick community college campus when a magnificent thunderstorm rolled in from the West. It was July on the Great Plains. The temperature dropped twenty degrees in ten minutes. The sky put on a light show of staggering proportions. Between the smell of ozone and the vastness of the storm, and the towering columnar thunderheads and the terrorizing effect of lightning and thunder at close quarters, I was suddenly alive again pixel by nerve ending. (This alone is reason to live on the Great Plains). I walked along an endless sidewalk that bifurcated two flanks of dormitory rooms, craning my face up to the vault of heaven and tripping, from time to time, into pitfalls. It was a storm that made you glad to be alive and, at the same time, slightly anxious about preserving that status. And yet in each room that I walked past, without exception, there was a flickering blue box and the sound of canned laughter. I wanted to knock on every door and pull the inhabitants, plains-piper-like, out into the pelting storm. But they were all filling the holes in their souls with cathode rays. (On most other nights, I would have been among them). They did not hear the rumble of the earth. "Oh what a falling off was there," says Hamlet: from an iron conviction that the sky is the domicile of Thunder Beings, to a sitcom misunderstanding about a polo shirt.

X

IN EACH OF THE TOWNS OF THE SACRED CORRIDOR there's a roadside café where the same drama is played out again and again. There's a good looking, very slightly overweight, waitress behind the counter, in her late teens or early twenties. She's efficient if perhaps a bit sullen to the usual customers, filling their coffee cups like clockwork and shrugging off the lewd remarks of a score of middle-aged men per day. Then comes in a trucker, or an oil field worker, or a construction worker from somewhere else, Anywhere Else, and he looks a little like Billy Ray Cyrus. He has a beard and a tattoo and he orders without checking the prices first, and he has more confidence than the local boys, and takes better care of himself. She gravitates toward him, and fills his cup more often than necessary, makes eye contact, and asks him where he's from, and before the eggs on his plate have congealed lets him know that there's absolutely nothing to do around here, that it's the dullest and most backward place on earth, and that she's fixin' to get out of here just as soon as she can figure out how— maybe go to Rapid City or Evanston or Salt Lake, maybe even L.A., where she has a girlfriend who works for a successful paving firm.

He listens to her story and only rains a little on her parade of imprecise dreams, makes it clear that he has seen it all. The older waitresses all witness this little semi-articulate drama as they bustle about their work. Some feel a rush of nostalgia for their own lost adolescence, some resent the way she is neglecting the tables assigned to her, some think he's cute, some that she can do much better, but they all know—and she does too, probably, at least in her head—that he's no damned good, that he drinks too much beer, and watches ball, and spends too much time fussing over his pickup, and he has a bad temper, and there's an imprecision that comes with his vast virility, and he hasn't read a book, not even the Bible, for many many years. You can see, as you look on from your booth, that she wants to reach across the counter and grab his shirt and shout, "Take me with you, take me away with you," and he is sizing her up twice, once for her short term potential (maybe I could linger here another day or two) and once for the possibility that she might be the one.

All this unspoken drama unfolds in thirty or forty minutes, amid a great number of distractions on both sides, because neither of them can let themselves be seen flirting openly, and each of them is rightly wary, for they have both been here many times before. Finally he gets up and leaves an ostentatious tip (a dollar more than usual), and maintains eye contact a half-second longer than usual, and then he walks out that door and gets into his rig and drives down the road.

In the end, maybe she marries one of these handsome strangers, but it is more likely that she winds up marrying one of the local boys, or that she drifts off to a bigger place and suffers all the slings and arrows of the country girl in the city, and marries there, or doesn't.

I have witnessed this moment a score of times in my life, in Goodland, Kansas, and on the Nephi death strip in Utah, and in Sydney, Montana, and most recently in Green River, Wyoming. The mating pool is small in such places, and most of the most promising young people leave young and leave forever, and come back only for the holidays and the funerals. Those who remain spend their best years trying to negotiate the gap between the fairy tale paradigm of true love we Americans cling to and the demographics of rural American in an age of decline. It is particularly hard on young women. They read *Seventeen* and

Glamour and *Cosmopolitan* and *Bride's* and they go to Julia Roberts movies, and they want a certain delicacy and romance in their lives, while the men see their fulfillment in fishing, hunting, drinking, sporting, driving, and pay-per-view.

XI

THE CORRIDOR IS ALSO SACRED because it was only slimly domesticated at its peak forty years ago and now the whole social structure, including all the buildings, is deteriorating. There's none of that Minnesota gumption—never more than once-removed from Babbittry—that actually endorses the small town paradigm. Almost everyone out here knows that the whole thing is a poor charade. The town fathers, by which one means the commercial elite, knows the new Economic Development Office (EDO) isn't going to lure a progressive company (like a 3M audio tape assembly plant) to the industrial park north of town, and that things are going to stay the same, at best, and probably worsen, but they dutifully pool their $5,000 so that Gwen can go off to the conference in Wichita about developing a town resume and a web site.

Unless something very remarkable happens, the population of this quarter will continue to decline rapidly, houses will be abandoned to beer-and-22-caliber vandals, the shelter belts will grow old and fall down, the leading edge of till will recede towards the 100th Meridian, the villages will board themselves up and even the larger towns will falter. Maybe buffalo and Indians will reclaim the place and the ingenious, vilified Poppers[†] of Rutgers University will be vindicated. The Poppers' argument—that the western plains are best suited to be a buffalo commons—almost

---

[†]For a discussion of the work of Frank and Deborah Popper of Rutgers University, see Richard Manning, *Grassland: The History, Biology, Politics, and Promise of the American Prairie*, 266ff.

certainly belongs more to the world of prophecy than prescription. The demographics of the Great Plains are fulfilling their vision sooner than anyone expected. It is a dream as old as Thomas Jefferson and the painter George Catlin, to designate some giant portion of the Louisiana Purchase as a permanent Indian and wilderness preserve and make civilization walk around it. Like so many other dreams, it is more likely to come to pass by default than by law. It seems altogether fitting and proper that things should tend this way, to the grand exodus of the European interlopers. And yet before that salutary macro-adjustment can take its course, a hundred thousand little tragedies must be played out in the corridor. I know and greatly admire a few score of the gritty lifers of the district, eking out a living in a hardtack place, flying to New York or London for three perfect days in the good years, seeing only an IMAX film and the botanical gardens in Denver in the lean, and I grieve for the inevitability of what is to come. It is a scene from Steinbeck, but there is no California to lure them to a new Eden on this time around.

XII

THE CORRIDOR IS SACRED because the people out here are closer to the macrobiotic than the rest of us. They know Thoreau's "grossest groceries,"[†] and are darned glad to be able to purchase them in the good times. Most of them have seen a calf pulled. Most of them have witnessed a fatal car accident. Most of them have hauled a bale of hay. Most of them have swept their refuse

---

[†]From *Walden*, "Economy": "It would be some advantage to live in a primitive and frontier life, though in the midst of an outward civilization, if only to learn what are the gross necessaries of life and what methods have been taken to obtain them; or even to look over the old day-books of the merchants, to see what it was that men most commonly bought at stores, what they stored, that is, what are the grossest groceries. For the improvements of ages have had but little influence on the essential laws of man's existence; as our skeleton, probably, are not to be distinguished from those of our ancestors."

off the back of the pickup into the pungent gash of the town landfill. Most of them have been to a foreclosure auction and conspired to let the owners bid low on a few carefully selected items. Most of them have dug open a drain field and smelled the smell of death and unbridled organicism at very close range. Most of them have seen a year's labor and investment blasted by a tornado that sought out their Jeffersonian rectangle, but spared that of their more prosperous neighbors a quarter of a mile away. Most of them have seen a farm wife rent an apartment in town and take a lover right under the nose of her beside-himself mate of thirty years. Most of them have played ball. Everyone can smell the feedlots (many who have been asked how they can stand it, lick their lips and retort, "Smells like money!") and everyone sees the corn and wheat sprout, grow, lie down, and die. Folks here know that an inch of rain is not a spoiled church picnic, but an unearned transfusion of economic blood, a one-year postponement of Chapter Eleven. When the horse dies they call up the rendering plant and then they smell the result as they drive on a Friday night to the VFW dance in the nearby market town. Everyone knows someone who lost a finger in a power takeoff accident. This is a landscape of fundamentals.

The sacred corridor knows death. The roads are littered with the carcasses of dead quadrupeds: skunks, foxes, cats, prairie dogs, deer, domestic dogs, porcupines, mice, and occasionally cows. Everyone who lives here runs over animals from time to time. The jobs of the district—rodeo, ranching, farming, oil rigging, trucking, welding, crop dusting, grading—are amongst the most dangerous of industrial civilization. Out here you see mangled or missing fingers on a daily basis. The cancer rates are abnormally high: herbicides and pesticides, even when they are not delivered by air assault, slosh around the district like Koolade in a jug. No town of the corridor is without its story of the wedding or high school graduation that was blasted by the news that a promising seventeen-year-old on his way to the ritual was in critical condition after a one-car accident on the county line. His girlfriend, who had just been accepted at Stanford, was killed instantly. Parents are always letting their underage children drive the pickup over to the "other place" for a tractor part. When they pull out of the driveway it is as certain that they will not return as that Patroclus will die before the gates of Troy when Achilles reluctantly sends him out to drive the Trojans back from the Greek ships. When I lived on my in-laws' farm in Kansas, we learned of a neighbor who had baled his wife. It was said to be an accident. Crop dusters auger in like mosquitoes on a windshield.

The young people grow up and leave. The rural essayist Teresa Jordan says seventeen million people have left the land since World War II. The parents of the young, who love them fiercely, advise them to leave sooner rather than later. And those who stay are narrowed by the experience and they get chips on their shoulders and say, endlessly, "well, it's a good place to raise kids." The whole Great Plains is undergoing an agonizing reverse Darwinism and nobody knows what to do about it. The answer would be revolution. Industrial gigantism would have to moderate itself at the same time the American people would have to choose Mr. J's pursuit of happiness over their addiction to getting and spending. Fat chance at either end. The whole Great Plains has begun to resemble a refugee camp. And the exodus is just beginning. My closest friend keeps saying, like a Greek chorus, "There's nobody out there now."

Almost all that matters is gone now. The buffalo are gone. There were sixty million of them when Thomas Jefferson took office on 4 March 1801 and by 1890 there were only about one hundred. For several decades they danced on the lip of extinction. Now they are making a slow incestuous comeback—if the ratio of two hundred thousand to sixty million can honestly be called a comeback. Virtually no plains county is without an entrepreneur who has decided to try his hand at beefalo or cattalo or, occasionally, buffalo *per se*. The grizzly bears are gone. Lewis and Clark encountered one south of Bismarck, North Dakota in 1804, and at one time they could be found scattered all over the plains country. Now there are perhaps three hundred in the lower forty-eight states. They live on probation among the garbage dumps at Yellowstone and up around the Canadian border along the Idaho-Montana line. In my daughter Catherine's lifetime they will probably slip like Sitting Bull into Canada, into the Grandmother's Land. The Elk are gone.

And of course the Indians are gone—or rather just doomed in their spoil bank concentration camps where the only light is the casino. The Indians were decimated to the point of genocide; the buffalo nearly exterminated; the wolves all killed off; the majestic rivers channeled, dammed, drained, and befouled; the ancient grasses plowed under and the good earth allowed to blow away; the organic curve of the earth trapped in the web of Jefferson's rationalist, rectangular survey grid—all this to make it possible for a few hundred thousand white people to try to carry wetland agriculture to a landscape that could not support it. And the fact is that they failed. They failed (on the whole) in the homestead era after the Civil War. They failed in the Reclamation Era at the turn of the century. They failed in the Depression-Dust Bowl cataclysm of the 1930s. And they have failed again in the petrochemical epoch of the post-war years (on the whole, through no fault of their own).

If they had just left it alone as Zebulon Pike and Stephen Long suggested, it might have been the world's most remarkable park— a homeland for the bison and the nomadic, free Lakota, among others, a homeland for the grizzled bear and the pilgrims of Bear Butte. If, on the other hand, all that destruction, all that European manipulation of landscape, all that certitude and righteousness and pioneer mythology had led to the creation of a great civilization on the Great Plains, it might have been worth the black karma that produced it. But even at their best moments, the Great Plains have never been more than a drama of marginality and provincialism. You can sense the insecurity as you drive the sacred corridor. No rusted out singlewide, no prefab, particle-board bungalow, no dilapidated two-story farmhouse is without its gleaming satellite dish to cut the boredom and pipe in something with color and spice. Most Euro-Americans don't want to live on the land. They want to occupy it.

To have seen the Great Plains as Lewis and Clark saw them in 1804, filled with fierce remarkable peoples who danced on ice cakes in the flood-swollen Missouri, who placed bits of food into the mouths of the skulls of the buffalo they killed to show gratitude and humility, who believed that the Medicines of the Cosmos and certain life skills could be transmitted by sexual intercourse (not original sin but original Spirit), who filched beans from the prairie mice, but left a small supply in the burrow so that their four-legged providers would not want through the long winter; to have topped a ridge and seen in a single valley 75,000 buffalo ruminating the plains grasses and drinking the creeks dry; to have witnessed the Missouri River when it was still a river, un-dammed, un-levied, un-channeled, un-tapped, un-tainted, shifting its course like a spoiled adolescent, grinding out its sluggish destiny over a windswept land, *that* would have been paradise on earth. Who would not have wished to visit the sacred corridor before we did to it what we have done to it? But of course, I would not have seen it in 1804, for I would not have been one of the "good hunters, stout, healthy, unmarried men accustomed to the woods and capable of bearing bodily fatigue in a pretty considerable degree" of the Lewis and Clark Expedition. I would have been a copy clerk in a Boston law firm or a penniless schoolmaster in the employ of the crackpot Federalist Noah Webster.

The paradox is not lost on me. I neither lived then nor live there, and whatever I have taken from the spirit of the place has come in those few moments when the windows were rolled down or when I stripped off my Vibrum-soled boots among the prickly pears and the buffalo grass. I can feel the keys and the credit cards in my pocket as I walk the ridges opinionating about the evils of industrial capitalism. Wolves and Indians are more romantic when they are no longer a threat. Those who actually live out where the wind blows in thoroughgoing pragmatism are— in almost every respect—more authentic than those who parachute in with a pack full of dried food and prophylaxis. I want my buffalo robe, but I would rather not chew it soft. I know enough not entirely to trust my nostalgia.

Still.

As long as there is cheap gas in America, as long as I can light out for the territories for a week or ten days every summer, when the pressures of more civilized places have become too great, as long as two trail dirt tracks promise some improbable mystery on the other side of the vanishing point, as long as I retain the impulse to cast my keys to the wind, as long as the coyotes nip and yip and howl at the moon, as long as the Thunder Beings continue to roll across the grasses in majesty and terror and I know enough to stop and listen to their rumbled voices, as long as there is licorice in the convenience stores, as long as there is a nymph who will sit with me on a pine ridge and dream of empires of the mind, as long as Indian FM radio blares out Neil Diamond followed by Kiss followed by the Red Willow Fancy Dance Drumers of Wamblee, as long as a U2 song is dedicated to Grandma Wanita Kills With a Lance on her eighty-fifth birthday, I'll drift in the critical times to my spot on the north end of Camp Crook, South Dakota. And read not.

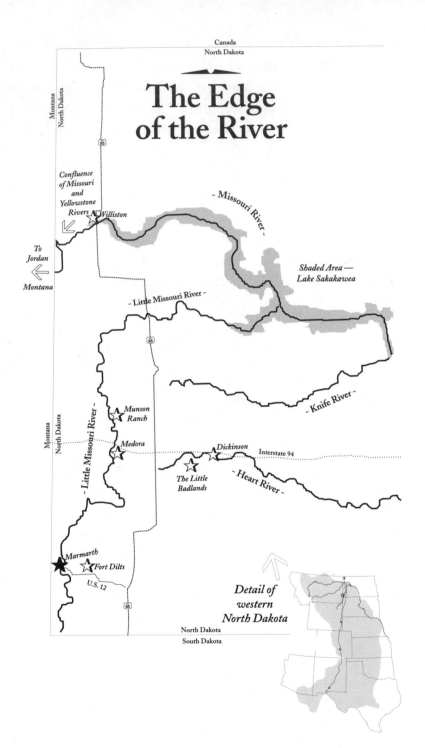

The Edge
of the River

Canada
North Dakota

Montana
North Dakota

85

Confluence
of Missouri
and
Yellowstone
Rivers ☆ Williston

- Missouri River -

Shaded Area —
Lake Sakakawea

To
Jordan

Montana

- Little Missouri River -

85

- Knife River -

Montana
North Dakota

- Little Missouri River -

☆ Munson
Ranch

☆ Medora

☆ Dickinson   Interstate 94

☆
The Little
Badlands

- Heart River -

★ Marmarth
☆ Fort Dilts

U.S. 12

85

*Detail of
western
North Dakota*

North Dakota
South Dakota

Growing Up on the
Edge of the River

Athene/Mentor

W HAT WAS IT LIKE TO GROW UP in western North Dakota?" I was asked the other day by someone who had never been there, and had no idea of the state beyond flatness, arctic weather, and low population density. "You mention it so often, and you speak of it with such a reverence. What's so important about it?"

It is true that if (say at a New Age conference) I had to make a list of the words that characterize me, in descending order of importance, my list would read: 1. Father, 2. Scholar, 3. North Dakotan, 4. Jeffersonian, 5. . . .

And yet, if one hundred people who know me were asked to make the same list for me, I doubt that North Dakotan would make its appearance in any but a handful of lists.

So, as my niece Jenny likes to put it, "What's up with that?"

North Dakota is an improbable backwater of no consequence to the nation's or the world's consciousness. It is far from the thoroughfares of anything that matters—socially, politically, culturally, economically, historically, demographically. It is in many regards the most rural and decentralized place in America. If North Dakota went to a New Age conference (the probability of which approaches zero) its list would begin: 1. Farm state, 2. Family, 3. Brutal climate, 4. Outback.

Actually, North Dakota is rather thin-skinned about the rigors of its climate in its dealings with outsiders, and somewhat too smug about those same rigors in internal discussion.

It is, among other things, almost impossible to separate my actual feelings about North Dakota from the conventions of rural romance. All North Dakotans are in some sense modest Jeffersonians. Somewhere deep in our souls we feel more virtuous than folks who grew up in less pastoral circumstances. Many Dakotans even regard Fargo (pop. 90,599) as the road to Sodom. Even so, there are plenty of people who consider the term "spirit of place" both pretentious and nonsensical. I meet hundreds of people every year. Nobody ever says, "There's something different about you. Are you by any chance from the Great Plains?" In outward respects I am merely an unmistakable American: in posture, language, consumption habits, education, and taste.

So how deep do you have to probe before you get to the North Dakotan in me? Or in anyone?

I grew up in Dickinson, North Dakota, when its population was about 12,500. Unfortunately, I did not grow up on a farm, though I spent holidays and summers on my grandparents' dairy farm in Minnesota. Dickinson was the kind of town you could walk out of in less than thirty minutes[†]. Depending on the wind, you could smell the stockyards or the sewage lagoon from anywhere in town. A couple of dozen trains whistled through every day. Until I finished college a few of them even carried passengers. Dickinson had all the amenities: a one-screen movie theater, a Dairy Queen, and a beach for summer swimming at the local reservoir. The town was divided between Catholics

---

[†]This, it seems to me, should be the definition of a Jeffersonian community.

(including some Ukrainians) and Protestants, with rival school systems and sports teams. This provided most of the dramatic tension in our village existence. Athletes in my school routinely accused our sole radio station of bias in sports coverage (the only "coverage" there was) because the sportscaster (Bob "Trinity" Weiler) was a known Catholic.

Because I was born in 1955, I entered consciousness on the cusp of the age of television. My parents had one clunky old black and white set. We received two channels—CBS and NBC. The transmitters were primitive. We lost the signal in any storm. A repairman named Bud was always squatting behind the set replacing vacuum tubes. During the great blizzard of 1965 (one of the best of the century) the receiving tower went down early and we watched a locally broadcast TV movie called *The Thing* a dozen times in four days. It was literally the only show in town. It was, appropriately enough, the story of a monstrous carrot-like man who thawed out of the Arctic ice and was, as a consequence, not well understood or accepted in polite society.[†] Our television set was boxy, hot, and it smelled of vacuum tubes. We did not even dream, then, of remote control.

My family consists of great readers, but because my parents were committed to the childrearing "principles" of the 1960s, I grew much more acquainted with Mr. Spock and Gilligan than with the characters in Dickens or Melville. I remember lazy Sunday afternoons watching Walter Cronkite's *The Twentieth Century*, Saturday night prize fights and *Have Gun — Will Travel*[‡], and the shock of the blackness of NBA basketball. We all celebrated the coming of color television (vivid on NBC, pastel on CBS) about the time of *Get Smart*, *Camp Runamuck*, and the

---

[†]*The Thing* (1951), starring James Arness, Kenneth Tobey, and Margaret Sheridan, produced by Howard Hawks and directed by Christian Nyby.
[‡]The series, starring Richard Boone as the "Paladin," began on September 14, 1957, and ran for six successful seasons.

Carol Burnett Show. We religiously watched the few programs broadcast in color not because they were good, but because they were bright. I saw my first color broadcast in 1965, at a friend's house, when the Minnesota Twins went to the World Series (they lost). By the time I was a teenager the television in our house was turned on most of the waking hours of the day. We ate around it. By the time I was 13 we ate at the kitchen table two or three times per year, at the dining room table on Thanksgiving and Christmas. We conducted our fragmentary family meetings under television's watchful eye. For many years on end my parents scarcely ever missed an episode of *The Tonight Show*. Johnny Carson influenced my humor, my mannerisms, even my sense of values more than any teacher, any preacher, of my youth.

The point is that my childhood was probably not very different from that of a youngster in Duluth, Detroit, or Manchester, New Hampshire. In the postwar decades, the great homogenization of American culture was effected by capitalism and mass media with a zeal and efficiency that suggests actual conspiracy. Not even North Dakota was immune.

My family ignored the landscape of the northern Great Plains as much as possible. In some sense, we were not even aware that we lived on the Plains. The only time we ever saw the countryside was during our quarterly visit to the farm in Fergus Falls, Minnesota, and then we looked upon the 350-mile journey as an ordeal, often undertaken at night to make the time pass more quickly. We preferred to align ourselves with the Middle West, which suggested stability, Main Street, and rain.

We were well aware of summer heat and the brutal cold of North Dakota winters, of course, and storm watches were common in every season. Hardly a winter went by that did not kill off a few people, often travelers from elsewhere, who broke down or went off the highway in a blizzard, or Indians who froze to death in the gutters where they had passed out upon leaving the bars of Mandan or New Town. We went on one or two picnics each summer in the badlands out near the Montana border, but only at the command of my father's employer. Nobody in my family ever said, let's go out this weekend and see the country. Let's go camping, hiking, canoeing, or even picnicking. My father looked upon hunting as a species of barbarism, and even fishing he dismissed as one of humanity's more tedious diversions. Even indoor hobbies were seen by my family as avocations of the dull.

Nobody in my family ever spoke of the beauty of the place, let alone spirit of place. Spirit didn't exist for my father—anywhere in the universe—and my mother boxed it into the church and perhaps, from time to time, private meditations. In another marriage she might have been a serious Christian. My sister and I were as secular and materialistic and addicted to American pop culture as it is possible to be in the middle of nowhere. If we reflected on being North Dakotans at all, it was undoubtedly to bemoan our fate in living so far from anything that was interesting.

My family had no interest in rural culture (bees, reunions, ball games, bazaars, church socials, outdoor sports, snowmobiles, ATVs, country western bars and dancing) and only a token interest in the Western in film or book. It is true that my mother, a speed reader, had consumed all of the works of North Dakota's prose-laureate Louis L'Amour, and that she once wrote to the producers of *Gunsmoke* to ask if what she had heard, but could not in good conscience believe, namely that Matt Dillon and Kitty . . . well, were intimate or something, but we owned neither cowboy boots nor horses, and we had never been to a rodeo, in spite of the fact that Dickinson has genuine historical links to the cowboy past, and it sits on the edge of some of the finest range in the world.

We were middle class, middle Americans abstracted from nature and climate as much as possible. We knew we were from an unusual place. There was virtually no crime. There were Indians in the vicinity, but we hardly ever saw them and we weren't then concerned about their culture or their problems. On welfare check day, used car prices went up all over town. Nothing more. There were perhaps a few seasonal Hispanic migrant laborers, most of them at the other end of the state. There was one black family in my town. I went to first grade with Rosaria Cobb. We were told not to notice that she was black. My parents warned us sternly that the common schoolyard rhyme, "Eenie Meanie Minie Mo," must be altered to catch a "thimble" by the toe. Out where we lived the few black families were granted the status of honorary whites so long as they didn't call attention to themselves. If they offended the law or the social structure, most white folks reckoned it was no surprise. The black population was slightly larger in Minot and Grand Forks, where the U.S. Air Force maintains Strategic Air Command (SAC) bases. No Asians lived in North Dakota. "Mase" Masad was our most prominent exotic—that is, Syrian or something. He had olive skin, sold hides and fur, and dealt in junk, and owned a motel cleverly called the Nodak.

Virtually all of us were northern and central Europeans. On the whole our demographics were homogenous—Norwegians, Germans from Russia, Germans from Germany, Bohemians. Almost every North Dakota town contained a Sons of Norway lodge. In Dickinson you could order lutefisk (Norwegian: briny, salty cod), borscht (Russian: beet soup), fleischkuechle (German: a deep-fried spiced burger), and lefse (Norwegian: potato pancake) in almost any restaurant.

We were virtually never mentioned in national affairs. When we were, North Dakota served more as a synonym for the end of the end of the universe than the heart of the heart of the country.

Even so, we took a perverse pride to hear ourselves mentioned—even as American Siberians—on the *Tonight Show* or in a *Superman* movie. We frequently won the contest for "coldest spot in the nation," though we in western North Dakota were quick to point out that we lived in the "banana belt," where temperatures were generally 5-10 degrees warmer (that is -5 F rather than -15 F) than in the Red River Valley to the East. Statistical note: average annual temperature in North Dakota, 42 degrees.

We were provincial enough to take pride in our state's best-known Americans: Peggy Lee, Louis L'Amour, Roger Maris, Eric Sevareid (opinion was mixed here), Angie Dickinson, and of course the Champagne Music Man, Lawrence Welk, of Strasburg. Keep in mind that all of these heroes left the state as soon as possible and never came back except to receive awards. Our superheroes were Theodore Roosevelt (1858-1919; we called him "Teddy" with a grating sort of familiarity) and the Marquis de Morès (1858-96), a French nobleman who squandered a fortune to build a meat packing empire in the badlands of the West, and gave us our most romantic narrative. His wife Medora gave her name to North Dakota's only recreational village. De Morès and Roosevelt were both outsiders who came briefly to North Dakota, before it was a state, but whose historical importance lies elsewhere. There is something pathetic in the way North Dakotans cling to these exotic visitors from a more glamorous, indeed less democratic, world beyond our borders. Decades later Roosevelt was kind enough to say if he hadn't spent those formative years in the North Dakota badlands, he would never have . . . etc. You can hear this mantra of borrowed respectability from almost any North Dakotan on demand.

We did not then know enough to prize Thomas McGrath, a major American poet from Sheldon, North Dakota, or the novelist Lois Philip Hudson, or Maxwell Anderson, a playwright of real distinction. Larry Woiwode, Kathleen Norris, and Louise Erdrich all came to prominence after my consciousness had been formed.

At the time I entered high school in 1969, I knew nothing of any significance about North Dakota. At no point in my education had I studied North Dakota history. The state-mandated study units on North Dakota history were routinely ignored in the schools. We took special pride in our massive production of hard red spring wheat and we begrudged Kansas for edging us in total production of all classes of wheat. No teacher had ever taught anything—save bigotry—about Native American culture. Nobody had ever informed me that North Dakota had a remarkable— and radical—political history. We knew Lewis and Clark had floated through in 1804-06, but I had never heard a single detail of their experience in the state. Men with unpronounceable French names had passed through in the 1830s and 40s, and the first pioneers had come shortly after the Civil War. We knew that George Armstrong Custer had headquartered near Mandan before he went out to Montana and got himself killed. I knew the state consisted mostly of Norwegians and Germans. We were, after all, the only American state whose capital was named after a German dictator. I knew that the geographic center of North America was located near Rugby, in the north-central part of the state. This fact gives North Dakotans the curious satisfaction of combating what they know to be their utter marginality with a purely statistical claim to centrality.

Thus far in my life, I had camped out exactly one night: at a wired, plumbed, and paved campground thirty-five miles from home, in a floppy canvas Sears tent (borrowed) so complicated to erect that it inspired in my brilliant but sedentary father a paroxysm of rage. So far as I know I had never been on a dirt road. I had never hiked on a trail that was not made of asphalt. I could not identify a single tree except a cottonwood. I had never caught a fish. I had never encountered a rattlesnake. I had never been to a community festival of any sort. Until now I had lived entirely in my house, our series of cars, my school, and with James T. Kirk and Little Joe and Hoss Cartwright.

I could not then appreciate North Dakota's simple virtues: its intense spirit of friendliness and cooperation, its restrained piety, its unpretentiousness, its equalitarianism, its commitment to fair play, community, decency, its economic fundamentalism, its willingness to be imposed upon in the name of national defense. Only years later did I learn to appreciate that quality of the North Dakota personality that leads its citizens in major airports to leave their purses lying about, to greet each other knowing that the other is surely not a complete stranger (there is a common friend or relative—or at least there is Lawrence Welk), and to compare the finishing work on each other's leisure suit. Break down on any North Dakota road, particularly the non-interstates, and natives practically compete for the honor of pulling over to assist.

My awakening came in 1971, when I met a man who turned my life upside down. I was 16. Of course, I survived other, more standard, awakenings during this period. They have their own poignancy, but they say nothing particular about North Dakota. I had gone to work for the *Dickinson Press* as a photographer and cub reporter. It was a newspaper so small (circulation 6000) and so hapless that in the course of four years I was able to dabble in every aspect of the newspaper business, except advertising. I even helped run the presses for a summer. The paper had recently been purchased by a Texas entrepreneur, who had decided to convert it from hot lead type to offset production. That technological revolution was one of the most interesting things I ever witnessed. Among other things, it recapitulated in miniature almost the entire industrial revolution in the western world: the giddiness, the uncertainty, the miracle of new machines, the fear of those who felt they would be left behind by the innovations, even some minor Ludditism.

My savior was a *Dickinson Press* staff reporter (he liked to say staff *writer*), an environmentalist, a political rebel, and— apparently—some kind of hippie. His name was Michael Jacobs. No one called him Michael. He was Mike or, more often, Jacobs, and he was clearly a man on his way to major achievement. He was tall, good looking, breathtakingly efficient at his work, and cocky. He could write like the wind and he knew it. The other reporter, an amiable buffoon, spent the whole day hammering out a few paragraphs of awkward prose. Mike would saunter in in the early afternoon, oblivious to the editor's outrage, make a few calls, knock out three or four stories in ninety minutes, hand them over without proofing them, and depart. He wore a moustache and his hair was a modified Beatles mop. He was married to his high school friend Suezette Bieri. They lived in a modest two-story bungalow on the east end of town. Their house was filled with books, some of them subversive, and exotic newspapers, some of them foreign and printed on onion skin.

Michael bailed me out of school eight or nine times a month to go on journalistic forays throughout western North Dakota. I wanted desperately to be a writer. He was my idea of prose elegance. He never wasted a word. He said what he had to say clearly and quickly and simply, and then he stopped writing. At a time when most stories in the *Dickinson Press* were barely literate, his work was always lucid, precise. Muscular.

Once the paperwork in the high school admissions office was dispatched, we'd stop to purchase sodas and licorice and drive out somewhere into the country to gather news. He asked me to take photographs to illustrate his stories, and he assigned me— mute inglorious apprentice—to write my own news reports of the same events. Over these I agonized as I have done over nothing clse in subsequent life except in Thomas Clayton's Shakespeare courses at the University of Minnesota. Writing involved so many variables about which I knew little or nothing—grammar, for example—and spelling, clarity, a good vocabulary modestly employed, an eye for detail, an organized mind—that I was more often than not simply filled with shame. I worried that I would never learn to marshal a narrative in plain sentences. For a long time Jacobs reinforced this fear. He provided scouring critiques of my puerile efforts to report and write.

I still have my typewritten copy of my first story, about a flood on the Little Missouri River; Mike's savage corrections in red ink; my revision draft; the story *he* eventually dashed off for the front page of the *Dickinson Press*; and my grainy photograph that ran beside his spare account of the flood. This little file is one of my relics. My prose was wretched: a sophomore's English composition. His criticism came from the Ayn Rand rather than the self-esteem school of pedagogy. We repeated this process a thousand times. I got better but never good.

I was abashed but thrilled by his mentoring. Nobody had ever taken me seriously before. No teacher had ever suggested to me that the native wit of an intelligent prairie boy was not a sufficient tool for adult life. Jacobs used to assert, with his swagger, that anything worth saying could be said in less than 500 words. He preferred short tight sentences. Above all, he knew how to coordinate language. When I read his articles late at night, in the incandescent printing hall, literally hot off the press, while Nick Morrell and his children, a squad of Dickensian urchins, kept the behemoth thundering and thumping out 6000 low-resolution, 24-page copies of the *Dickinson Press*, or under the dim streetlight in the alley of the nearby bakery where we waited for the night crew to bring out fresh hot pumpkin muffins, I thought, "journalism doesn't get any better than this." I always looked for my photo credits and cutlines first (I even agonized over these), then I read every word Jacobs had generated for that morning's edition. In many respects, on the other end of decades of indefatigable reading from Plato to T.S. Eliot, I still think Mike Jacobs the finest writer of unself-conscious prose that I have ever met.

Michael's greatest service to my mind was to turn to me in the car one day and say, "Scoop," for such he had nicknamed me, "you are interesting, but I don't want to be your friend unless you read books." This was an unexpected blow. I never read books. Not even school textbooks. I had probably not read a book through voluntarily for half a dozen years. What did books have to do with anything? More to the point, what did they have to do with good journalism or friendship? What an odd demand, and an unfair one.

There was a long silence. I knew even then, in my dim adolescent consciousness, that I was standing at a crossroads, and that I was about to take the road less traveled by. I was so enamored of Michael's talent and so grateful for his friendship that I agreed, sullenly, to read. I was determined to do whatever it took to impress him. I accepted his Faustian bargain. Soon enough, he put books into my hands: *Slaughterhouse Five*, *The Teachings of Don Juan*, *Trout Fishing in America*, and (one that would survive the 60s) *Walden*. I never did get through Richard Brautigan, but I dutifully slogged my way through the others. For years afterwards I ladled tags from Kurt Vonnegut into my letters: "Listen!" and "so it goes," and "unstuck in time."

It was not very long before I learned to read with some pleasure. In the first Christmas of our friendship Michael and his wife Suezette gave me a package that included a copy of Ambrose Bierce's *Devil's Dictionary* and Strunk and White's slim masterpiece, *The Elements of Style*. It was the treasure of that

Christmas, one of the few gifts I can recall from a lifetime of splendid materialism. I caressed the two slim volumes (still on my priority shelf thirty years later) as if they were rare medieval manuscripts. Jacobs' gift eclipsed many more expensive gifts my parents had sacrificed to provide that year. No doubt they were hurt by my indifference to their generosity and my obsession with a couple of paperbacks Mike had probably bought *en passant*, but they never said anything. That was their style.

I have, since 1971, been trying to catch up as a reader. It is a chimerical, at times a tragic, quest. I'm sure I read vastly more than the average American, but it is still much less than the top 1% of readers, not enough even to keep up with the best that is published annually, even in my "fields," and I know now, in mid-life, that I will never be able to catch up, never read even through the old discredited canons, never overcome the habits and the setback of my illiterate childhood. My library runs to over 8,000 volumes now. My book purchases were one of the greatest sources of tension in my marriage (to a reading intellectual), but I feel permanently stunted, in spite of a career of hectic bibliophilia. In the presence of serious intellectuals I sense that my poverty of culture must show like dandruff on a blue suit. I am, moreover, the slowest of readers. My mind actually mouths the words that I read on the page, though at least I have learned to keep my lips shut. My classmate Odie taught me that. Not only did he read with his mouth open, but his breath smelled of peanut butter. Michael handed me a memo one day and, observing my plodding study of its contents, told me that I was too slow a reader to accomplish much. That still rankles after thirty years. He awakened me as a reader and as a fledgling writer in those desultory journeys. He also opened the door to my political consciousness.

Mike Jacobs found himself shouldered with the burden of Jeremiah in the early 1970s. In a sense, his journalism had to yield to his ideology. The nation was facing for the first time the limits of its resource base. Analysts had wrongly projected that energy consumption would continue to grow at the historically aberrant rates that followed World War II. There was a national hunger for new energy reserves, particularly after the Arabs ceased to sell oil to the western world for a pittance. Since the easiest pools of domestic crude oil had long since been exploited, coal was being promoted as the most abundant and most easily accessible energy source for the future. The northern plains were coal-rich. North Dakota had a virtual monopoly on the supply of one of the most attractive coals for electricity production—a sub-bituminous variety called lignite.

Energy production companies were circulating grandiose plans to build dozens of coal-fired generating plants, coal gasification plants, liquefaction facilities, and coal-slurry pipelines to carry North Dakota's resource to burners as far away as Arkansas. Mineral speculators were quietly buying up lease rights to tens of thousands of acres of North Dakota crop and rangeland. State governments in Montana, Wyoming, Colorado and North Dakota were being lobbied to keep environmental reclamation laws painless to development. Boosters promised boom times on the northern plains: population growth, economic stabilization, malls, McDonalds, increased property values, better roads and airports, windfalls for the gumptious and a rising tide of prosperity for all Dakotans. Meanwhile, a zany irrigation scheme known as Garrison Diversion was being promoted—and in part built—to irrigate (unnecessarily) a few tens of thousands of acres in central North Dakota and to provide water for municipal and industrial use throughout the state, and beyond. Every day, we were being told that the dynamo, not the wheat farm, was the future of North Dakota.

It was the last gasp of industrial gigantism in twentieth-century America. A generation later such massive projects seem unthinkable. That era in American history is over. Back then, when the concrete on North Dakota's two Interstate highways was still drying, the sulphurization of the plains was widely promoted as the solution to the historical dependence of the region on agriculture. Presidents of the United States were seen turning down the White House thermostat on national television. North Dakota was eager to comply with the national thirst for energy, if only because we suddenly felt indispensable for a change.

The governor of North Dakota, Arthur A. Link, was a husbandman with a powerful love of the land and the agricultural heritage of his people. He played his fiddle at county fairs. He rode spirited horses in rodeo grand entrances. He danced at powwows, an honorary member of every North Dakota tribe: Chief Charging Eagle. He spoke in the half-assimilated European accents of Dakota people. He had a kind of reticent spirit of place. He urged caution in the face of the energy promoters, but he was a gentle man among earthmovers, and he had the unfortunate habit of falling asleep at many of the meetings he attended. In one of his memorable speeches, he wondered aloud if a state that had grown so much corn and wheat should engage now in a "one time harvest" of fossil fuels. That became the title of Mike Jacobs' book. Even so, it seemed as if North Dakota would be unable—or unwilling—to resist the rape of its swelling landscape. The boomers called it "mineral extraction," and they blandly promised something called "reclamation."

Jacobs was not alone in opposing coal development in North Dakota, but he became the most energetic and effective spokesman for restraint. He championed conservation, even preservation, in a series of carefully-researched articles in the *Dickinson Press* and in state and regional journals. He spent hundreds of hours in the dank basements of county courthouses documenting the pattern of mineral leasing and proving that industry assurances about the modesty of its intentions were bald lies. He attended dozens of legally-mandated impact hearings all over the northern plains. He lectured, including at my high school, about the way North Dakota could expect to change if we let the developers have their way with us. Eventually he wrote a superb book, *One Time Harvest: Coal Development and Our Future* (photographs by his young friend Clay Jenkinson), which nearly broke his spirit and his marriage, and which established him as the most articulate voice of a new generation of Dakotans. He founded and edited the *Onlooker*, a left-of-center occasional newspaper that served as the bulletin board for environmental and social virtue in North Dakota for several years. He was the only young Dakotan confident enough to tell the state how to think, and to challenge the long-standing patriotic passivity that led Dakotans to acquiesce in whatever absent men of power told them was their duty.

I was in awe of his talents, his character, his power, his politics. He was the first charismatic of my life. He subscribed to *Rolling Stone* (not then a music industry shill), listened to the Nitty Gritty Dirt Band and Bob Dylan, drank wine at a time when this was seldom done in rural America, and experimented with the lesser drugs. He had first appeared on the North Dakota stage as an articulate opponent of the war in Vietnam, which he denounced—amid great controversy—from his platform as the editor of the student newspaper at the University of North Dakota at Grand Forks. My parents were principled left-of-center Democrats but, except for one tepid anti-war rally in front of the post office in Dickinson, they expressed their politics only in the voting booth and over the dinner table at the local Elks club. They were exceedingly normal. My father was a banker, my mother a school teacher. Michael was a cultural malcontent. They lived quietly. Michael was as outspoken as it was possible to be and still hold a job. He had extraordinary friends who lived eccentric lives. All of them seemed to have had dark adventures elsewhere. They talked about Che Guevara and, occasionally, Trotsky. They had been to Woodstock or the 1968 Chicago convention. They read Noam Chomsky. They smoked dope. They called policemen pigs. They hugged each other tightly at each greeting, each departure. They strategized endlessly about the draft laws. Several of them lived outside the official American economy. They were honest, engaged, profane, opinionated, carnal, hopeful, as well as deeply cynical.

Mike and Suezette took me to a wedding once, north of Jamestown, of two of their friends I barely knew. The wedding was held in a barn. Perhaps 300 people attended. The adults looked like tolerant 60s Lutherans in their suits and summer dresses, and the young people looked like Grateful Dead groupies who were doing their best to clean up their act for just one day. Corki wore a gorgeous wedding gown—perhaps the frills were gone, but none of the traditional adults had reason to be displeased. After the service—performed by a with-it young minister and characterized by homemade vows and guitar interludes—was over, there was a reception in the barn with cake, a receiving line, petite sandwiches, toasts, and the usual beer and champagne. *De rigueur.* Then, precisely one hour later, the hundred or so adults left as if on cue within the space of ten minutes. The instant the last of them passed through the double doors of the barn, collars were loosened, ties and shoes were sloughed, the champagne ceased to require glasses, the guitarist was joined by two barefoot men who played a tub and a washboard, and the barn was suffused with the sweet haylike smell of marijuana. It was a metamorphosis worthy of Ovid: the scene had changed from respectability to sweet misrule within minutes, and nobody had been offended. I had been to very few weddings, none so remarkable as this. I enjoyed both portions of the afternoon, and I especially admired the graceful way in which the adults yielded to the inevitable. Corki dancing in her white dress, barefooted on the wooden floor of the barn, lifting the hem to the middle of her calves to the sound of the washtub jam, delicate beads of sweat glistening on her forehead, was one of the most erotic images of my adolescence. We all felt a new age was dawning.

I worshipped Jacobs' world through an adolescent fog. I knew I would never be a genuine exemplar of counterculture—indeed I was routinely reminded by Mike's friends, if not by him, that I had been born too late to know the golden age of the 60s. Looking back on those long evenings of drugged-out music, tendentious conversations about the war and the "establishment" (if ever a word dated a generation, this was it), the tatterdemalion crew that drifted through Mike and Suezette's household to eat lasagna and pass a jug of wine unwiped from mouth to mouth, I feel the same flush of affectionate embarrassment that comes with watching *Easy Rider* from a twenty (er, thirty) years' retrospect.

Even so, I know that my time in the circle of Michael Jacobs set the patterns of my adult life. I learned to tolerate and even celebrate eccentricity. I discovered that hippies were not merely shallow Epicureans. A thread of idealism was woven into my soul. I learned to suspect men of authority in all walks of life. I learned to resist—and often reject—received truths. I learned that there are many paths to the Great Spirit. I learned to get my facts right. Above all, I learned what disciplined prose can be. I have never found that mix of simplicity, candor, and modest thoroughness in my own writing, but it remains a standard against which I judge all that I read and write. It was all alive in the soul of Mike Jacobs. My life's goal was simple. I wanted to be like Michael.

All this I might have learned in Madison, Wisconsin, or Orlando, Florida. What I have been describing, after all, is waking up in the early 70s. It is true that Mike Jacobs was an extremely unusual North Dakotan, and that the outback innocence of the state enabled me to enjoy a mobility and freedom that my parents would not have permitted in New Jersey or Los Angeles. But my story so far is not much rooted in the land.

Michael's greatest gift to me was that he awakened my soul to North Dakota. He took me out into the countryside and taught me how to read it. He introduced me to the badlands, to the paleontological heritage of the Hell Creek formation. He taught me the history of the state, a history similar to, but in some regards much more strange and fascinating than, the standard Norwegian pioneer story I had heard a hundred times. He introduced me to landowners, government range supervisors, old, well-known Dakotans, American Indians. He showed me secret places that he had discovered in his wanderings. He took me to Marmarth, in extreme southwestern North Dakota, a magical oasis in the Little Missouri River valley, perhaps the most remarkable place I have ever seen, a town of about 100 railroad retirees, ranchers, people marginal in the economy, poachers, oil patchers, black market truckers, genuine desperadoes, and about fifty others who simply find it congenial to live out on the other side of where all the grids break down. He initiated me to the sacred places of North Dakota—some historically sacred like Killdeer Mountain or Lost Bridge, some sacred only to Michael, like the little badlands south of South Heart, or some obscure campsites on the Little Missouri River.

He used to spring me from school one or two days per week, more if my parents didn't squawk. Eventually I had to get special dispensation from the school board in order to graduate; my countless absences had broken a school record. Fortunately there was an enlightened vice principal at my high school, who realized that I was getting a first rate education under the tutelage of Mike Jacobs, and a third rate education from the public educational system. He signed absence slips for me, and he winked at my contrivances for skipping school. Later he quit his job and became an interstate trucker, and he removed the radios from his rig. In his indirect way, he was as good a school mentor as I have ever had.

Jacobs and I explored the whole western third of North Dakota together, dirt road by dirt road, sometimes two-rut track by two-rut track. "You know you are west of the Missouri River," he'd say, "because you don't have to look both ways when you get out to pee by the side of the road. East of the river, you have to look first." We hiked endlessly, in silence, he in front, I behind, across most of the vistas of the region. I'd never walked the plains until I met Mike Jacobs. At the end of a ten-mile hike overlooking the Missouri River, he'd say, "You know what I really want to do right now? Wash my face."

He taught me how to think and argue in hundreds of informal Socratic dialogues on every possible subject. We often went out to some lonely place alongside a sluggish river and just sat—a few score of words exchanged in five hours, or spread across a whole day. We were inseparable. Some people thought it odd that he would find a boy half his age interesting, and some thought it bizarre that I would want to turn away from proms, homecomings, ball games, beer, and the endless process of trying to become a sexual initiate, to spend my time with a no-nonsense intellectual who chose to spend his time to reading and hiking in godforsaken places. It didn't seem odd to me. Michael was the first person who ever sought a relationship with my soul. It was like leaving the larval stage and getting wings. I had never been alive before. One day he gave me a copy of the *Dream of Chuang-tse*,[†] in which a man, waking from a dream, wonders if he is a man who has been dreaming he is a butterfly, or rather a butterfly now dreaming he is a man. That was how it was.

[†]Zhuangzi (Chuang-tse) c. 286 BCE.

Eventually he and Suezette moved to Jamestown, across the state, and from his new pivot he taught me to appreciate glacial lakes and potholes, the rolling prairies out near Chase Lake and Harvey, and the Sheyenne River Valley in southeastern North Dakota, the odd drainage system of the Devils Lake region. Wherever we drove on those endless days of my childhood, Michael knew the most interesting characters. He was intimate with the official and the quirky history of every place. He knew the geography. He had read the often tedious local literature. He studied the weekly newspapers. In every town he knew the person who knew what there was to know about the place. It was invariably a newspaperman or a public official of the second tier. He knew where to find the best caramel rolls in every village. He knew historic sites that the State Historical Society had never catalogued. He radiated a respect for the heritage of North Dakota, though it had little to do with the usual pioneer and political mythology that Dakotans prefer to the truth. I learned to understand something about the Sioux, the Ojibwa, the Mandan, the Hidatsa, the Assiniboine, and the Arikara. They were no longer just Indians to me.

It is clear that I adored Mike Jacobs in a diffident boy's way, but through him I fell in love with the Great Plains and North Dakota with a passion that has given me more heartache than all of my subsequent relations with humanity. I learned to appreciate the contours of buttes, breaks, badlands, coulees, bench lands, grasslands, scoria, pine ridges, and geosynclines. I learned the history of the great migration of Europeans into the American heartland after the Civil War, and its impact on the indigenous peoples who were thriving in their fierce and minimalist way in the Missouri River Valley. He gave me a copy of Dee Brown's *Bury My Heart at Wounded Knee* and taught me that the decimation of the Indian peoples of America was not a necessary evil or a cultural inevitability, but the fruit of a worldview and a set of policies that were chosen not destined. I learned of North Dakota's radical political past, a source of embarrassment and perplexity to most respectable citizens. There was a time when farmers took control of their destiny and North Dakota was— briefly—a socialist soviet. That was 1917. Now we were a colony again, and it looked as if it were going to get worse.

I learned to read the weather, the wind, the clouds, the color of sunsets, the phenomena of night (auroras, moon crystals, moon shade). I learned to walk for hours on the grasslands, to pluck a stalk of grama grass, square it off, and stick it between my teeth as a meditational rosary. This was Jacobs' habit, and I aped it. I learned to lie still under the wind and listen to the grass. I learned to befriend the wind. I learned the value of silence in wild places.

In later years I came to understand the second great migration of our history, the exodus of the young people of Dakota (of the Great Plains, of rural America) for better climates, better jobs, better mating prospects, better access to the tangible fruits of life. When I was growing up there were 55,000 farms in North Dakota.[†] When I went off to college there were approximately 40,000. Today there are fewer than 30,000 remaining. To paraphrase Mark Twain's famous syllogism about the industrial shortening of the Mississippi River, if this trend continues, by the year 2050 there will be only one farm in all of North Dakota.

Mike took me once to the little badlands south of South Heart on a heartbreaking gray autumn day, when it got dark too soon, and the landscape was defined by a kind of slate sameness, sky and soil. We leaned with our binoculars against the warm engine fenders of his pickup. The engine creaked and groaned as it cooled. We absorbed what heat we could from the vehicle and listened to

---

[†]North Dakota farm density peaked around 1930 when there were at least 85,000 farms in the state.

the nighthawks swoop. I had never noticed them before. It was chill. There was a melancholy in the air. It was that first day in the autumn when one feels the seasonal death of the earth. We were silent for a long time in wonder at the poise and dexterity of the nighthawks, soaring and diving and pulling up with a boom a few inches from the ground. This was the first time I had ever given birds a chance. I had not figured that they did much more than fly and brood their eggs. Now I saw that the ingenuity of things finds marvelous and subtle expression in every species. Jacobs taught me to discern godhead in a grain of sand.

On the way home in the car, Michael, a constitutional melancholic, turned to me and said, "Scoop, what's the purpose of life?" I had no answer. I had no idea such questions were ever posed, even in the Congregational church I attended a handful of times per year. I was shy and tongue-tied. Blood rushed to my head. Nobody had ever asked me such a serious question before. I felt deflowered somehow. I wanted to have something profound to say in reply, but I had no matrix with which to make sense of his enquiry. Eventually he relieved me of the burden of the moment and offered, "The purpose of life is to get through it." Then we let it be.

Months later, after a heady first year of college, after encounters with T.S. Eliot and Hamlet and Pico della Mirandola, when I had recovered my composure and thought about it a little, I insisted that the purpose of life is to get through it with dignity. But we could never agree what that meant. And from this vantage point, in early middle age, such a notion as dignity in life seems merely absurd. My adult life has been a series of attempts to recover dignity. I believe it is possible. I can close my eyes and see the path. When I open them it is all strip malls and insurance policies and super bowls.

We took two professors from the local college, once, to the badlands north of Marmarth. One of the professors had been plunked down in Dickinson because there was a job there. As far as he was concerned he might have been in Cincinnati or Mobile. Indeed, he would have preferred to profess in a more prestigious locale. North Dakota was merely a place in which he had been— temporarily, he hoped—marooned. He was more than a little agoraphobic, even in the presence of his reassuring friend Jacobs. I felt smug. My own comfort level with the breaks country and unmarked roads was now high, though I probably would never have ventured into the countryside without having been taken there first by such a mentor.

We stopped to observe an antelope community as it drifted over the plains like a gust of wind. The herd of about forty buff and white pronghorns sprinted up to the fence on our right, and *mirabile dictu*, all forty creatures went down on their flanks, slid like baseball players under the barbed wires, and rose again to their delicate feet, without ever appreciably slowing down. They ran off to the east and disappeared over the ridge in less than a minute. It was a miracle of coordinated energy and elegance. We all gasped audibly at the sheer beauty and mastery of the thing, and Mike's academic friend literally could not stop exclaiming over it for the rest of the day. We stopped for coffee at Mert's Café in Marmarth. The professor wore the appearance of one who had seen God—which, of course, he had. And Mike was the holy spirit with whom He was well pleased. To see such a sight as fence-skidding antelope is rare and delightful. To see it with Michael was sublime, for he was the only person I knew who could explain it and fully appreciate it.

When we had known each other for more than a year, we camped one night at the Munson ranch on the Little Missouri River. It was a working ranch in the breaks north of Medora, but the owners lived somewhere else in the valley and kept only an old line cabin on the site. We drove down an impossibly eroded road to get to the ranch. I was a little scared. The slope was dangerous, the car flimsy, and I did not particularly like the idea of trespassing, even though Michael assured me that the Munsons wouldn't mind. We parked in mid-afternoon at the log cabin. Outside there was a huge chest freezer, unlocked, full of beef. A sign on the door said, "Go ahead and take what you need, but make sure you close the lid tightly when you finish." We left Munson meat alone. We went down to the river and waded across it. The Little Missouri River is seldom as deep as one's chest. Except for a couple of weeks of late spring runoff, it barely propels its giant load of silt along. At times it is virtually intermittent, and its banks are always perfumed with cattle urine and feces. Still, it is an intensely romantic river—especially because it is unknown to most Americans, including, except in name, to most Dakotans. Our friendship had begun on the banks of the Little Missouri, in one of its exceedingly rare floods. Now we were ambling its contours in the dog days of summer. It was Jacobs who taught me what "dog days"[†] meant.

The Little Missouri takes its source in the shadow of Devils Tower in northeastern Wyoming, runs north by northeast past the western edge of the Black Hills, enters North Dakota in its extreme southwestern corner, then cuts its way through badlands country to its confluence with the Missouri in the west-central part of the state. You do not drink from the river unless you are dying of thirst. You do not bathe in it unless you are hopelessly besmirched. The Little Missouri supports no watercraft—save an occasional canoe—but you can drive your pickup through it in a hundred places, if you are lucky and brave. There are only three towns on the river: Camp Crook, SD; Marmarth, ND; and

---

[†]The part of the summer that occurs when the Dog Star, Sirius, rises at the same time as the sun. Usually July 3-August 11.

Medora, ND, named for the young wife of the famous Marquis de Morès, the French cattle baron. The entire human population of the Little Missouri Valley might run to 500. There are ten cattle in the valley for every person. Maybe a hundred.

We sat in the river for a long time loafing and talking. The water was chocolate brown, warm, gurgly. Uterine. There is, in the middle of the channel of the Little Missouri, in so stark and broken and lonely a place, so far from everything that matters to most Americans, a sense of hopelessness so powerful that it liberates the most interesting sorts of conversation. The river is a brown provocation to absurdist meditations. Conversation came in lazy clusters, between long bouts of gazing at the clouds and the cottonwoods. We talked about coal and oil, Custer and Crazy Horse, the utter badness of the badlands, the need to create an American civilization worthy of the landscape of the continent. It was a talk in which I did most of the asking and Jacobs did most of the thinking. In a sense, all of our conversations were about the same three issues.

1. What was the future of North Dakota, a small, out-of-the-way, undercapitalized farm state that cannot persuade its young to stay, and whose economic diversification—were that even a possibility—would degrade the strange semiarid ethos of the place?

2. What is a life of integrity, and how does one achieve it, and what is the mix of nature and culture, books and badlands, in that quest?

3. Whither our friendship when my apprenticeship at the *Dickinson Press* ended and the structure of adult life began to make its claims on me?

We talked about these things with delicacy and even beauty. Each of us felt a powerful nameless melancholy. The dog days, they cannot last forever. Meanwhile, the river sought the sea with its usual patience. It slid past us down the spine of the continent.

Had we stayed there long enough it would have carried us with it. But when our feet were prunelike and our necks sunburned, we stood up and shook off the river like sheepdogs.

Then we threw down our bags near a corral by the cabin, not far from an artesian well that filled a steel basin, and overflowed to create a considerable mess in the direction of the river. Michael had brought fine cuts of beef, potatoes, and onions. Plus wine and a small quantity of marijuana. I did not share the marijuana with him. He never in our long relations pressed me to take on that agreeable habit. I drank a little wine. He cooked. He wrapped the potatoes and onions individually in tin foil and placed them in the coals. I had never heard of such a thing. I assumed the potatoes would be burned, and I had considerable doubts about the onions. We crouched by the open fire like characters from *The Grapes of Wrath*. He fussed with the food. I asked him questions. He said with an affectionate sigh, "Scoop, I have no wisdom about such things." He said, "You know what I want to do? I want to wash my face."

We ate in the dark by firelight alone. The beefsteaks were outstanding. We were hungry from a day of wandering. The potatoes were moist and steamy. I ate mine skin and all. And the onions were heavenly, sweet, and slithery in our throats. As the night grew darker we talked in lower and lower tones to honor the spirit of the place. Crickets, night birds, and occasional coyotes punctuated the solemnity of the night. We could hear water trickle out of the artesian well, and when the cottonwoods were quiet we could hear the river gurgling towards the Gulf. From time to time unspecified creatures moved through the scene. We were not afraid. When the fire ebbed to waves of red/orange/gray, we spread out our bags three feet or so apart. It was chilly now. After a final pee, we slipped into our bags. At the end of a day in the canyon country of the Colorado in 1869, John Wesley Powell wrote, "At first we could not sleep, as the excitement of the day had not yet worn off." Indeed. Although we were both tired, we did not wish to relinquish so perfect a day. It was, at any rate, not much after nine p.m.

We lay on our backs looking up at the stars, trying to fathom them—failing—trying in another way—failing again—talking about it—ratcheting ourselves in popular scientific terms up for a run at the vault of heaven—failing. To understand the cosmos for a single moment would be the ultimate enlightenment, but we could press our souls no farther than wonder. The heavens were huge, spangled, quicksilver, mysterious, palpably close, infinitely far, punctuated by planets and satellites, indecipherable, familiar in four or five constellations, the most amazing sight that any human can ever experience. From time to time a satellite zipped across the firmament. Occasionally, stars shot to the earth.

We lay thrilling to the cold night air and the sounds of wild things nearby, especially the coyotes, the genii of the place, and waves of fatigue, friendship, and wonder swept over us. The ground was hard, the good earth warm, the air caressive. The river flowed nearby. This was as close as we were ever going to get to the rightness of things. Eventually he said, "Good night, Scoop." I replied, half asleep, "Good night, Michael." We tried to stay awake to fathom the mystery of the stars, but eternity won the battle and the organic yielded as gracefully as possible.

We both knew that this day could never be recalled. The inevitable drift was as unrelenting as the current of the Little Missouri River. In a few weeks I would go away to college. Nothing would ever be the same. Nothing should ever be the same. I have tried—all my adult life—to be a generous mentor to others, to nurture unselfishly, to know how to catch and release, and I have kept my eyes open for the young man or woman who would enable me to do for another by grace alone what Mike Jacobs did for me. My adult character, my adult achievement, my adult vision are all unthinkable without the teachings of Mike Jacobs. It might have been south Florida, but it was not. It was North Dakota, and he was the quintessential child of the Great Plains. I cannot dream of happiness without the Munson ranch and the Little Missouri in it, though—it is one of the primary mysteries of life— I can now imagine it without Mike Jacobs.

We woke to the sun and a cow bellowing in for a drink. The hills and breaks seemed near in the morning light. The dawn was rosy-fingered on the broken hills. We were stiff getting up and stretching for the day. We packed in silence. We drove slowly up the river road, windows open, I dozing, the dust pinching our noses, grasshoppers catapulting over the hood. At a bend in the river he saw horses wading and drinking up to their knees. He woke me up to take a look. We got out and took pictures. Mine were fine, his mediocre. That upset him for a long time. Whenever the words "Little Missouri" are voiced anywhere in my earshot, I think of those horses knee-deep in the bend of the badlands, at the center and at the margin of the universe. Timeless.

We did not say much that day as we drove back to Dickinson, but the pickup carried us through a valedictory landscape.

We drove once on a fool's adventure to the Missouri Breaks country of Montana. A window of opportunity had suddenly opened for us, and we decided to drive somewhere to camp and explore—it was that vague. This trip precipitated concern among my parents, and considerable hostility from Suezette, who thought that Mike should be finishing his book, or perhaps vacationing with her, rather than wandering the West with his youthful ward. So our little adventure had the added satisfaction of having been stolen from the claims of our lives.

One of the joys of Dakota that Michael taught me was our proximity to Canadian radio, CBC Canada. CBC programming was infinitely more interesting than the top-forty and country-western fare of the United States. We listened to CBC Saskatchewan, and the nationally produced program *As It Happens*, a more thoughtful and less pretentious magazine than the newly-created American *All Things Considered*. We smirked our way through Elvis retrospectives, reports of crimes harmless by U.S. standards, gentle interviews, profiles of the genial small heroes of Canadian prairie history, debates about policy questions that would not come to the U.S. for decades, and, most interesting, broadcasts of British radio (BBC) programming.

Our favorite BBC program was something called *Just A Minute*. It featured the British equivalents of Kitty Carlisle and Bill Cullen, that is, men and women whose job description was "radio game show personality." Clement Freud, a famous British gourmand, and Kenneth Williams, a comic monologist, were two of the regulars. The rules were that the moderator picked a topic, and the designated guest-contestant tried to speak to that subject for sixty seconds without pausing, without repeating anything, stammering, or saying what was nonsense. The British were so adept at language that they not infrequently succeeded, in spite of hilarious and impertinent challenges from the other players, including, once, a challenge to one participant's laugh: repetition of "ha." A successful challenge or a verbal slip passed the word for the remainder of the minute to another guest. The idea was to consume the whole minute oneself, or at least to be the last to speak. We played the game between ourselves on those long stretches of road along U.S. 2, the High Line. At first we could not sustain discourse even on our pet subjects for more than fifteen or twenty seconds. Eventually we (mostly he) learned to speak in informative complete sentences for thirty seconds, forty-five seconds, even a full minute. Our challenges were not witty like those of the Brits. Nor did we try to trip each other up. Michael was the best user of the language I had ever encountered. His vocabulary was immense without ever being ostentatious. I was a mere novice: apprentice, beginner, fledgling, neophyte, novitiate, rookie, tenderfoot, cub, greenhorn. . . . The combination of *Just a Minute* and Mike Jacobs was my Dale Carnegie course, sans patriotism, boosterism, and the capitalist ethic. We would suspend the competition only when the landscape was especially beautiful.

We stopped at Jordan, Montana, one of the most wonderfully god-forsaken places in America, to buy gas and licorice. Michael, in an affectionate tone, asked the gas station attendant if this were the end of the world. "No," he replied on cue, "but you can see it from here." In the course of ten minutes this mustachioed Montanan spat out four or five additional apothegms, all apparently unrehearsed. He had all the characteristics of a *Just A Minute* champion except loquacity. He could never have sustained a conversation on any subject, even his favorite, for more than fifteen seconds, but what he said was the epitome of a western verbal tradition as finely wrought as British Ciceronianism.

After an endless drive, in which Jacobs got a severe headache, we camped at a place called Cow Island Crossing, somehow important to Lewis and Clark. We threw our bags down late at night in what turned out to be a bad spot, and both of us were grumpy. The next day we wandered aimlessly around a place called Bowdoin National Wildlife Refuge, studying pelicans. What was the point of this trip? What was our destination? What were we looking for? Should we press on for Portland to gaze into the Pacific? Should we drift up into Canada to see what kind of landscape produces CBC radio? What would become of our friendship in the long run? More to the point, what would happen when I went away to college? How long could we safely be gone? How much money do we have in our pockets?

We kicked around such stuff all day long and then gave up and limped home to take our licks from parents and spouse.

Those were the days of miracle and wonder. I learned to see North Dakota through the eyes of its most alert consciousness. I learned to feel the soul of the plains as I lay on my back on river banks and buttes on spring days. I stood out in the middle of thunderstorms half wishing to be scared enough to wet my pants, more vaguely wishing to be struck by lightning and devoured a day later by coyotes. I learned to understand our history, our potential, and our failed potential as industrial agrarians. I learned to become a North Dakotan, a project quite different from simply being one. I felt the spirit of the place in the grasses and in the wind. And like Carlos Castenada, whose *Teachings of Don Juan* had awakened me, as the Bible had never done, to the sacredness of things, I found my spot. It was north of Marmarth on old state Highway 16, a road not only not paved, but not particularly passable except under ideal conditions. About ten miles north of Marmarth, on a trail that I would never have discovered without the guidance of Michael Jacobs, the river comes in close to the road below the aptly but bathetically named Pretty Butte. If you look north you see only endless badlands, an eerie landscape that violates every convention of beauty, but which is nevertheless the essence of strange magnificence. If you look south you see the breaks drop into a cottonwood oasis with a lonely water tower standing above it. That is Marmarth, the middle earth of the Great Plains. To the west lies Charlie Russell's Montana.

It is the loneliest place on earth. I wish to be buried there on a scaffold, Lakota style. My mother, who has followed me into true North Dakota citizenship, wishes her ashes to be scattered there. Both are probably illegal acts, but I trust my friends Patti Perry and Merle Clark to find a way to bring it about, out there where the grids break down. There is nothing Patti cannot bring to pass.

Eventually I went away to college, first in Minnesota, then in Britain, where I learned to play the verbal games of Just An Hour, or perhaps Just A Lifetime. Michael, meanwhile, was seduced into one form of respectability after another. We tried to keep up—and did pretty well for a time—but the old intensity could not be sustained, not for a dozen reasons. It was the kind of friendship you can never forget, can never duplicate, and can never fully rekindle. It leaves a hole in your soul that nothing, including its own diminished form, can ever fill. Michael and I somehow disappointed each other without ever quite knowing how. Our friendship survives, even grows and develops in a spasmodic way, but there will never be another night like ours at the Munson ranch. We can never be so young again, and the stars will never quiver endless and infinite in the sky the way they did then, fueled by the river and sweet onions, and all those singing coyotes, that night long ago.

Marmarth

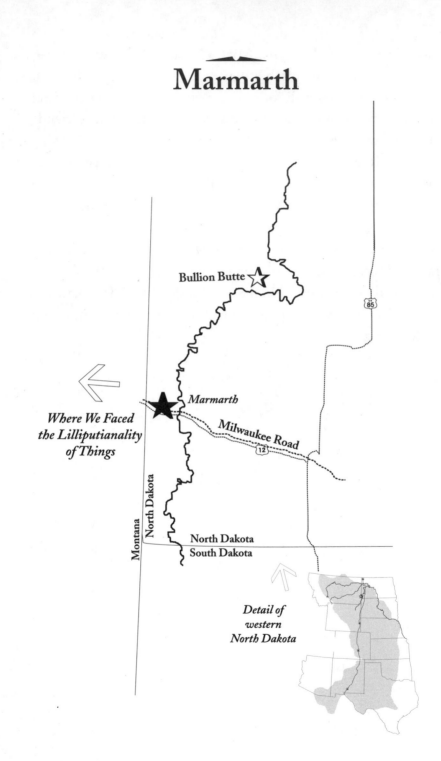

Bullion Butte ☆

Where We Faced
the Lilliputianality
of Things

★ Marmarth

Milwaukee Road

North Dakota
South Dakota

North Dakota

Montana

85

12

Detail of
western
North Dakota

Rampal, Opus 47, in Marmarth

The Lotus Eaters

MY FRIENDS AND I WERE IN MARMARTH conducting a weeklong humanities program called Chautauqua. Think of a huge blue and white tent, a public audience of 350, and history offered up in a way both scrupulous and at the same time delightful. The modern tent Chautauqua was partly my invention, and I was the field director, and Marmarth was one of my favorite places in the world, so I had invited friends from all over the country to join me there. It was to be a reunion of people who cared about the humanities, had a strong sense of the absurd, and gravitated toward adventure. This, for me, has always been an irresistible cluster of virtues.

There are four things you need to know about Marmarth. First, it is a ghost town set in the badlands of North Dakota along the Little Missouri River. It is not one of those ghost towns that have figured out how to market their ghostliness. In some ways it has not yet fully recognized its decay. Second, although it was historically a railroad town, the westernmost point on the Milwaukee Road in North Dakota, its railroad days were all but over by the 1980s. Now its economy depended on oil patch drifters and local ranchers. In fact, if you figured out the minimal economic activity required to keep a very marginal village afloat on the northern Great Plains, then subtracted the work ethic and divided the whole by two, you'd have the gross domestic product of Marmarth. When it rains plentifully for a couple of years, when there is plenty of oil extraction in the Williston Basin, when the state highway department works on U.S. 12 in Slope County, there is just about enough cash in the Marmarth economy to keep the place on a minimal drip. Third, there is a certain roughness to Marmarth. Given the choice between opera and mud wrestling, it's mud wrestling, or better yet, opera descending rapidly into mud wrestling. Fourth, behind the tough façade Marmarth is a great-hearted place. If I were in serious trouble, if my life were in tatters, if I were crosswise with the law, if I needed to be salved in the most fundamental ways, and had nowhere else to turn, I would turn up at the ramshackle home of Patti and Gary Perry in Marmarth, certain to be fed, patched up, and protected without fanfare and without judgment for as long as it took, no questions asked. Usually, it's your mother who performs this penultimate rite. But I'm talking about real trouble and serious tatters.

We were staying in the old broken-down bunkhouse, now a fundraising enterprise of the Marmarth Historical Society, which as far as I can tell, never talks about history at all. My friend the former mayor, Patti Perry, calls it the Marmarth Hysterical Society. The members meet once a month, and if Merle Clark isn't out of town, or busy with his auctioneering (no one has ever accused him of being busy with his ranch), everyone listens with wary fascination to Merle's monologues on old-time rodeo (his father was Elmer Clark, the only man who ever rode the famous horse Tipperary), classic automobiles, or—more recently—dinosaurs. Marmarth is the epicenter of a dinosaur alley much frequented by paleontologists of the second tier. Strangely enough, there are more triceratops in the badlands of North Dakota than people. In the absence of Merle, who is beloved in spite of his notions and obsessions, members of the hysterical society pretend to squabble (wit, in Marmarth, lives at the brickbat end of the spectrum), and ask themselves if they are up to mounting a theater production in the historic Mystic Theater, which, aside from the bar and the quick shop and the town hall Quonset, is the only intact public building in Marmarth. Usually they decide it is not worth the trouble, or they water down whatever playbook they have into a rough and ready farce.

One year they performed *Hamlet* with six-guns. It was a remarkable moment: equally notable for thespian ambition and a determination not to leave out violence and buffoonery altogether. In this part of the world, Hamlet is seen as a bit of a whiner. Fortinbras gets high marks. Horatio doesn't even register. And every adolescent girl is, of course, Ophelia.

They have dreams of getting the old Barber Auditorium restored, of creating a dinosaur museum in Marmarth (not talked about in Merle's presence lest he be off and running), of turning the bunkhouse into a hunting lodge, and of getting the old Milwaukee Road depot off its wooden supports on a side street and onto a concrete pad. That would require Merle, its owner, to exert himself, and everyone knows that that is the unlikeliest prospect in the world. Merle is well over six feet tall, lean as barbed wire, a mere creature of anecdote, and easily the most cosmopolitan citizen of Marmarth. When the writers come around they invariably find Patti first, and then Merle. He's the historian of Marmarth. Half of that history is held in his capacious mind, the other half in the sheds and barns and garages in which he stores his vast collections.

Patti tells the story of the discovery of some dinosaur bones on an Indian sacred site in Slope County. Because he was the region's resident expert on paleontology, Merle made some long distance calls and managed to import an Indian medicine man (from great distance and at considerable expense) to bless the site and sign off on the dinosaur dig. But on the day of the ceremony the weather was lousy. According to Merle, the shaman was by now heavily inspired by the kind of "medicine" that is locally called by the name of Southern Comfort. He approached the sacred site, started in on what promised to be a rather elaborate prayer, then said, "Oh the hell with it, go ahead and dig all you want." Now whether this story is strictly-speaking true or not is impossible to ascertain. One never quite knows whether Merle Clark is a short-grass sage or something of a BS artist, but somehow it doesn't matter. He's a master of his craft and nobody can be in his presence without smiling broadly and often.

My group of curious adventurers had been hiking and horseback riding, holding informal seminars on top of buttes, musing and meditating and talking on the banks of the Little Missouri River, eating jumbo beef burgers at Mert's Café, driving the lonely badlands roads, and letting our sobriety set with the sun. We also milked goats with Patti Perry, who owned about two hundred French Alpines, plus pigs, a few sheep, a head or two of cattle, and a mélange of exotic birds. Bumb lambs in Marmarth invariably find their way to Patti's yard. She tends to spend money she doesn't have to acquire exotic animals she then grumbles about and can never quite bring herself to eat. We had managed to erect the big Chautauqua tent in the rodeo grounds on the edge of town before misrule was loosed among us, and now our only duty was to keep the tent up through the afternoon thunderstorms until the Chautauqua programming began on Wednesday night.

On about the third day of sweet listlessness we all drove out to a butte west of Baker, Montana, and took a picnic lunch with us, and some local rotgut wine, and we sat for a long time in the hot wind looking off into the broken country in every direction. We talked and mused and walked and regrouped in small clusters of intimacy, and got lazy and lay about studying the clouds and our navels and just finally getting quiet enough to sense, for an instant, the utter infinitude of the place. When the size of things—

including our own Lilliputianality—swept in on our silence, each person made a separate peace with it, but there was evidence of both awe and some uneasiness in the eyes of everyone. Endless marginal land sagged away to the rim of the earth in every direction, and brought on a sense of helpless isolation so profound that you could hear it in the grass. The wind blew like a sonofabitch, as the local ranchers say. It was a vast bowl of land and sky that never was and never could be settled. It made you shudder to be there, and even literally shake your head. Each of us experienced a kind of barren inflowing of the sublime and not everybody was happy about it. Our one true philosopher, Gerhardt Ludwig, looked as if he was about to belt out "One Hundred Bottles of Beer on the Wall," or sing snatches from old sitcoms, and though his companions all would have frowned, nobody would really have been sorry. Gerhardt was smoking more than usual just to fight off the emptiness of the place. The silence was appalling.

Recently it has become fashionable to speak of the Great Plains and the desert Christian fathers (like St. Anthony) in the same breath. Much of this discourse seems forced, a pathetic attempt to compensate for the collapse of the social structure of the region by hitching our bleak experience to one of the world's greatest spiritual traditions. Having failed as capitalists, we refashion ourselves as prairie mystics. The trouble with mysticism is that it pays so little. Meanwhile we lobby to house the cruise missile at our now-and-probably-always pointless Strategic Air Command (SAC) bases, and beg Congress for more farm price supports, and we worship—and depend upon—the industrial paradigm more thoroughly than at any previous time. We have been an industrial landscape for just one hundred years and yet we cannot imagine what might lie beyond it.

Now we had chosen to walk off the grid for an instant, and it was clear that this was the kind of afternoon that was going to open up a new place in everyone's soul—forever—and yet not leave any monuments on the new slate. The question we kept working, when we fell into conversation, is how one comes to terms with a barren like this, a place so huge, empty, and void of all that hums in the world. When we finally scrambled down the butte to the car, I could see an O.E. Rolvaagesque flaw in every visage. A perfect day. Emptiness is the seed of all virtue.

But the day was far from over. We drove slowly back to the bunkhouse not talking much. When we pulled up in the drive, everyone exploded out of the car and ran to find something— anything, a blow-dryer, a razor, a radio—to plug into the grid. Over dinner at the Pastime I reminded everyone that Anne Rawlinson had agreed, at last, to provide a flute concert before the night was done. Anne was at once the most silent and the most cheerful member of our little club, and she had been fretting about the performance ever since she arrived. She was a serious student of the flute. Probably she would not have agreed to give the performance had she known what to expect out on the windswept plains of Dakotah, if she could have anticipated the absurd geography of her performance hall, but I was not letting her off the hook at this juncture, and the sense of everyone was that if the solo did not occur tonight, it would probably never take place at all.

So, after a spell of mumbling, murmuring, diffidence, and scrupling, Anne finally sat down with her flute on the rough wooden steps at the north end of the bunkhouse. It was a dark night in a not very well lit little village at the end of the earth. There were some kitchen lights on in the middle distance and from time to time headlights pierced the darkness on U.S. 12, which bisects the village east to west, but the principal light by which the scene was illuminated dangled a few feet over Anne's head. It was a single forty watt light bulb in a metal fixture that resembled an inverted flower blossom, the kind you see on top of the old light poles in farm country.

Her audience, which consisted of about six of us, all sweetly but powerfully intoxicated in one way or another, sat on the nearest silvery rail of the Milwaukee Road. It wasn't exactly comfortable, but it was better than the barren ground, and we found it exotic to be sitting on a spot that, sometime in the next few hours, would be crushed by the weight of a hundred thousand tons of steel.

The audience consisted of:

Timothy Billings, popularly known as Youthful Timothy, an absurd and beautiful young man, so full of himself that it had gone right over annoying into a kind of delightfulness. He possessed a brilliant and at that time undisciplined mind. He was at once virile and uproariously effeminate. He cut a mighty odd figure amongst the horny-handed sons of toil in the rangeland of western North Dakota. Not that he noticed, or cared overmuch. He had read and memorized scads of literature, and he walked, ate, talked, and no doubt made love with a mincing affectation that delighted everyone it did not appall. He affected a slight lisp, and he spoke with an Elizabethan formality. He was, of course, trained in several of the martial arts and from time to time he executed kicks that carried his foot artfully over his cranium. He was always dusting the top of a doorframe with his toe. He made it clear that he could kill a man with this maneuver if necessary, but in fact he was a youth of pacific temperament. He had a huge boyish laugh, almost a guffaw, which he honked into the world at the most inappropriate times. He sprinkled his discourse with allusions to Spenser and Yeats and Tennyson, and never stopped to consider that nobody had the slightest clue about what he was trying to say. He had long red hair and long fingernails, and he drove an orange Datsun with fins in the rear window. We called it the Shark. He considered himself a man fatally alluring to women and the hint was that no woman was ever quite the same after he made love to her, but in fact he tended to be helplessly in love with this or that pure virgin, and he spent much of his time pining and punning and penning missive verses to his mistress' eyebrows. You get the picture. He was as alien to the world of Marmarth as Mike Tyson to high tea. He was enormously cheerful and resilient. In short, in the words of his beloved Shakespeare, I loved him for the dangers he had passed, and he loved me that I did pity them.

Gerhardt Ludwig was then in his early fifties. He was a professor of humanities at the University of North Dakota, the creator of an experimental college within the university called Integrated Studies. So far as anyone knew he had never published anything, or indeed undertaken any publishable research, but he was always reading through Spengler and Schopenhauer and nobody doubted that he had mighty things on his capacious mind. The problem was that—German educated—he was seldom capable of articulating his philosophical thoughts. He was, however, as fascinating as anyone I have ever known in routine conversation. He was a large, life-affirming, goatish man, with a tumescent gut, who had once radiated an Aryan virility, and by now was still attractive, but essentially harmless. He had a huge holy goof smile. He was a man wholly given to appetite except when cogitating, and unapologetic about his lust for life. In addition to being a serious intellectual, he was a great-souled man with a Homeric laugh that could turn any situation into comedy. I remember lecturing once to a crowd of four hundred in a darkened tent in eastern North Dakota and uttering something absurd. The audience sat in bewildered silence for a second or two and I— suddenly uncomfortable—was not sure where to take my discourse. Suddenly there was a vast life-affirming laugh—heh

heh heh haaaaaaaaaaaaaaaa, the last ha on a high hilarious pitch—
that pierced the darkness. It was one of the most gratifying sounds
I ever heard, the platonic response to which I have ever since
aspired in public life and never again achieved. Gerhardt was
breathtakingly selfish, which (except perhaps to his wife) made
him all the more delightful. He was game for anything and he
could take an absurdist conversation to profound heights. I have
known better men, better scholars, even better friends, but I have
never felt so wonderfully alive in the presence of any other person.
He smoked—anything—and he drank wine in vast quantities
and he possessed a constitution equal to his immense hedonism.

Rita Ludwig had once been Gerhardt's student. In a sense, that
tells you everything you need to know about her. Rita was
remarkably intelligent and sensible. Every performer's wife must
endure a fair amount of repetition and bombast (Rita would call
it bullshit), and Rita had heard more than most, but she loved
Gerhardt with all her heart, and—more remarkable still—she
loved his mind. They spent countless evenings together talking
the issues: books, music, politics, philosophy, parenting, university
life, literature, the law. I had never before witnessed marriage
partners who actually still found each other interesting after more
than a decade of shared life. They still loved to buy a bottle of
wine, a couple of packs of cigarettes, and spend the evening alone
together reading and talking. Rita had a tremendous sense of
humor—I would describe it as seeing through the bullshit without
feeling the need to cut through it too—and a laugh every bit as
infectious as Gerhardt's. Like Gerhardt she was equal to any
adventure, from butte climbing to end-of-the-road flat tires, and
unlike Gerhardt, she never complained about physical exertion.
In spite of her invariable cheerfulness, there was an air of deep
sadness in Rita's eyes, the kind of ancient nameless sorrow that
made you want, somehow, to take care of her. Rita was, at any
rate, the sort of person you want on a road trip. If she drank

enough wine, she could become positively assertive, not to mention drop-dead funny. Then and then only she spoke of her love of literature, particularly Charles Dickens. I loved her.

Pat Sanborn was a professor of humanities at the University of North Dakota. She was a New England Brahmin Yankee puritan trying not to be a New Englander, a Brahmin, a Yankee, or a puritan. She was easily the most intelligent member of our troupe and at some earlier phase of her career she had written learnedly about Sartre. But there had been a conversion experience of some sort and now you couldn't get her to talk about Sartre under any circumstance. She was tall and thin and beautiful, but she steadfastly endeavored to ignore her beauty. She wore her sandy hair long in the way that women do who claim not to give a damn about their appearance. She wore no makeup. She wore plain but elegant clothing. She told me that ten years ago or so she had wrestled for many months with the idea of ceasing to shave her legs. At last she had decided to try it for a while and see what sort of response such a political gesture would receive. She was both relieved and hurt when nobody noticed one way or the other.

Somewhere in her being was a large and serious core of emotion, but she did everything in her power to be a mere creature of reason and good sense. She didn't waste language. She didn't gush, even when you could see her gushing beneath the character armor. She was the least judgmental person I have ever known. She seemed to look upon humanity as a collection of interesting specimens in a felt-lined box. It wasn't clear whether she found our badlands wanderings enchanting or just willed herself to affect enchantment, but there was a level of energetic weariness to everything she did. She had a son who was the cleverest whippersnapper in five states, whom she had named Eagle in some moment of breathtaking audacity. And he soared! She adored him in a kind of reserved way and rebuked him constantly for his uninhibited exhibition of his superb mind. Pat was the kind of person who can dispatch a hundred tasks before noon and not break a sweat. Gerhardt and I would wrestle with one or two of the easiest chores and then take a long break. Pat never complained even when she was in pain.

Anne Rawlinson had been my college student once in another life. And though she tried always to blend into her surroundings as much as possible, nobody could doubt that she had remarkable gifts and the kind of quiet competence that would eventually outdistance every one of us and perhaps all of us together. She was then still a girl-woman or a woman-girl. She was androgynous. She was lithe and healthy and disarmingly innocent, and filled with the kind of unselfconscious physical energy one sees in month-old calves. It was not clear where her shadow was, if she had one, in a group that self-consciously prized the shadow and dissected it in Jungian terms, and—in Gerhardt—made love to it day and night. Anne had a streak of persistence that might break out into stubbornness, though no one had ever seen it do so. Her only fault was that she mumbled, but even though this forced her to express virtually everything she said twice, she still talked less than any member of our troupe. She possessed what the English cavalier poet Robert Herrick is said to have possessed, "a tough reasonableness beneath a slight lyric grace." Unlike the rest of us, she was musically talented (though Timothy affected madrigals, of course), and she was artistically disciplined (Timothy had just enough self-knowledge not to try to trump that) and she had agreed, long distance, to provide a flute concert. Now her moment had come.

So what have we here?

Two college professors in their fifties, one who never called attention to herself and one whose every fart drew a bemused crowd, both marginal figures in their university's life. A professor's wife in her thirties, not yet willing to move out of his shadow. Youthful Timothy, a recent immigrant, admired by them all, making his adolescence the theme of his existence. Anne, not romantically linked to Timothy, but somehow living in his wake. And I, who had the good fortune to bring them together in the most improbable place in America.

Rita and Gerhardt and Pat had driven down from Grand Forks, North Dakota, the university town, four hundred miles away. Anne had come in from Des Moines, where she was a recruiting officer for Drake University. Timothy was still a student at Pomona College in southern California, biologically in his fifth, academically in his second year, but he was serving as the tentmaster for Chautauqua that summer.

So we sat on the silvery rail mumbling and laughing and celebrating this holiday from mundane life while shy Anne blew a few warm-up notes into her flute. She was at once eager and unwilling to give her concert—I had pressed for it for months by long distance—and she was, I think, the only completely sober person in our company. She looked frail on the bunkhouse steps, but she knew her music perfectly and, partly because she was the most diffident member of our group, she was eager to show us her own brand of mastery. She sat 25 feet away.

It was concert night in Marmarth.

I was sorry that Patti Perry was not with us. She had some late chores to attend to at home. I wanted to share her with my friends. In many ways she was the most remarkable of us all, a strange irresistible combination of the local and the universal. She was a big-boned woman whose whole life had been a bad hair day. She was highly intelligent, a kind of living embodiment of the Foxfire arts, at once mayor, goatherd, cheese and sausage maker, butcher, historic preservationist, gardener, midwife, mother and grandmother, grantwriter, actress, rodeo director, cook, canner, reader, building contractor, bus driver, trucker, agricultural fair contestant, bartender, and much more. A woman for all seasons. She was tough, practical, no-nonsense, generous, sometimes gentle and sometimes coarse, sometimes both at once. She could strip a car engine, plumb a bathroom, or rewire a restaurant kitchen. She could drink any man under the table and knock him down if he deserved it. She could drive a herd of fifty goats across the country to Fresno in 48 hours, if necessary, and I had seen her patch up local feuds with astonishing deftness, or testify before a state legislative committee until the seasoned pols were wiping away their tears of laughter.

Somehow she had taken a liking to me. When we had first met, years previously, after a few drinks in the bar, I had said, "Patti, if you couldn't live in Marmarth, where would you live?" She called it the damn-foolest question she had ever heard, and she reminded me (and anyone handy) of the idiocy of that inquiry every time I ventured into town. I still don't know why she found the question so explosively nonsensical. Over the years she had come to consider me a bookish nitwit and a naïf, but arguably possessed of some redeeming spirit of adventure. She had done me enormous favors, including heal my bone-deep back sores with goat salve when I staggered into town after a two hundred mile hike on the Little Missouri River: "What in Sam Hill possessed you to do anything so damned foolish as lug an 80 pound pack up that poor excuse for a river?" When she found out I had been carrying five books in my pack, one a Dickens novel, she pronounced once for all that I was beyond redemption. Our roles, by now, were well established. I said naïve and romantic things. She wrestled them to the ground with a huge relish. We filled some kind of niche in each other's souls. Among other things, we entertained each other. We had become real friends, across some pretty considerable barriers.

I had invited her to come to the concert at the bunkhouse, but she had gone home right after dinner and she said she wasn't sure she'd be back until the morning.

So everyone settled down on the Milwaukee Road rails and Anne played her flute. There was a winsome tentativeness to her performance. The notes of her flute were thin and a little raspy on the vast plains of the American West. It was not an audience accustomed to silence or reverence, but no one said a word during the fifteen minutes that she piped. The only sounds we made were small sighs of appreciation and animal pleasure. Her music was as pure as the song of the meadowlark, and just as innocent. It was painfully beautiful. Everyone was transfixed. It was music that had been born in a drawing room on the other side of the world, a world of perukes and décolletage and dangerous liaisons. Now it was fulfilling Thomas Jefferson's great dream—high culture amid populist demographics in northern Louisiana.

Once or twice we heard a dog bark two or three pro forma notes somewhere across the village. If you listened carefully you could hear the faint hum of lonely highway traffic off to the West. It was Jack Kerouac's landscape: "Whither goest thou America in thy shiny car in the night?" Someone staggered out of the Pastime a hundred yards away and for a moment we could hear the click of pool sticks, the flick of the guitar from the jukebox, and the traveling remnant of a slurred argument at the bar. Then the door closed and all was still again. The few licks of sound only deepened the immense silence of the place. Anne played on. She was John Donne's "nimblest crocheting musician." The motion of her small, delicate fingers was almost as impressive as the lovely music she created. She exhaled her soul through a perforated metal tube and her soul that night was the music of the spheres.

Anne played her classical flute solo as far from the centers of high civilization as it was possible to be. When was the last time

Marmarth had heard such a concert? Indeed, when had North Dakota last heard music so finely articulated? Everything was intelligible then. It was one of those rare moments when all the energies of a group of people and a place gather and flow together and create a meaning and a music that is as glorious as it is ephemeral. Nothing muddled the scene. Life was endless, and every day in every way we were all getting better and better. That was before everything fractured and the center ceased to hold and the inevitable drift sent us all down different corridors of time. Anne wafted her lean flute notes to an amphitheater of the cosmos: low badlands hills in the near distance, the rails gliding off to the vanishing points on the eastern and western horizon, gelid night air, the bright silhouette of the bunkhouse and the fainter shadow of the deserted Barber Auditorium behind it, the Pastime, and the clapboard and stucco houses of Marmarth. You could see the whole town from where we sat. It was the world in miniature. Middle Earth. Most everyone had settled down for the night. The only hub of activity was the bar, where a half dozen fogged consciousnesses lost another night of their brief existence. There was no one among us who was thinking, when will this end? Everyone was thinking the same thing: like every other ecstasy in this sublunary world, this too must end.

In the middle of Anne's concert, I heard a car door slam far away. Someone started an engine. All sounds are poetry from a sufficient distance. At first I thought some local Huck Finn had lit a cluster of firecrackers on the other side of town, but then I realized that it was the backfire of a car engine without a muffler. It was Patti Perry! She was coming after all! She'd been complaining about the carburetor of her pickup for several days, said she'd asked, then told Gary to fix it, and he hadn't gotten around to it yet. It was an old "toy" pickup—not the full-ton model preferred by the ranchers in Marmarth—which she used to haul milk from her goat barn. If the Perrys ever spent more than $100 on a vehicle, I'd be surprised. And yet with gray tape and bloody knuckles Gary Perry could squeeze a last hundred thousand miles out of any car.

I whispered to my colleagues, "Listen!" and for a second we turned our attention from Anne's exquisite solo to the pop and spit and flutter of Patti's pickup threading its way through the streets of Marmarth to the bunkhouse. It sounded like a funny car in a rodeo or circus clown act, and for a moment I envisioned a club-footed back wheel lurching the pickup into the air and smoke blowing out of the radiator cap, and Patti in size thirty red shoes. The mayor was coming after all. We all followed her trajectory in the cosmic silence of the night.

This was one of the greatest single moments of my life: the quality of the night breeze (breeze is too strong a word for the gentle wafting and soughing of the air), the sound of rustling cottonwoods, the gorgeousness of Anne's music, the sensuous buzz of intoxication, the faint vibrations of the rail on which we sat, as if they were announcing a train just starting out from Chicago, the serenity of deep friendships all the way around, the stupendous array of stars, the ghostly light flickering over the north end of the bunkhouse and Anne's frail form bent over her flute, and now—and now—one of the earth's great women snap-crackle-and-popping her way in the cab of a once-proud vehicle, late, to the edge of town and Bach's haunting flute music. If I had to choose one moment to explain my wayward life—of books, adventure, friendship, the West, North Dakota, Marmarth, the Great Plains, and the sheer unpredictable zaniness of experience—this would be it. It was a moment that could not have been planned—Croessus could not have bought it—and it could never recur.

Patti sputtered up and skidded to a stop on the dirt street. She shut off her lights in the haze of dust she had kicked up as she approached. The driver's side door had been wrenched somehow and it shrieked when she forced it open. Then she slammed it home, glanced over at Anne, and padded her way quietly over to the tracks where we sat. She guided herself to the track by the pilot star of Gerhardt's orange-glowing cigarette. Muttering at the foolishness of sitting on the railroad tracks, she nevertheless joined us, and we all turned our full attention back to Anne and the lovely music she was creating. I touched Patti on the shoulder. "Glad you made it." She smiled.

When the concert ended, Pat Sanborn said: "Anne, that was really fine. We all thank you for sharing your talent with us."

Timothy: "Prithee, sweet Anne, playest thou another on thine oaten reed."

Gerhardt: "If my ass didn't hurt so much I'd ask you to play it again."

Pat: "Gerhardt! Really!"

Rita: "Say 'prithee,' Gerhardt. Anne, that was really good."

Gerhardt: "Goood? It's greeeeaaaaaaaaaaaaaaaaat!"

Timothy: "If Tony the Tiger could play like mistress Anne, my friend, he'd not be marooned on commercial television, methinks."

Gerhardt to Timothy, "Boy are you weird."

Timothy, offended, "After some careful observation, I believe the correct local riposte is, 'You should talk, barf breath!'"

Patti gave him a long look, then glanced at me, then gazed at Timothy with the "around here we eat guys like you for breakfast" look. But she said nothing.

Then in one unbroken sentence Patti Perry said,

"Anne, thank you, I'm sorry I couldn't come sooner,"

and

"Clay, if you'd told me what you had in mind I could have opened up the city building and brought some chairs for all of you. What the hell are you doing squatting on the railroad tracks? Geeeeeeeeeeeeeeeeeeeeez. You make me crazy."

There was a long silence while we all craned our necks to see the stars. We were all content to be outside on such a night with the cool air laving us almost delicately. A meteorite streaked across the eastern sky. Then Timothy said, "I shall hope that I will not be belittled for asking if there is any veracity to the hoary Indian tradition of being able to put one's ear to the track and hear a distant train approaching?" "I'd be skeptical of that one," I said, turning knowingly to Pat, but avoiding eye contact with Gerhardt. "Most 'Indian traditions' turn out to be white man's lore, often racist lore."

Gerhardt said, "Timothy, did you ever hear the story of the origins of the famous Fukari tribe?" There was a start of a nervous laugh all around, except in Timothy, who was about to take the bait, when Rita snapped out a "Gerhardt!!" with sufficient voltage to return us all to silence. Timothy said, "Tedious lore or no, methinks I feel the distant rumble of yon train." We listened. Sure enough, the tracks had begun to vibrate. I said, "The train is still a couple of miles off to the east but I suggest we move to safer ground." Patti burst out with, "Well, it sure wouldn't do you much damned good to sit here while it passes!"

Transcriptions of Patti Perry's insults do not do them justice. Both her tone and her affectionateness are lost when her colorful talk is reduced to print. For one thing, she had a remarkable speech pattern. The first half of each of her one-sentence outbursts piled up as on the edge of a cliff, and then the rest of it tumbled down in an instant, with a very strong emphasis on the last word or two, when the insult splatted on the valley floor of the victim's consciousness. None of us was used to blunt and aggressive language—especially when it was intended comically. Moreover, no one ever laughed harder at Patti's humor than Patti herself. Samuel Johnson's definition of laughter as "convulsive merriment" fitted her precisely. Her whole frame shook with joy whenever she fired off the blunderbuss of her riposte, and her chemically hypercurled hair whipped around like a shield. No one ever mistook her humor for rapier-like wit, but she had a remarkable talent for puncturing absurdities and exploding illusions. She found all of us wanting in common sense and practical knowledge. She had the disdain of one who can weld a trailer frame for those who prefer to theorize about—as Timothy put it—"industrialization at the garage level."

So we got up and moved. We could hear the whistle of the train as it penetrated the endless lonely night of the American West. Timothy turned to me and said, quietly, not wishing to trigger another burst from Patti, "How close might one stand and not be sucked into either the empyrean or the caboose?" The train was just coming into view half a mile to the east. I said, "Stand next to me and hold on to me if you get scared." Youthful Timothy and I approached the track cautiously.

The train was hurtling towards us rapidly now and we were both a little frightened. The agreeable clackedy-clack clackedy-clack we had been hearing for a couple of minutes had become, with proximity, an ear-splitting screeching and thumping. We were about to have our most visceral encounter with the Industrial Revolution. We began to realize, what of course we knew in the abstract, but had never previously experienced, that several hundred tons of unyielding steel (and all the produce of America) were about to thunder past us. However much we may like to think of ourselves as the "beauty of the world, the paragon of animals," we were, in fact, nothing but inconsequential impedimenta. The same mass that could crush a quarter or half dollar into a wafer of "airy thinness" would, for two or three minutes, be hurtling past our frail bodies at sixty miles per hour, and the gap between us and death like a mosquito on a windshield would be no more than four feet. In the last second before speech became impossible, I turned to Timothy and said, "Scream as long and hard as you can."

We held hands and emitted the loudest and most sustained noise of our lives. And yet our primal screams were swallowed up by the train like mere hors d'oeuvres of sound.

Even from four feet away, the train pummeled and buffeted us, blasted our faces with hot industrialized air, sucked us into its vortex and blew us backward almost off our feet. It was difficult to stay planted on the ground. I gripped Timothy's hand hard, but not as hard as he was gripping mine. It is not clear whether we were dancing with death in Marmarth or just bellowing our vitality there on the rail bed—or perhaps investigating the boundary between the two. It would have been so simple to throw ourselves under the train, Karenina-like, if only to confirm Thoreau's, "We do not ride on the railroad. It rides on us," or to have proved Iago's irrefutable logic, "'Tis but a man gone." To have perished in this way, leaving mere gobbets to surrender to our parents, would have given Marmarth a world-class story to pass around the Pastime, and it would have confirmed all of Patti Perry's prejudices. We were not tempted. But we were tempted to be tempted.

Life is so hard, so tedious, so nonsensical, so full of the DMV and the IRS and ATMs and OBGYNs, and so lacking in poetry, that it only takes one jejune Milwaukee Road freight train to call it all into question. Jefferson reported to John Adams that one of his friends was willing to die merely because he had grown tired of putting his socks on in the morning.

Long ago in a hopeless roadside motel room on another pointless journey, I heard Joseph Campbell tell Bill Moyers that the word

"Buddha" means "the man who waked up." But waking up is hard to do. It is painful. Life lived is as often raw as exhilarating. There is a joyful side to the absurdity of life and then there is mere absurdity. We struggle to wake up against habit, fear, toxicity, institutions, family, friends, even (perhaps especially) lovers, and when we finally lift the veil and see life in its magnificent starkness, the pain can be excruciating. Meanwhile all the Lotus Eaters are pleading with open arms to call us back to mediocrity and quiescence and habit. As usual, Hamlet says it best, "Who would fardels bear when he might his quiescence make with a bare bodkin?" Nor am I terrified by the "something after death."

But Youthful Timothy and I were only flirting with death, not proposing a full-blown affair, which is perhaps why several members of our company turned away in quiet disapproval. By the time half of the empty coal train had shot past, Anne had joined us, and Gerhardt and Rita. Pat Sanborn had remained on the bunkhouse steps with Patti, who was either predicting or inviting the sudden death of one or more of us.

We all screamed at the top of our lungs, and laughed the laugh of elemental experience, while the others looked on in bemusement and horror. We did not back away. But the coal train had miles to go before it slept, and promises to keep, and eventually it left us behind, ravished like one of Zeus' conquests among the mortals. Even Timothy only managed, "*Kein wunder* that the Sioux saw the Iron Horse as considerable Medicine."

When all the shouting stopped and we had begun to catch our breath, Gerhardt said, "Now at last I begin to understand the physics of *Roadrunner* cartoons." He walked towards the lamp-lit steps. Pat said, with her usual cheerful smile, "How was it?" Timothy, speaking for the group, said, "Pat, it was positively orgasmic."

We all turned instinctively toward Patti.

"Hell, only someone who's never had one could say something like that!"

Timothy took his beating well, though he later confided to me that he wished he'd used the term "sublime" instead of "orgasmic." "Yep," I said, "that would have turned it around."

By now it was late and we were all tired and for the most part talked out, but nobody was ready to let go of such a night. Each of us felt, already, that this was one of the most remarkable days of our life.

A coyote howled, one two three yips in the middle distance. I could not help my impulse, "That is the most beautiful and remarkable sound there is."

Patti lost no time in reflection. "You couldn't talk that way if you owned a cattle ranch."

"I'll grant you that and yet I've heard that coyotes don't kill many calves."

"You're dead wrong. And even one or two kills per year is enough to take the profit out of a few of the smaller outfits."

"Surely this country is big enough for a handful of *canis latrans*."

Timothy: "Wouldn't the plural be *canes*?"

Patti: "There isn't room here for a single damn coyote. Every time a coyote takes a lamb or a calf, there goes what little cushion the ranchers are working on."

Clay: "I would think that every rancher factors in a certain small percentage of loss to such natural predators."

Patti: "Well they do, for Christ's sakes, but just because you expect a flat tire now and then doesn't mean you puncture the damn thing yourself. Geeeeeez."

Timothy: "The sound of the coyote is very eerie, like a banshee woman of Gaelic legend."

Patti, not deigning to look at Timothy as he balanced—delicately as a dancer—on one foot on the opposite rail: "Banshee, baloney, it's all the same to me. They're pests, they're vermin, and we don't want none of their kind out here."

I could see that Timothy, wounded, was trying to remember just what a banshee was, exactly. Uncertain pedantry took him briefly out of the conversation.

Clay to Patti: "Ok, I understand why ranchers might not relish coyotes in their midst. But leaving economics aside for a moment, Patti, don't you agree that the coyote is a living symbol for the entire West, what is called a barometer species, that the sheer survival of the coyote is a monument to something that we all prize in this landscape, the very thing, Patti, that keeps you living in so unusual a place, and that the silencing of the coyotes would destroy something that we all take for granted and indeed cherish about the American West?"

"No."

"So there is no part of you that thrills to the call of that coyote?"

Patti, laughing from the belly: "Only if I have a thirty-ought-six handy."

Gerhardt to Patti: "No kidding, Patti, you've shot coyotes?"

Patti to Gerhardt: "Well of course I have! You're not prepared to kill vermin, you'd better stay in sidewalk and espresso towns. I haven't killed many, but I've done my best to kill every one I've ever seen."

Clay to Patti: "You love to talk tough, Patti, but I bet you wouldn't kill that coyote if it walked past us now."

"That's a bet I believe I'd take."

Clay to Patti: "When I was walking the Little Missouri last year, no night passed when I didn't hear coyotes howling, sometimes quite close. So I decided to try to call them in. The usual method, employed by hunters, is to blow into a "dying rabbit" call. But that doesn't seem very respectful to me. It may be effective, but it's not cricket. It's cheating. I don't want to trigger their appetites. I want to communicate with them. So I tried to speak "coyote." Every night when they made their appearance known, I called and called, trying to sound as much like a coyote as possible. Every time I'm out in the wild places, I wonder all over again at what makes them howl as they do. They are a symbol of the almost unbelievable loneliness of the West. At first all I did was make them go silent, but towards the end of my trip I felt certain that some of them actually began to call back to me, as it were to talk with me."

Patti: "Well, now I've heard everything. If you felt that, you must have been smoking something out there. You go talk that way in the bar, you'll have to fight your way out, if the boys don't just roll on the floor laughing at you. Now I know why I keep coming back for more from you. You say the damndest things I ever heard. Jesus, are you planning to teach a course in "coyote" back at the university?"

She could not restrain her mirth. Gerhardt was laughing too, enjoying the delicious absurdity of the conversation. Rita looked concerned for my feelings. Pat Sanborn was just wishing I would put an end to the debate. Timothy was still musing on banshees he had known. Anne studied her flute.

Patti carried on. "If I'd known you were out there howling at the moon, I wouldn't have wasted my goat salve on you. I've got to live in this county. All we thought you were doing was reading your Charles Dickens and your Shakespeare."

Clay, acquiescent: "Well, I don't begrudge the ranchers their historic antipathy to the coyote, but I have just two more things to say about this. First, there is something comforting in the fact that no matter what we do, the coyote survives.

I could hear Patti muttering, "comforting to you!" It was the plains equivalent of Prospero's "'Tis new to thee," in the *Tempest*.

She spoke her mind. "Look, my friend, this is ranch country. We raise sheep and cattle. That's what we do. That's how we pay our bills. Anything that kills our critters from disease to coyotes is unwelcome here. This is who we are, like it or not. We cannot afford to be romantic about any conditions that bring us loss. You come here to visit and you're always welcome, all of you, but your income comes from somewhere else and it doesn't depend on the environment, on weather, on predators, on market prices. If you had grown up here and not in a town you'd understand. We love this land, but we love it as realists who actually live on it, not as theorists or readers or cultural tourists."

Clay: "Touché, my dear friend. Who could ever argue with that? But I have to speak from my experience too, and we all know that four-fifths of this territory is public not private land. I agree that this country is primarily an assemblage of ranches-for-profit. But it has other purposes, some of them mandated by government and some mandated by a much higher law than that. It seems to me that cattle and sheep production must be willing to co-exist with things that either produce no profit, or even slightly impede the business of making money. I cannot help it. I love coyotes. Hell, there are coyotes in Los Angeles, one of the greatest conurbations on earth. When everything else has been poisoned or vaporized, there will still be cockroaches, ants, and coyotes."

Patti: "Are you going make the case for the cockroach next? Come, give us your cockroach call."

Clay: "I guess I don't mind people shooting coyotes. That's never easy and coyotes frequently elude even the best hunters. What really offends me is the use of strychnine guns."

Timothy: "What do you mean?"

Clay: "The cruelest way to kill a coyote is to use a strychnine gun. You put some rancid meat on it and when the coyote tries to eat it, the gun shoots a jet of strychnine into the face of the animal. It dies a terrible and agonizing death. Fortunately, it is banned in most states."

Patti: "There is no cruel way to kill a coyote. The point is to kill it. Do you think a coyote kills lambs humanely? I don't know if with all your vast education you've ever heard the word "Darwin" mentioned."

Gerhardt: "heh heh heh haaaaaaaaaaaaaaaa."

Timothy, innocent, admiring: "Clay, haven't I heard you say that if you have to die, the way you'd like to go. . . ."

Clay to Timothy, in the whisper of command: "Perhaps another time, Youthfu. . . ."

Timothy: ". . . is to be struck by lightning and then eaten by wolves or coyotes?"

Gerhardt: "Geezus, talk about weird. I'm hoping to die in a hospital, heavily sedated, bathed by bosomy nurses in crisp white uniforms, with a plastic tube up my ass."

Rita: "You'll have to remove your head first, Gerhardt."

Clay to Patti ostensibly via Timothy: "Well, youth, there are perhaps times when each of us is carried away by poetic fancy. What sounded romantic and charming in the cloister. . ."

Patti: "Cloister, bull! That kind of talk wouldn't sound charming in a lunatic asylum. I believe I'll call it a night. You make me craaaazy. Meet me at my goat shed at dawn and I'll try to rustle you up a five-iron you can carry out with you during the next thunderstorm."

She turned to Anne. "That was really lovely, Anne. I'm sorry I interrupted your solo. In spite of being taught by the defender of coyotes here, you obviously have a lot of talent and discipline."

She wrenched open the door of her truck, backfired in the parking lot for a while, and sputtered off into the night, while Gerhardt, having the time of his life, scrounged his coat pockets for something to smoke.

Anne played a little half-tune of doubtful provenance. Pat Sanborn said something about paradigm collisions and excused herself for the night. Rita was awash in some deep introspection.

As I drifted off to meditate the sheer glory of life, Timothy came up close and asked me to teach him a few coyote conjugations before the dawn.

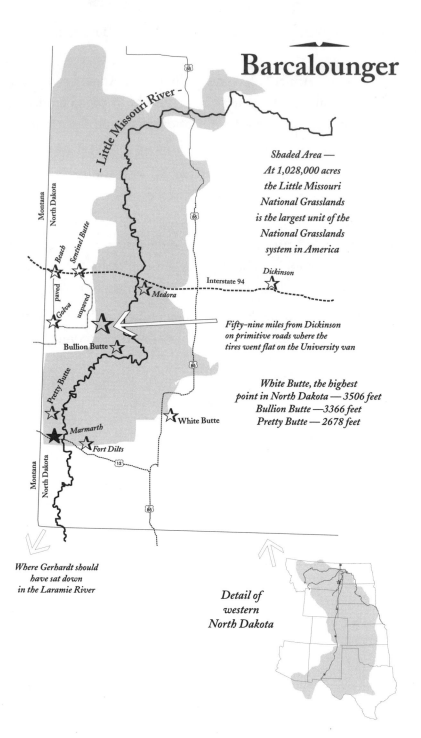

Barcalounger

Little Missouri River

*Shaded Area —
At 1,028,000 acres
the Little Missouri
National Grasslands
is the largest unit of the
National Grasslands
system in America*

Montana
North Dakota

Beach

Sentinel Butte

paved

unpaved

Golva

Bullion Butte

Pretty Butte

Marmarth

Fort Dilts

Medora

Dickinson

Interstate 94

*Fifty-nine miles from Dickinson
on primitive roads where the
tires went flat on the University van*

*White Butte, the highest
point in North Dakota — 3506 feet
Bullion Butte —3366 feet
Pretty Butte — 2678 feet*

White Butte

Montana
North Dakota

*Where Gerhardt should
have sat down
in the Laramie River*

*Detail of
western
North Dakota*

Barcalounger

Cyclops

MY PROFESSOR FRIENDS FROM THE UNIVERSITY were out in my neck of the woods in their official university van, fender decal and all, with a university credit card, and we were on official university business, though none of us knew exactly what it was. We'd had brunch with my parents in Dickinson: coffee, regionally famous sausage, scrambled eggs, English muffins, toast, orange juice, and—for Gerhardt Ludwig and my father—a chain of cigarettes. I think we were out scouting for places to take students on university retreats, and we were inspecting the lay of the land to try to determine if there was something called "spirit of place." We had vague plans to climb Bullion Butte, the premier grass mesa in North Dakota, a butte so massive that it has forced the Little Missouri to make a forty mile detour around its base.

Our reconnaissance party consisted of Gerhardt Ludwig, philosopher and professor of humanities; his wife Rita; George Frein, professor of religion; Pat Sanborn, professor of philosophy; and me, *johannes factotum* and guide, consultant to the new Integrated Studies Program we were trying to invent at the university with a grant from the National Endowment for the Humanities.

We were driving and talking and laughing and observing the countryside, and everyone was wondering where the heck we were, and Pat and George were asking me to slow down, especially at the cattle guards, and Gerhardt and Rita were thinking the same thing but unwilling to raise the issue, and I was pointing out this and that feature in the landscape, a herd of antelope here, a recognizable butte off on the horizon, and doing commentaries on the history, geology, and economics of the place, with some glances at things of the spirit, and it was, generally speaking, the kind of day you have with people of great good will and more than a little agoraphobia, when they are all mature and sensible and you are a young whippersnapper feeling your oats.

Gerhardt and I were taking turns regaling the others with the story of the time Gerhardt and Rita had driven out to meet me at Sidney, Nebraska, and we had explored the country around Fort Robinson and together had read out loud John Neihardt's "Death of Crazy Horse" on the side of a pine ridge on a hot dusty day in July, and then had driven off with cold sodas to find the Laramie River. When we found it, we all took off our shoes and socks and got into shorts and waded into the river, which ran about six inches of clear cool water.

After getting accustomed to the pebbly bottom of the river, we had discovered that it was full of minnows. This frightened Rita and didn't do Gerhardt much good either, and to tell the truth I was not at first wild about the idea, until I managed to stand still long enough to discover that the minnows were as curious about us as we were about them. This led to the usual pointless discussion about whether they considered us gods who had suddenly decided to visit their watery world, and just how they were communicating this interesting information to each other. In the midst of this humanities patter, I discovered that if I stood still, the little fishes actually came up to the extremities of my feet and explored my alien presence with their only tactile instrument, their wee mouths. If I didn't shoo them away with my pale feet, they would actually kiss and nibble me on every surface they found in the shallow water. Once I overcame my fear, it was in fact a wonderfully sensuous experience, not to mention a delightful one, to close my eyes and feel the two-inch creatures sucking the tips of my toes and probing the vulnerable flesh between my toes, all the while whisking their tails back and forth in the water to propel their little piscatory voyages of discovery. When I had become accustomed to the idea, I managed to talk Gerhardt into trying it, and both of us in turn convinced a slightly more hesitant Rita to let the fish have their way with her feet. And what feet they were!

Gerhardt took over the narrative at this point. "When I got back to Grand Forks, I told the whole story to my introductory humanities class on Tuesday morning. I was describing the experience in some detail, dwelling on how agreeable their little mouths felt as they sucked on my toes, when a girl who had never spoken one word through the whole course looked up from her notebook for the first time, and said, 'Why didn't you just sit down?'"

The van exploded in laughter.

Everyone was getting a little edgy about where exactly we were, and I couldn't exactly tell them, but I was trying to explain that thanks to Thomas Jefferson's Rectangular Survey Grid System, we couldn't really get lost. One of the perpendicular roads would inevitably lead us out to an asphalt road and then I'd know exactly how to get us where we needed to be. In the meantime, take a look at that old windmill on the side of that hill. There was a fair amount of skepticism about the reliability of the survey grid even among those who understood the concept in the abstract, and several of our members were as perplexed by the idea of a rectilinear gridwork as they were by the idea of being a half game out of first place in a pennant race. I was trying to explain correction lines when we hit a poorly constructed cattle guard at an odd angle, and the van began to drag and veer on the right side.

"Looks like we have a flat tire," I said as I pulled to a stop. Some glances were exchanged at my expense. I got out. I walked around to the passenger side of the vehicle and was about to say, "Yep, here's our problem," when I discovered that we had not one but two problems. Both right tires were entirely deflated. "Trouble, Gerhardt," I said. "We have two flat tires, and I'm guessing that there is only one spare in this van." Everyone piled out to inspect the damage and make pronouncements that teetered on the edge of judgment.

"What shall we do?" Pat asked.

"Well, I said, we passed a ranch about a quarter of a mile back. I think we should pony the van into the ranch driveway and get some help."

"Won't that ruin the tire?"

"Probably not, especially on a dirt road. I'll drive slowly. There should be at least a small cushion of air still in the tires."

So we did it.

We drove to the access road. I tried to glean a name from the mailbox for the purposes of flattery, but there was nothing there. So we pulled up in front of the house. I shut off the engine. I could tell instantly that nobody was home.

I had spoken of entering the house with bravado for the sake of my guests, but now that I was about to do it I felt considerable trepidation. North Dakotans are sometimes particular about their private property. What if the owner returned while I was trespassing in his living room? What if he had a gun? Of course he had a gun! What if he used it? And what if there were a dog inside poised to tear out my throat or at least gnaw my calf muscle? Besides, even if nothing bad came of it, I didn't particularly like the idea of entering another person's private space. It felt like an invasion even though it was a bonafide emergency. I had grown up hearing stories of North Dakotans who leave their doors unlocked and the keys in the ignition of their tractors and pickups as a courtesy to anyone who needed help. It had to do with trust and with every Dakotan's realization that prairie storms can be deadly. We live in a climate that kills. But this was the first time that I had ever actually "made myself at home" in someone else's digs.

I knocked on the door. Again. And again. I opened the door a crack and said "Hello," in that realtor's tone that suggests confidence but not familiarity. No reply. Again. I walked in.

It was a squat two story house that had been built in the thirties or forties. The outside was covered with a tan-yellow siding from the cheap throw-it-up-one-fall-to-avoid-having-to-paint end of the spectrum. It was a two-story house, but from the outside it looked as if the upstairs was cramped, mere dormer space. The downstairs consisted of four rooms: a kitchen with ancient linoleum and the first refrigerator, but a state-of-the-art dishwasher; the living room, with old spring-loaded window shades, yellowed at the frayed spots, and a grandma-hand-me-down industrial strength carpet, brown, with white and gray flecks, electroluxed almost to the pad; a bathroom with homebrew shower stall and cheap wall fixtures; and a bedroom with an old four poster bed, a matching dresser with a two-inch marble top, cracked in the middle, and clothes strewn in every direction.

I was looking for the phone.

The entire furniture inventory of the house consisted of:

√ The two-piece bedroom set;

√ A chromium kitchen table with an early version of gray-white Formica on its surface and two mismatched chairs;

√ A cheap K-Mart toaster;

√ An early—giant—microwave oven;

√ A sink full of a stained assortment of dishes;

√ Eight or nine pairs of boots of different sorts, most of them grubby, a couple of them newish;

√ A pocket calculator with outsized number pads next to the telephone, which was a beige plastic wall model with a rotary dial.

But it was the living room that was remarkable. As I stood in the doorway scanning the room, I realized that the 20x30-foot space was entirely bare except for a giant-screen television set, a brown Barcalounger, a half-eaten bowl of popcorn, some of which was scattered on the carpet near the bowl, one empty and one half-filled bottle of beer, an overflowing ashtray, and two dog-eared copies of *Playboy*.

I thought, "I'm just guessing that this is a bachelor's house."

It was not exactly Thomas Jefferson's rural America. This was not the dwelling of a man who worked moderately hard in his garden by day and at night read Homer in the original Greek. I had a sudden picture of loneliness, boredom, isolation, and temporariness. Not to mention a perfect vacuum of female energy. There did not appear to be a book in the house, though I felt certain I could rustle up a Bible (in the *Good News for Modern Man* translation) somewhere in the bedroom if I were willing to snoop.

By now my colleagues were all standing in the doorway looking uncomfortable, surveying the simplicities of the room. "Looks as if another proud alumnus of the University of North Dakota lives here," I said. Tepid laughter.

I found the telephone and called home collect. I was worried that nobody would be there, but in fact my father answered and accepted the charges. He was a bit surprised that I was calling collect, but he merely said, "What's up?" I started by asking if Mother was home, knowing that she would be infinitely more useful in any crisis than my father. She was gone. Wouldn't be back for hours. He didn't know where she was.

My heart sank. Mother would have considered it an adventure to come rescue us. Dad was another matter entirely.

I spoke breathlessly, like a disc jockey or a television commentator, not wanting to pause long enough to be interrupted until I had communicated everything my father needed to know. "Dad, I need your help. I'm with Gerhardt and the UND group in their university van. Somehow we got two flat tires at the same time in the badlands south of Sentinel Butte. Yes, it *was* a cattle guard, so far as we can ascertain. We managed to limp into a ranch yard, but the owner is apparently gone and we can't find the tools we need to repair the tires in his shop."

"Sounds like you've got yourself a problem," was my father's contribution.

"Dad, I need you to do me a favor. If you go down into my file cabinet and look in the first drawer under Maps you will find a copy of the Little Missouri National Grasslands map. It's folded in a five by eight inch format and it is clearly marked. It is wider and less colorful than a North Dakota state highway map, which wouldn't do you any good. In fact, there should be a couple of Little Missouri maps in the file. If you get a pencil, I'll tell you how to find us and you can go ahead and mark the route on the map. It's not at all hard to get here, but I'll need to show you where to make your turns. Getting to Sentinel Butte is a simple thing—just take the interstate. No, west. But then you'll need to follow grasslands and forest service roads until you get to the ranch. I'll have someone stand out at the driveway so you cannot miss us. Then we can take the tires to Golva, get them patched, and return to the van."

"These are unpaved roads?"

"Yes, unpaved, Dad, but they're very good roads. It has been a dry summer and there is a fairly fresh coat of gravel on most of them. It's almost impossible to get lost." I lied.

"We're in a pretty serious jam here, Dad, but fortunately the remedy is a simple one. Can you drive out and save your prodigal son one more time?"

There was a pause. And my father, with whom I have been, all of my life, exceedingly close, the man whose intellect I most admire of all the people I have ever met, a man who loves me to the verge of adoration, an intellectually fearless man, said,

"No."

Now I spoke with infinite gentleness. "What do you mean, 'no'?"

"I mean I would not be comfortable driving out there. I've never been there before. I'm not sure I could follow the map and Bob Stribel tells me that the forest service roads are badly marked. Besides, I'm not eager to get my windshield pitted with all that gravel."

I said, "Dad, this is not exactly a yes or no kind of situation. I can certainly understand your reluctance, my dear Padre. I think you know that I would not for any routine problem seek your help, *mein Vater*. But you have to admit that this is a pretty knotty problem, and I'm really not sure what to do unless you can find a way to come out to help us, *mi amice*."

"I tell you what," he said. I'll give you the number of Dinsdale's Texaco. You can give them a call and explain where you are and I'm sure they'd be willing to send out a wrecker to help you."

He put down the phone without waiting for me to respond and I could hear him rattling around in the cupboard for the phone book. I thought, "Well yes, I'm sure Dinsdale's *would* be happy to come out to get us. We're only 59 miles from the gas station on a Saturday afternoon during college football season. We're on a private drive off a spur of an unmarked gravel road in the middle of nowhere. I feel certain that some high school grease monkey with a walnut-sized brain or—worse—some thirty-year-old who has decided to make his career in pumping gas, would be glad to roar out like Hercules to save us, not without a few deficiencies in cartography and listening skills. Indeed, **FATHER!**, I'm sure we could hire a rescue helicopter to fly in from Denver, or we could dig the airbags out of the van and try to construct a hot air balloon, or we could find a cutting torch and melt down the van into a cryogenic shelter, or we could vote to see which of us we butcher and broil first, or we could dig a cave into the side of that hill over there and wait for the next car to pass through the district, or we could tear down this guy's house and use the lumber for firewood or. . . ."

My frail elegant father was back with the number. I said, "Let me ask you one more question, Dad. I take it there is no room for negotiating here?"

"No," he said, as nonchalantly as if I had asked him whether he wanted another ice cube in his soda. Then he said,

"Good luck."

There are times when a hard truth rolls into our beings with such purity that we cannot be angry. Naturally, in a Platonic world I would have chosen a man for all seasons to play my father. The father from whose loins I swam into life was a wholly sedentary man, a creature of habit, a phobian, a contemplative, a town dweller. He could add a dozen four-digit numbers in his head, or read the corpus of James Boswell or Shakespeare or Mark Twain, or cross-reference the Watergate testimony over the course of the winter, or solve the most sphinx-like crossword puzzle before breakfast, but he could not replace the washer in the kitchen sink. He eschewed all but one of the arts of virility. He folded in a crisis. He was wry and ironic, witty and thoughtful, sensuous and stupendously literate. But he was a moron with a pliers. I had known from the moment he answered the phone that our chances of securing his help were minimal. And if he had fetched the map and tried to come out and find us, I would almost certainly have wound up rescuing him, and—truly—it would have wounded him to have lived through the experience even if it had been successful. He had never pretended to be anything else than what he was through my whole life, and I could not blame him for being so true to himself.

Among other things, my father taught me to retain a soft spot for the frail ones of the world. That they are sometimes overwhelmed by the unexpected is not a weakness. It is just how they are wired. At the same time, I have tried all my life to become a man for all seasons, or at least a couple of seasons, to rise to the occasion, not collapse under its weight, to be willing to undertake the unusual. I want my daughter, all of her life, to say, "My daddy is equal to anything." If one could only blend the cerebral and the witty with gumption and adventure, weld by day and study Sanskrit by night, go to rodeo on Tuesday and the ballet on Saturday, think like Henry Adams and move through the world like Shane. . . . I suppose Theodore Roosevelt was as great an exemplar of this balance as the American West has produced, but Wallace Stegner was another, and Edward Abbey—at his best— was a third. Patti Perry of Marmarth exemplifies the Aristotelean balance. She might not choose to read the *New Yorker* after a long day of goat-milking, but if she did, she would bring as much sense and sensibility to the enterprise as anyone I know. But my father was none of these folks. He was a man in a chair with the English language, and he was not going to be much use to us in our little crisis. I was disappointed, but I judged him not.

With a good deal of hesitation, I went out to face my friends knowing that it would be difficult for them to understand why my father was unwilling to assist; that they would wonder as much as I how there could be any genetic link between such a father and such a son, between the contemplative and the active life, and that they would hear my news as a certain death sentence.

And they did.

I was immediately bombarded with a sharp barrage of questions: "What will we do?" "Why can't he come?" "Where is your mother, anyway?" "How often does a car pass through here?" "What if the rancher doesn't come back?" "How long would it take to walk to the nearest real ranch?" "Is there anyone else we can call?" "So what if we have to spend $300 bucks for a tow, it beats the alternative, doesn't it?" "Why were you driving so fast?" "Do we have any food in the van?" "Aren't there any buttes along paved roads in this area?" "What if we run out of cigarettes?"

Gerhardt Ludwig took control. He said, "Hold it, everyone. Let's not panic, ok? Let me just say, as the leader of this retreat, and I believe I speak for everyone, that I have complete confidence in Clay. Clay, I have just one question." [Stage pause.] "What the *hell* are we gonna do now?" This brought a cathartic laugh all around, but it was what James Joyce calls a mirthless and malicious laugh and I could see that I would be blamed for this mishap for many years to come.

I said, "First, I apologize for the situation we are in, but I want you all to know we are in absolutely no danger. Second, there is nothing to fear but fear itself." Nobody laughed. "Third, the thing to do is act, do something. If that doesn't work, we'll just try something else. One thing is certain. We're not going to solve this problem by wringing our hands. The van contains about half the IQ of the Great Plains. We ought to be able to solve a picayune problem like this. The worst case scenario is that we'll be here for a few hours, and then the owner will show up and get us back on the road. Meanwhile we'll flip coins on the *Playboys* and make some popcorn." Nobody laughed. I looked around. There were at least twenty "vehicles" in the ranch yard.

"I suggest that we simply borrow a wheel from one of the vehicles here, drive to Golva, get our tires fixed, and return with the borrowed wheel. I know the owner wouldn't mind and I doubt that he'll be back by the time we return. The problem will be in finding a wheel that matches the one on the van. Take a good look at the placement of the hubs, and let's fan out and see if we can't locate a wheel we can throw on temporarily." There was some fairly serious protest over this, mostly on the grounds that we did not have the right to mess with someone else's fleet. But most of the vehicles hadn't been moved in months, if not in years, and when I made it clear that I would both take all the responsibility and do all of the grunt work of removing the cho-sen wheel, lugging it to the van, mounting it, and reversing the entire process once we returned from Golva, everyone agreed to my plan, more or less.

Unfortunately, none of the hubs seemed to match ours. In the end, without much hope of success, we removed two or three wheels and lugged them over to the stricken van, but there was no fitting square pegs into round holes. Then I had to lug them back and reattach them to vehicles under which they might never roll again. This was time-consuming, and soon I was sweating like a pig and the others were sweating from fear itself. The frustration level of our troupe was getting pretty high. Several appeared to be close to genuine panic, and I didn't fancy having to slap them in the face and then hear them say, "thanks, I needed that," or whatever one says after being whacked by a very close friend in the middle of nowhere.

Gerhardt said, "OK, Plan A did not work out very well. Perhaps you could give us a sense of what Plan B might look like."

"I'm just guessing," I said, "that you don't want to just sit tight until whoever lives here comes home? If you were willing to do that, we'd find a place to sit together and have a little dialogue, perhaps read from the dozen or so books we are carrying between us, and, when the rancher returned, he'd simply take us to town and everything would be a simple business after that."

My guess was correct.

"Right. If we cannot wait, then we have only one choice left. We've put the spare on the van. That leaves one flat to worry about. I suggest that we simply fill up the tire as full of air as we can, and make a rush for Golva. It's at least fifteen miles away and possibly as many as twenty-five. There is a significant chance that we will damage, possibly even ruin, the wheel in question. That's going to be rather expensive, but it will not, I think, do any essential damage to the vehicle. [I lied.] Since I got us into this scrape, I'm perfectly willing to pay for all the damages."

There was a consensus that this was only appropriate. Everyone got in and buckled up gravely as if we were the crew of the Challenger. I filled the tire as full as I dared, ran the air hose back into the tool shed, shut the door quickly, took a quick look at the tire, jumped into the driver's seat, and put the van into motion. So far so good. I drove about ten miles an hour for a minute or two, got out, checked the tire, discovered that it was still apparently full, and jumped back in the van.

"Good news," I said, "It looks as if it might actually hold the air."

We drove twenty miles per hour for five or six minutes. I made another inspection. Aeolus, the God of Inflation, was on our side today. We drove thirty miles per hour for ten minutes. I inspected the tire. Then we simply drove to Golva at 45 miles per hour, though, like a school bus, I slowed virtually to a stop at every cattle guard as an act of public contrition.

When we finally rolled off the scoria gravel and onto asphalt there was a choral sigh of relief from my colleagues. Gerhardt looked like he might break out with, "Free at last, free at last, thank God almighty. . ." Everyone started to talk again, and there was even some laughter and some semi-serious back-slapping of the driver. Golva is a tiny town, and the Standard station is more or less the whole town center. I pulled into the station. We drove over the cable that sounded a clanging bell in the service bay. Everyone got out and stretched and relaxed, and stopped glaring at me.

Pat Sanborn marched into the office with an uncustomary air of command and blurted out, "You sell tires?" and when the pimply boy nodded, she barked out, "I want four new tires, top of the line, balanced, as soon as possible. Put the best of what you remove on the spare. We'll walk up the street to the café. I've got a University of North Dakota credit card here. There'll be a considerable tip if you can get this done in the next hour. And fill it up to the brim with gas, and check the oil and everything you can think of!" The pimply boy tucked into his assignment like a civilian recruited into a CIA mission of global importance.

We ate like refugees from a Jack London short story. Burgers, malts, fries, onion rings, sodas, even slices of raisin sour cream pie arrived and disappeared with dispatch. I was embarrassed to have been reckless. They were embarrassed to have panicked. I bought lunch. Everyone thanked me with a kind of strained formality, and we walked back to the gas station in silence. The total for the van came to $543. We slapped the whole business on the university credit card. Pat said she would submit the bill and see if anyone challenged it, but that it seemed to her to be a university matter and no one in that Byzantine bureaucracy need know that an unauthorized person was driving the vehicle at the time of the mishap.

I took this little insult without comment. Pat drove the van the fifty miles to my house in Dickinson while I slumped in my seat watching the hills recede. If I could have persuaded my colleagues to comply with my wishes, I would have had them merely slow down to about 20 in front of my house and I'd have tucked and rolled onto the lawn. They did have enough grace to make their farewells at the curb. There was no lingering that day. I shook hands with everyone and even hugged great-hearted Gerhardt Ludwig, but I did not invite them in to pay their respects to my dear father.

Dear father was reading in his chair. He didn't ask many questions and I didn't volunteer much that night. When Mother arrived, I gave her a sharp look to stave off her questions and likely responses, and waited to tell her the full story when Dad went up to perform his endless evening ablutions. I resolved to drive out one day to find out who the ranch hand was, to explain why three of his vehicles had been tampered with, and to thank him for leaving his door and his shed open. Who knows: perhaps he formulated an alien abduction story out of the experience. It is more likely that he never even knew we had visited his precinct. If I had known his rural route mailing address, I might have sent him a subscription to *Playboy* or at least *TV Guide*, or a dozen jars of Orville Redenbacher's popcorn. But way led on to way and I never went back.

I often wonder what the half life of a Barcalounger is in that part of the world or if he eventually convinced a school marm to live with him and be his love and with him stately pleasures prove, or if he moved to Denver or Billings to take up a trade. I think of him at the end of the day sitting exhausted, sock-begrimed, and beery, watching his giant television screen under the constellation Orion, and I wonder, sometimes, if my father, in his tender calfskin slippers, with his jingling tumbler of Walkers & water, his *New*

Yorker or *New Republic*, and his pack of cigarettes, is half-watching the same television program 59 miles—and a world—away.

And so I entered again the growth of innocence

And writing —

Now! — I am furry with animal light.

I enter the ecstatic

Round dance of the fox and the field mouse on the scarred, warring
Hills,

the rites of passage toward the sacred city of birdsong,

The tunnels of morning hunger and the ancient rivers of night. . .

Thomas McGrath
Letter to an Imaginary Friend, Part Two: IV

Let Them Be Rock Stars
and Scholars and Such

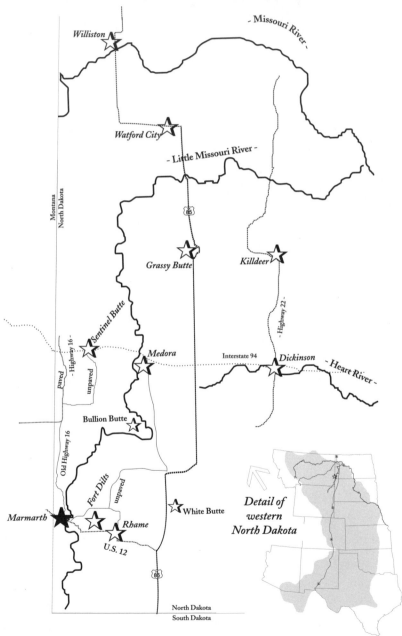

Williston

Missouri River

Watford City

Little Missouri River

85

Montana
North Dakota

Grassy Butte

Killdeer

Sentinel Butte

Highway 22

Highway 16

paved

unpaved

Medora

Interstate 94

Dickinson

Heart River

Old Highway 16

Bullion Butte

Fort Dilts

unpaved

White Butte

Detail of
western
North Dakota

Marmarth

Rhame

U.S. 12

85

North Dakota
South Dakota

Let Them Be Rock Stars
and Scholars and Such

Penelope & Telemachus

MY MOTHER IS A GREAT READER. For years she had read everything she could get her hands on about the American West, especially novels, and she had developed theories about the development of cowboy and ranch culture. I was frankly skeptical of her theories, which seemed to me to be too dependent on Fenimore Cooper, too obsessive about the proper "conventions," but I was glad to have a mother who had theories about such things. The fact that I had never actually read Fenimore Cooper made it difficult to engage in debate with her, though the same liability did not stop my sister Leslie from weighing in authoritatively at will. She had built a persona based on having extreme opinions that were seldom, if ever, propped up by homework.

Mother took it all in stride and devoured books about the cattle industry. She was helplessly in love with some Platonic cowboy of the mind, a fact that her cerebral and elegant husband, a banker, looked upon with wry bemusement. My prejudice was decidedly for the farmer in his simple work boots, not the rancher in his spiffy cowboy boots and buckles. One afternoon when my mother was singing the praises of the ranch world, my sister walked into the room, instantly picked up the thread of the conversation, and said, "So what's so interesting about a rancher? Put a bunch of cattle in the fields. They make babies. At the end of the year round them up and sell them at auction. Repeat. And this is a noble pastoral way of life?"

From time to time Mother would tell us that she was tempted to apply for a grant from the state department of higher education to interview the cowboys and ranchers of western North Dakota and produce a slide program for use in her classes, and perhaps those of other teachers. Whenever she indulged in this agreeable pipedream, I'd pledge to take the photographs for her and chaperon her on her travels. My father only smiled and raised an eyebrow a hair's width or two, knowing that the best way to discourage her was not overtly to discourage her.

My sister Leslie had, over the years, turned sibling rivalry into a high comic art. She barely tolerated my love affair with the Great Plains, but she found Mother's interest in the North Dakota outback appalling, because she ascribed it to some kind of baleful influence I had gained over a grown woman who would not be even slightly interested in such nonsense were it not for me. This was wrong, and cruel, particularly when one considers that my mother had read at least a hundred times more than I had about the West. When Mother would begin to daydream about conducting such a research project, Leslie would step back a few paces, wait for a convenient interruption point, and say in her most mincing tone, "Polly want a cracker?" Mother did not find this amusing.

Leslie piped these sweet words once too often. Without informing any of us, Mother applied for a small research grant, obtained it, and began to lay in a supply of audio tapes. Leslie continued her career of deep sarcasm. Dad swallowed hard and tried to suppress his chagrin. I tried to figure out how I was going to find the time to accompany Mother on these journeys. It was clear that she was going to hold me to my promise.

In the end, Dad bought us an old $250 clunker of a car, a tan

1966 BelAir, with a tube-type radio better than any silicon receiver I have ever heard, with a couple of extra spares in the massive trunk. We called it the Beast, I cannot remember why, and in its broken-down hull Mother and I explored western North Dakota together.

For two long summers we ventured forth as often as we could beat back other claimants on our time. We interviewed more than fifty ranchers and half that many cowboys. We took thousands of photographs. We collected maps, pamphlets, county and township histories, memoirs, historical photographs and postcards, and several hundred hours of audio tapes. By the time we finished the project—we called our enterprise Shoebox Productions—we had visited every town, every village, every combination gas station and café west of the Missouri River in North Dakota. We had been on almost every road—some of them treacherous—and we had been seriously lost at least a dozen times. I'd changed a half-dozen flat tires and the Beast's old clutch had nearly marooned us in a place you would not want to have to walk out of. We ate a thousand cheeseburgers at Mert's Café in Marmarth and at Walker's Wheel Inn near Grassy Butte. It was on the wall of Mert's Café that I first read the delightful Rodeo Cowboy Prayer:

As cowboys, Lord, we don't ask for any special favors,
We don't ask to never break a barrier,
or to draw a round of steer that's hard to throw,
or a chute fighting horse,
or a bull that is impossible to ride.
We only ask that you help us to compete
as honest as the horses we ride.

So when we do make that last ride
that is inevitable for us all to make,
to that place up there,
where the grass is green and lush and stirrup high,
and the water runs cool, clear, and deep —

You'll tell us as we ride in
that our entry fees have been paid.[†]

Who can resist smirking at this?

We camped out at least thirty nights, more often than not in the same place—a barely developed forest service one-holer just off U.S. 85 near Watford City. I showed my mother every secret place I knew.

We had looked in vain two or three times for the celebrated Ice Caves, a crevice on the National Grasslands where you will find sick-looking ice chunks twelve months per year—a reminder, one is told, of the nearness of the Arctic Circle and the last ice age. All this I take on faith, for the Ice Caves were to us the Holy Grail we were forever approaching and never quite grasping. We had listened to hundreds of hours of Canadian Broadcasting Corporation (CBC) radio programming. And we had some of the best talks we ever had—some of them about extraordinarily personal and volatile subjects.

When we camped I usually made something we called Remarkable Stew. My sister, who joined us just once, and ruined the experience, said it was neither stew nor remarkable, and she abused my mother for pretending to find it delicious. It consisted of sautéed green peppers and onions, carrots and potatoes, cubed beef and Durkee gravy mix, rice and beans and plenty of water. I cooked it on my old Svea stove and we ate it at dusk so hot that the first dozen bites burned the tops of our mouths. I cannot make Remarkable Stew even now, two decades later, in my solo journeys through the American West, without welling up in emotion at the memory of mother and son, Mother and Son, in the heart of western North Dakota, dividing up a bar of Baker's

---

[†]This is how I remember it. I have heard versions of this prayer at dozens of rodeos around the Great Plains over the years. It is virtually a staple of the rodeo circuit. I believe the original prayer, somewhat longer and more formal, was written by a man named Clem McSpadden.

chocolate and a couple of slices of sharp cheddar cheese, reviewing the adventures of the day far from the madding crowd, and saying, "I hope Dad's not worrying too much about us," before saying good night, Mother disappearing into her tent, I to my sleeping bag beneath the endless stars. If I could only keep one set of memories of my mother, these would be they. The Christmases and the confirmations, the anniversaries and the awards, the funerals and the fussing—all that is dross by contrast.

Opening the curtain of western North Dakota to my mother, showing her places she would never have visited without me, passing on some of what my mentor Mike Jacobs had taught me to her, so loving and so willing a student, was one of the supreme pleasures of my life. We have been through good times and bad, my mother and I, through periods when we were in perfect harmony and others in which we could barely stand to be in the same room. Through thick and thin, the bedrock of our relationship has been the experience we shared as adults together in the Little Missouri country—the mutual respect, the shared creativity, the uncomplicated affection, the fund of joyous memory. We enjoy that rarest of family commodities: an adult friendship formed from adult adventures. There is much in my adult experience that I would cheerfully give up, some that I am desperate to discard, and some that I would be willing to yield were the pressures significant enough. But I would not under any circumstances agree not to have experienced those two delightful summers with my mother. Among other things, I helped to keep alive in her a spirit of adventure that my father could not appreciate or support. Among other things, she filled my soul with a pool of confidence that has served me through life, that indeed may be said to have kept me alive on a couple of occasions when it seemed that my life was essentially over.

Beyond the confines of our housebound relationship, my mother and I had conversations that neither of us could ever have expected. We had wandered off the grid, and we were liberated therefore. We talked about our dreams, our doubts, our fears, and our perplexities. We talked about the West. We talked about my frail father, my mother's relationship with my frail father, and my own. We talked about mating, about friendship, about parenting. We talked about our values. We talked about literature. We talked about religion. And we talked about God. Sitting on the banks of the Little Missouri River, gazing out into the middle distance, we found a conversational candor we could never have sustained at the kitchen table. We probed each other's souls and sensibilities in a way that I think is unusual between parent and child, mother and son.

We never stayed out more than two nights in succession, to keep the lid on Dad's anxieties about coyotes and rattlesnakes. Mother lined up the interviews. I drove the car, took the pictures, and served as the security blanket of the operation. I always insisted on factoring in some padding time, loafing time, see-where-that-two-trail-road-might-take-us time. Mother was perfectly willing to indulge my wanderlust, so long as I assured her that we would get back to blacktop alive more or less within the framework of our time constraints. We'd load up the Beast with cameras and film, a tape recorder and spare batteries, and an old yellow Green Stamp cooler filled with blue-ice packs, cheese, fruit, bread, Baker's chocolate, hard candy, licorice, and plenty of soda.

My mother is not much of a camper (I'd give her 1.5 on the wilderness consciousness scale.[†]) Given her druthers, she would have preferred a couple of motel rooms. Or a highly-developed public campground with showers, or at least flush toilets and running water. She was willing to stay at unimproved

---

[†]See "Learning to Hunt with the Wally Brothers," beginning on page 171.

campgrounds, so long as there was an outhouse of some description on the property, as long as the car was nearby and she got to sleep with the keys. She chose not to camp out in the middle of nowhere. In the mornings, no matter how badly she had slept on the hard ground, she was invariably cheerful and ready for action.

II

WE ALMOST ALWAYS TRAVELED TOGETHER, but on one or two occasions I went out alone, when some professional or domestic imperative kept her off the road. It was unfortunate that she could not join me at the Old Timer's Rodeo in Medora, in the summer of 1976. It was her kind of event. It was a hapless celebration that did not even make the hapless local papers, but it really was the last time that several serious North Dakota rodeo men competed: Alvin Nelson, who won the 1957 National Saddlebronc Competition at the Cow Palace in San Francisco, and not only brought home the trophy but a trophy wife, Kaye, the 1957 Miss North Dakota Rodeo Princess; Jim Tescher; Duane Howard; Joe Chase; Walt Neuens and others.

The announcer was an outstanding third-rater named Syd, with a baritone voice full of TV and radio aspirations, carefully glued jet black hair, and a winning smile. He came equipped with a mouth full of patriotism, the purity of the Nazarene, the code of the West, pastoral pieties, anti-urban, anti-environmentalist, antifeminist, and anti-intellectual humor, and some hints of bigotry. He was, in short, the epitome of the cowboy philosophy of life. After an ear-splitting, soul-numbing rendition of Chris LeDoux's song "Rodeo Cowboy," performed by the beefy runner-up of something in a pink leisure ensemble, we settled into a dog day's competition designed to let the old timers show the right stuff one last time.

The old boys were modestly competent at calf roping, and on the whole abysmal at everything else. If it required young legs or a finely-wrought sense of balance, the competitors looked like bandy-legged, middle-aged ranchers, who did most of their cow work from the cab of a pickup. Poor Syd found himself doing a great deal of excusing and even apologizing. "Ladies and Gentlemen, you have no idea how difficult this sport is. What you see before you are gen-u-wine ath-a-leets, some of the finest this great country has ever seen. In their prime, there weren't nothing these boys couldn't do on the back of a horse." This was not prime time. By the time the rodeo ended, everyone in the audience, and especially the competitors, were glad this was the last time these old timers would have to strut their stuff.

So it was with heightened alertness that we heard Syd say, "Ladies and Gentlemen, boys and girls, we have a special treat for you this afternoon. We all know that before the Knights of the Prairie came to this great grassland of ours, there were Indians living here in God's country. While it's true they didn't know quite how to use this land, we all have shed common tears for their unavoidable submission to the forces of human progress. Without getting too religious, I want to say there was a Manifest Destiny in the white man's conquest of the plains. We can comfort ourselves that we fought them fair and square on their own ground. It's been said, Ladies and Gentlemen, that the Sioux under Sitting Bull and Crazy Horse were the finest light Calvary [sic] that the world has ever seen. They're gone now, but their ghosts still haunt this great land of ours. I don't know a single working cowboy—and folks I've had the honor of meeting most of them—who doesn't feel a sense of sadness for the West that is no more. They were buffalo hunters from time immemorial, those old Indian bucks, and they done it with beauty—never wasted a sinew or a bladder, ate their buffalo hooves and all. We could all learn from that. What some folks don't know is that they were natural-born cow punchers too, these red men, at least when they were sober. We all know that Indians haven't fared too well in the modern world—it's a long leap from your bow and arrow to civilization in less than a hundred years—but quite a number of our Indian, may I say our Native American, friends have gone on to be serious rodeo competitors. You are fortunate today because you're going to see one of the best of them. He's a red man with a white heart, and he hails from White Earth, North Dakota. I've seen him ride many times, and I can tell you he's a Christian gentleman and a credit to his race. Ladies and Gentleman, competing today in the calf roping event as a special tribute to the old timers' rodeo is Mr. Marvin Eagle Soldier."

The crowd of two or three hundred onlookers turned their gaze to the chutes on the west end of the Medora rodeo arena. There was a long pause, as if the universe had been placed momentarily on hold. Everyone quieted down. The chute sprang open. A calf burst into the arena. Everyone tracked the calf, but kept an eye open for the majestic entrance of Marvin Eagle Soldier.

Marvin Eagle Soldier did not appear. Something was wrong. Several seconds passed.

And then Marvin Eagle Soldier made his appearance on top of a majestic bay horse. Unfortunately, he was not fully in control of the moment. He was, in fact, performing a virtually perfect reenactment of Lee Marvin's famous entrance in the film *Cat Balou*. Marvin Eagle Soldier was drunk. He was very drunk indeed.

His horse rolled into the arena on his own recognizance, entirely unguided by the red man with the white heart. The crowd went totally silent. Marvin seemed to realize that he must take control of the situation. He pulled himself up to a sitting position and began to chase the calf, which by now was listing at the far end of the arena waiting to be released to a holding chute. Marvin closed in on his prey, lifted his lariat from its cradle with that hyper-precision that only a drunk man needs to employ, notched the lariat, twirled it around his head in a series of beautiful loops that promised to redeem this awful moment, and then hurled the lariat forward like a man who had roped ten thousand calves.

Alas.

Marvin Eagle Soldier somehow roped the head of his own horse.

Marvin Eagle Soldier's horse panicked.

Marvin Eagle Soldier's horse pulled to a stop, threw its head forward to get out from under the errant lasso.

Marvin Eagle Soldier pitched like a salmon over the head of his magnificent horse and dropped like a sack of potatoes unto the dirt at the center of the Medora rodeo arena.

Then for good measure the horse stomped Marvin Eagle Soldier in the abdomen. And bolted to the other end of the arena where it stood looking nervous and guilty as Marvin Eagle Soldier lay flat on his back, motionless, like Hector or Patroclus before the walls of Troy. He fell thunderously, and his armor clattered about him.

There was a very long pause. The crowd stayed stricken to silence.

Finally the professional, Syd, took control.

"Well, Ladies and Gentlemen, boys and girls, if you ask me, it appears that Marvin Eagle Soldier might have imbibed a bit too much Fire Water before today's competition."

There was another pause.

Then the assembled multitude broke into unquenchable, Homeric laughter. They laughed loud and long. They slapped their thighs. They slapped each other's backs. It was the funniest thing they ever heard.

Spotters rode out and hauled Marvin Eagle Soldier off the field. Syd provided unwelcome updates on Marvin's condition for the rest of the afternoon.

White-Indian relations on the northern plains were set back—again.

It was, so far as I know, the last time that Marvin Eagle Soldier rode in a rodeo.

All things considered, I was glad my mother had not made the trip with me to see the last great ride of the old-time rodeo heroes of North Dakota.

III

MOST OF THE INTERVIEWS MY MOTHER CONDUCTED were interesting but not remarkable. Cow folk are hopelessly romantic and hopelessly taciturn at the same time. One always senses that they have something profound in their souls that they are unable or unwilling to articulate. So most of the hundreds of hours of our interviews are basic stuff—invaluable as data points, but not much use as humanities perspectives on the theme of American pastoral. Once or twice only we managed to open the shutters onto the sublime.

The first of these moments came in an interview with Bill Adams, an old old man who lived with his old old wife on a tiny rented spread west of Killdeer Mountain. We spent an afternoon with him a year or two before he died. He had been in North Dakota forever—almost from the beginning of its pioneer history—and he had peaked as a cowboy back when there was no mechanization of ranch agriculture whatsoever. He told us of a line cabin deep into the breaks country, far from the ranch homestead, that he used to stay in a couple of times each year. It was a low log shack, nothing more, always cold, tiny, not much more than a cot and a stove and a windbreak, without electricity, without easy water, and without a road to its door. He told us how he used to rise well before the dawn on winter mornings out there, alone, and make some hot coffee in a blue-mottled ceramic pot, and then saddle up in the fierce cold dark morning, and ride along the ridge checking on the cattle. Bill Adams had a soft and gentle voice, filled with unself-conscious nostalgia for a lost era of American life.

I could feel those raw dawns as he described the days of his youth, and I could feel the hot bite of that eternal coffee, with the coyotes making their last calls of the night, scores of miles from the nearest habitation, when the country was new, the Indians barely herded away to scrabbly reservations. I wanted to have been riding alongside him, quiet, ears perked, listening to the creak of saddle leather and the snorting of the horses, hoping he would stop soon and pull out that jar of coffee. He was as authentic as anyone I ever met. He was utterly obscure. His immortality consists of a few dozen photographs distributed among his kin, and a few seconds in my mother's audiovisual program. His voice was so nearly inaudible that we could use almost none of his interview, the richest of all that we ever conducted in all that landscape.

The other sublime moment was when we ventured out across the line into Montana to interview a remarkable ranch couple we had heard about. Ty and Heather Russell lived in a cinder-block house embedded into the east bench of a badlands tributary of the Yellowstone near Sidney, Montana. Ty had done a fair amount of rodeoing in his youth and he was an officer in the stockman's association, and Heather's beauty was a matter of legend in twenty counties. She had grown up in Denver, the daughter of a surgeon, and the story was that she had turned Ty's head in the way that only a fatally attractive woman can. He had nearly lost the family ranch to roses and jewelry and plane tickets—and a holiday in Jamaica that was still the subject of rumors twenty years later. But at last she had yielded to his entreaties and married the cow man from Montana, and had tried to bring a bit of civility to a marginal ranch that didn't even get telephone service until 1969.

Heather Russell was a remarkably attractive woman, and she knew she was still a remarkably attractive woman. Ty was wiry and gnarled, still virile after a thousand low-level ranch accidents and decades of meager success in the pastoral economy. When we arrived at the appointed time, Ty was resting. He had been up most of the night fighting a grass fire with his neighbors. He was exhausted. He won my mother's eternal affection by showing her his cowboy hat, blackened by smoke, with a couple of dollar-sized holes burned through it by the flying sparks of the fire, the sorriest looking cowboy hat you ever saw, and telling her, apparently in earnest, that it looked as if he could wear it for another year or two after all. Heather served bad iced tea in the living room, which had the gray luminosity of the isolated ranch house about it, with a few dozen hardback books on the dusty shelves, many of them L'Amour and the rest Zane Grey as far as I could tell from where I sat. Heather looked splendid in her jeans and white blouse, her blonde hair tied in the back. At the end of the interview, I said, "I'd like to take a few pictures of you and Ty at the back of the house overlooking the river."

Heather was surprised, almost shocked. She wasn't prepared for the idea of photographs (we had called *and* written with this specific request). She could not see what good photographs would do. Why not photograph Ty, he's the one you came out to meet? Why, she hadn't been photographed for years, perhaps not since 1959 when she was the princess of the Cherry Creek Junior League Ball. She had been urged to compete in the Miss Denver contest—people said she was much prettier than the girl who won the title—but she was not sure that Christ looked favorably on beauty contests, and she started junior college instead.

I persevered with as much patience as I could muster. Heather said she thought we had better just give up the idea of photographs, and she excused herself for a minute while Mother finished up her interview with Ty. Half an hour passed. Then it was forty minutes.

Suddenly Heather Russell appeared—like Penelope among the suitors in the *Odyssey*, when Athena has stepped in to heighten her sexual gravity, and stirred the suitors to unquenchable lust and distraction. She was wearing a green rodeo ensemble, with the crispest whitest pleated blouse in human history, and she had made up her face like a professional model, with magnificent red lipstick, which glowed in the semi-gloom of that July afternoon, and she wore a pair of beautiful, expensive, white and black-flecked cowboy boots, and she had done up her hair in some impossibly alluring manner. She looked stunning. She knew she looked stunning. She could have been Elizabeth Taylor reappearing after changing into something more comfortable in *Who's Afraid of Virginia Woolf*. She stood in the doorway with the luminous white light enveloping her from behind, and she said, "Are you sure you need photographs of Ty and me? Wouldn't it be better if we did it another time?"

So I took a thousand pictures of the Russells standing stiffly like Grant Wood's American pastoralists. They were not good photographs, did not really serve Mother's purposes, but I look at them sometimes with deep amusement, Heather spectacular standing next to the crumpled and bent Ty, their modest house slumping behind them along the banks of the creek.

One of the greatest moments of my life came as Heather Russell sat—after she had suited up for the photo shoot—answering my mother's sometimes stilted questions about daily chores on the ranch, her aspirations for her sons Ty, Jr. and Cody, her view of the relationship between government and grazing rights, her favorite place on the ranch, the meaning of the Yellowstone River, etc. Mother asked something innocuous about why Heather had chosen to marry a rancher. Mrs. Russell gave a kind of Christian-formulaic answer, full of the usual pieties, but then she paused and looked Mother straight in the eyes, and said, "You know, I could never have married a man who was not good in the saddle."

I had to get up and leave the room.

IV

WE WERE UP IN THE NORTH COUNTRY listening to CBC Saskatchewan when the news flashed to the world. It was August 16, 1977. The King was dead. Elvis Presley had fast-fooded and over-the-countered himself to death in his bloated mansion in Memphis, Tennessee. He was 42. Neither Mother nor I had ever found Elvis endearing—when he was young and gorgeous his music had not appealed to us (it's Ginger or Mary Ann, Elvis or the Beatles, and we were solidly Beatles), and in his premature dotage he was a mere hog in our eyes. He weighed more than 300 pounds at the time of his death. I find it easier at century's end to watch *Easy Rider* or *Vanishing Point* than footage of the late concerts, when he slurred his lyrics, gasped for breath after a single tune, and had to be removed from his jumpsuits by the Jaws of Life. So far as I know I had never seen an Elvis movie.

Still, you cannot hear of the death of Elvis Presley without a pang for the golden age of the 50s and 60s. As the CBC system scrambled to cover the momentous story, the Saskatchewan affiliate played a series of Elvis' spirituals, which—to my mind—

are the finest music he ever recorded. All his Grammy Awards were for gospel.[†] We listened to the early reaction interviews and the hushed Canadian commentaries with half-grins on our faces, not knowing where mirth bumped over into blasphemy. We were in the middle of cattle country, in a place the King never saw, but a place where he was revered like an Apollonian god. We had, for the moment, forgotten all about cowboys and ranchers of the American West.

Then the hosts of *As it Happens* decided to go to the source itself, to ring up (to use the quaint Canadian phrase) Wolfman Jack. Is there anything finer than live radio? The Wolfman was called. The Wolfman was home. The Wolfman answered. And the interview began:

As it Happens (AIH): Wolfman, thanks for taking our call. We are sorry to intrude upon your busy shed-yule at such a difficult time. We're calling to get your reaction to the news.

Wolfman Jack (WMJ): Heeeeehhhy, no problem. What's hap-pen-ing, man? The Wolfman is ready to tell all.

AIH: Well, sir, we'd appreciate your reaction to the tragedy.

WMJ: I have no idea what you boys is talking about. Speak English, man.

AIH: Is it possible that you don't yet know? Elvis Presley died at 2:30 p.m. this afternoon.

WMJ: Hey, man, don't jive me about a thing like that. That's not funny.

AIH: Sir, I'm quite serious. Elvis Aaron Presley passed away at Graceland earlier this afternoon.

[†]Between 1959 and 1974, Presley was nominated for fourteen Grammy Awards. He won in 1967 (Best Sacred Performance) and in 1972 and 1974 (Best Inspirational Performance). He had three Platinum Records, thirty-five Gold Records, and one hundred and six Top 40 hits. He appeared in thirty-three films.

There was a long pause.

WMJ: The King is dead?

AIH: I'm afraid so.

The Wolfman wept on Canadian national radio for more than two minutes. And nobody interrupted. It was Canada. He was, it turns out, speechless. He had nothing to say. He needed time to think. He needed to be alone. He had some calls to make. He just wanted to say that an era of American history, no, an era of the history of the world, was over. The Wolfman wept again. The Wolfman rang off.

CBC Saskatchewan played Elvis' masterful rendition of "Amazing Grace."

It was one of the loveliest moments of our lives, mother and son. We never talk about those happy golden summers without recalling the death of the King and the Wolfman's public grief, the day the music died.

V

MY MOTHER WAS WELL-READ, ENTHUSIASTIC, AND EAGER TO LEARN. But she was pretty green in cowboy country and she made some delightful mistakes. My favorite was near Killdeer, North Dakota, at a small horse-training spread. We watched a couple work together to break a horse: patting it, throwing a blanket over its shoulder, placing a tiny saddle on its back and removing it, again and again, stepping up into the stirrups for a couple of seconds and dismounting, with a dozen intermediate steps. We watched in fascination for a couple of hours. As we were about to drive away, mother asked about a contraption that stood next to the corral. It looked like a merry-go-round. It had a dozen metal radii, with ropes dangling down to about three feet from the ground. I didn't know quite what it was either, but I was not about to ask. "Well, said the horse breaker's wife, "the horses get pretty well lathered during the training, sometimes, and we use that rig to cool them off real slow." It took me a few seconds to realize that the horses are simply bridled to the dangling ropes, and made to walk slowly round and round as they cool off from their exertions. Then I turned to Mother.

Her eyes were the size of silver dollars.

I realized instantly that she had missed the point a little. It was clear to me that she had in her mind's eye a picture of the horses being lifted off their feet by the power of the whirligig, and whisked around and around in the air, their nostrils flaring, their manes flying like guidons, their legs rising higher and higher until they were perfectly parallel with the earth. Her mental picture of tired horses being whirled by centrifugal force until they were dry as the plains wind, in a glorious travesty of a carnival ride, was as delightful as it was ludicrous. Still, I gave her the whatever-you-do-keep-your-mouth-shut look that every child perfects, and waited until we were safely down the road to set her straight. This became my father's favorite story from our travels. Mother still gets defensive when she makes me tell it.

The one time we took my sister and her boyfriend camping, in a paved and plumbed campground in the north unit of Theodore Roosevelt National Park, we arrived late in the day, with about an hour of sun remaining, and I was worried that there would not be a campsite, for it was the height of the tourist season. When we entered the odious one-way loop road system favored by campground designers, I saw that there was one still-unoccupied site near the end of the ¾ mile loop. I was afraid that it would be taken by the time we could circumnavigate the loop, so I simply drove in the wrong way, violating the one-way principle of the egress road, and parked at the place we coveted. Forty minutes later a park service ranger appeared. I knew immediately that we were in trouble, since we could only be parking in the direction our car faced if we had violated the park's traffic code. I was prepared to go to jail or pay an enormous fine or at least be booted out of the park for the night. The jig was up, as far as I was concerned. There is nothing more righteous than a national park cop.

The ranger got slowly out of his car and walked up in the swaggering way of men with badges. I walked out to meet my doom. The others walked a dozen steps behind me. He said, "Sir, were you aware that this park uses a system of one-way drives to the individual campsites?" I was prepared to take the fall for my family when my mother pushed past me and said, "Officer, of course we are aware of the traffic system here. We're from Dickinson. You don't understand. It's just that to make things easier for unloading our gear, we *backed* into our campsite." I tried to prevent my dear mother from completing this lie, but there was no stopping her. She would not be interrupted. Even my sister began to blush. The ranger looked quizzically at mother. He looked at my sister. He glanced at me. He looked again at my mother. He started to open his mouth. Then he said, "Well, ma'am, may I say, that was a very nice piece of driving you did to get into that spot." And he left.

It took about half an hour to explain to Mother that the only way her pathetic lie could have made sense would have been for us to have backed our BelAir ¾ of a mile around the one-way asphalt road and into the campsite, a feat as tedious as it would have been pointless; that the only person who was even remotely taken in by her story was Mother herself; that the ranger must be, in fact, one of the choice ones of the earth, a man with a sense of humor as well as Christian charity. We giggled for hours over that, and Mother hid in the trees every time an official pea-green ranger truck drifted past on patrol.

VI

No MATTER WHAT ELSE WE DID, we tried always to finish up by driving out of Marmarth around five p.m., up ND 16, surely one of the most marginal state highways in America. To say it is unpaved does not do justice to its meagerness. It has been the grave of many cars and all RVs (there is a God!) As the sun began to cast shadows on the low butte country to the west, we'd meander up the dirt road, without a care in the world, negotiate ND 16's two washes, get out to take pictures, and talk about how fortunate we were to live in such a place and to be working on such a project together. Over the course of time we came to depend on that improbable road. Two precincts between Marmarth and Golva were etched permanently into our souls. First, there is a place where the river swings in to greet the road. We'd get out to stretch there and check the depth of the river—a game of inches. It looked like a scene from a *National Geographic* study of the savannah of Africa. One day when all had been serenity I told mother I wanted to be buried there on a scaffold, Sioux-style. After she rebuked me for harboring such organic and morbid thoughts, she agreed to do it so long as my Marmarth pals Patti Perry and Merle Clark handled the illegalities and someone helped her obtain the buckskins and construct the scaffold. Later she told me she wanted to be cremated after her last ride in the arena of life and her ashes strewn in the Little Missouri River right there below Pretty Butte. That one should be easy enough—one day deep into the next century. I hope I'm strong enough to hike the ashes in to the site from Marmarth—a distance of 18 river miles.

The second spot we never failed to honor is farther north on ND 16 by twenty miles or so, north of Pretty Butte where I got married, not far from Bullion Butte where I spent the Millennial moment alone with the coyotes and the cosmos, on the astoundingly cold and star-spangled night of 31 December 1999. After threading its way through breaks and bluffs and miniature buttes, through the dinosaur alley, through washes and cutbanks, ND 16 finally climbs out of the badlands country and up onto the smoother shelf of the Great Plains. We always stop there, at the top of that climb, on the orange scoria road, and look back to the south and west into the most jumbled landscape in North Dakota, one of the least likely places on earth, a place sacred to me and to us. We sometimes take pictures there, sometimes of ourselves in a kind of same-time-next-year commitment to record-keeping. Once we sat for a long time and observed a magnificent thunderstorm move through the jumble country to the south. It was late summer. It was late afternoon. I was still a college student then. Mother remembers me saying, as I eased the car back into gear, "Homer is right, as always. Zeus of the golden thunder must actually exist. The Greeks had it right with their sky gods. That's the last time I'll dismiss mythology." I was young then, enchanted by literature and not yet in need of *re*-enchantment.

Mother's slide-tape program was a hit. She wrote the outline. She assembled the photographs. I spent two weeks spread out in the family living room editing audio tape the old fashioned way, with an exacto knife and adhesive tape strips. Mother dutifully tried to stay awake through the three all-nighters that were required to meet our deadlines. We were up against the clock. I was about to go back to college. She had to submit her research report. We put the lid on Shoebox Enterprises. Her work went on to win awards, to give her school and her fellow teachers and even her daughter pride. It made my father cry.

When my father died, a few years ago, and we had fulfilled the socially-mandated rituals, Mother and I drove the great loop again—I would say "one last time," but we will, I know, make the journey again, and again, and again until one of us succumbs—and we stopped in the usual spots and prayed in a kind of informal manner there. We might have scattered my father's ashes in our secret place on ND 16, but he would not have liked to be so far from town, in a place he never saw, in a countryside he did not admire, in an ethos he did not appreciate. So we scattered him in the trees near the green of his favorite hole at the golf course instead.

The King has been dead these twenty years. It is hard to imagine him in his sixties, doing interviews on country cable, wrapping his bloat form in cling wrap and larding up to fit into his white leather jumpsuits, appearing on *Politically Incorrect* to denounce drugs and Arabs and gun control. Still, his death in 1977, as Samuel Johnson said of the death of the actor David Garrick, eclipsed the gaiety of nations.

I know only this. Whenever I hear Elvis croon his lonely gospel hymns on the radio, I can see the butte and the blacktop, the ridge and the skyline we had in view when the news flashed to the world that August afternoon. (Heather Russell is in there somewhere, too.) And I can still see my mother's quizzical expression as she tried to decide whether the moment called for solemnity or mirth. And I know this too: When Elvis made that last great ride up to the arena in the sky where the grass runs stirrup high, and the waters cool, clear, and deep, I feel certain that he was told that his entry fees had been paid.

Are you lonesome tonight? Of course you are. This is America.

Well — money talks. It's hard
To say "love" loud enough in all that mechanical clamor
And perhaps the commune must fail in the filth of the American night —
Fail for a time. . .
                          But all time is redeemed by the single man —
Who remembers and resurrects.
                          And I remember.
                                              I keep
The winter count.
                          And will remember and hold you always although
Fortuna, her heavy wheel, go over these hearts and houses.

Thomas McGrath
Letter to an Imaginary Friend, Part Two: II

Learning to Hunt
with the Wally Brothers

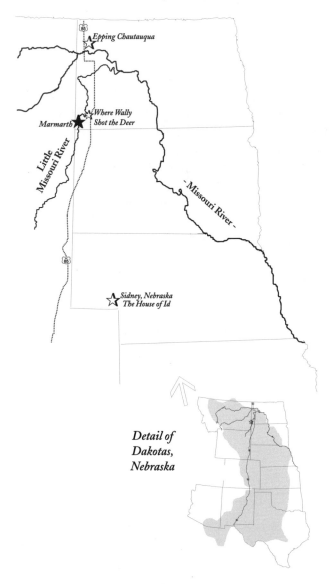

Epping Chautauqua

Where Wally
Shot the Deer

Marmarth

Little
Missouri River

- Missouri River -

Sidney, Nebraska
The House of Id

Detail of
Dakotas,
Nebraska

Learning to Hunt
with the Wally Brothers

Telemachus

*A*LTHOUGH MY FAMILY LIVED BY THE MYTH OF LIBERTY, and the notion that we were each free to make our own choices in the world, my father made it clear just what he approved of and what he condemned in virtually every aspect of life and—in spite of his grand gestures of disinterest—nobody ever crossed his will without paying a price for it. He was too middle class and too enlightened, for example, to have a "favorite chair" of the kind that overtly patriarchal houses featured. We all were taught to laugh at that kind of Pavlovian territorialism, the stuff of the working classes. It was nevertheless the case that my father always sat in precisely the same chair day after day, year after year, and when anyone else occupied his chair, by accident or by design, he fretted and paced and sighed until somehow things were righted again. But he did not, I repeat, have a favorite chair.

So we never listened to country music.

We never attended rodeo.

Never camped.

He was a quiet, intellectual, distant man sitting alone with a cigarette, a whiskey and water, and the *Diary of Samuel Pepys* or *The Life of Samuel Johnson*, a man who never participated in the joyful confusion of family life in any meaningful way, but who sat in tacit judgment of all that we did and thought, and who had somehow accumulated veto power over every decision of our household. A certain amount could be done around him, but his power over anything he knew about was enormous. I adored him and thought of him as a semi-divine figure.

I often wonder whether I gained or lost more by having such a father. He was a man of great mind and sensibility. He could trail his way through a dense book of nonfiction like Natty Bumpo through the forests of the Hudson. He was thoughtful, elegant, well-spoken, abstractly compassionate, and supremely well-organized, not to mention a good provider for a family of large material appetites in the heart of the 1960s. He was as clear and direct a writer as I have ever met. Even his handwriting was perfect. He paid his taxes on time (early), never cheated anyone, and in his whole life he never had a brush with the law. There was no one who could compete with him in learned wit, social decorum, or judiciousness in conversation—so long as he was sober. In a town where Babbittry is so universal that it doesn't even have a name, where public conversation typically runs along the dreary sports-babes-barbecues axis, this was profound enlightenment. It would, in fact, be enlightenment anywhere on earth.

He was, on the other hand, frail, unavailable, and constricted. He never showed any interest in outdoor activities except golf, and that was something he pursued with his buddies until I was an adult. He traveled for his work most of the time until I was 12, and then—when he was home long enough to be observed—he sat alone in his chair most of the time until I moved away. His parenting principle was, do anything you please, so long as it doesn't make any demands on me, but be prepared for my scorn or my veto if it doesn't suit my tastes. Thus it was fine, when we traveled as a family, to listen to "The World Tomorrow with Garner Ted Armstrong" on radio as a kind of fascinating absurdity, but if we had suggested that we wished to go hear a gospel singer, he would have sneered openly. He might laugh at a perceived absurdity until he cried, but if you laughed a microsecond too long at anything, even at something he found funny, he'd look at you as if you were an embarrassment to decorum.

Perhaps I might have been better off with a less cerebral, less insightful father, some sort of amiable buffoon who wanted to throw or kick the ball, go for a boat ride, catch a walleye, or attend the state fair. I longed for such a father through much of my adolescence, even though it seemed undeniable to me—even then—that I was the son of some sort of natural aristocrat. I am proud that I had a father I could be proud of. If my father had been a typical Dakotan, I doubt that I would myself have become a reader and eventually a scholar, but there is in mid-life a time when all appears to be vanity, and one would, or thinks one would, trade everything for a fund of happiness or even contentment.

So there was no possibility that any of us would ever go hunting. The gospel according to Sir Charles (for such we often called him), was that hunting was a barbaric ritual of Neanderthal men, that it was a cruel, mindless, unconscionable activity, and that nobody worthy of respect would shoot at a deer or an elk. From an early hour I imbibed this liberal philosophy and, like an automaton, spouted condescension at anyone who would admit to enjoying the hunt. This was, needless to say, a highly unpopular stance in a rural district where, on any autumn weekend, one could not escape seeing sedans dripping with blood and draped with eviscerated carcasses tied down with baling twine.

My prejudice against hunting had ironically been deepened by a lecture I heard at least twenty times (once by choice). A philosophy professor of Dickinson State College gave a public talk about hunting based heavily, which is to say totally, on the famous essay by Ortega y Gasset. In his *Meditations on Hunting*, Ortega wrote:

> To the sportsman the death of the game is not what interests him; that is not his purpose. What interests him is everything that he had to do to achieve death—that is, the hunt. Therefore

what was before only a means to an end is now an end in itself. Death is essential because without it there is no authentic hunting: the killing of the animal is the natural end of the hunt and the goal of hunting itself, not of the hunter. The hunter seeks this death because it is no less than the sign of reality for the whole hunting process. To sum up, one does not hunt in order to kill; on the contrary, one kills in order to have hunted.

Ortega's argument, I now admit, is provocative and at times profound, but through the mediation of a narcissistic college professor, who appeared to be "sucking up" to the base passions of the local hunters, and who seemed to be casting a threadbare metaphysical blanket over a form of licensed cruelty against creatures as innocent of human baseness as they were vulnerable to it, it appeared to be so much nonsense. The professor's audiences approved of what he had to say, not because they listened carefully to his arguments, or Ortega's, but because he seemed to be sanctioning their favorite fall activity. (Later, when his career was in the doldrums, he became a legendary local softball referee, and professed to find the beer-guzzling grandees of the softball circuit more real than people who read books from time to time.) His endorsement of hunting was worse than Babbittry. At least the local hunters' zeal was sincere.

The opinionatedness of my father, coupled with the infantile hypermasculinity of virtually all the hunters I ever met, left me nothing to doubt for thirty years. Even now I see no reason to challenge Dr. Johnson's judgment: "It is very strange, and very melancholy, that the paucity of human pleasures should persuade us ever to call hunting one of them."[†] The "arguments" of the hunters on behalf of their blood sport were no more convincing to me than the "arguments" of the National Rifle Association for libertarian gun codes, and the "arguments" of miners whose love affair with the "Jeffersonian" 1872 mining law serves as a

---

[†]Mrs. Piozzi, *Anecdotes.*

justification for a Canadian gold extraction corporation obtaining rights to ten billion dollars worth of minerals for a filing fee of $125. But then Mike Waldera came into my life and I could no longer keep my mind closed.

MIKE WALDERA WAS THE MIDDLE OF THREE SONS. Between them they contained about half of the testosterone of the Great Plains. They were the sons of academic parents, the mother an actress and theater director who resembled Nefertiti more than a Norse Dakotan, the father a man so handsome and virile that he looked like an extra from a Kirk Douglas movie. The sons were described as "hunks," "studs," "hoses," whatever the most fashionable term for sexual charismatics, by the legion of girls who mooned about them wherever they went. They had muscles and massive confidence. Mike was the middle son. Since my comfort zone was far from the testostcronic side of the spectrum, and since the Walderas were all a good deal younger than I, I did not know any of them well, until I spent a couple of summers working with Mike. He was the road manager for a tent-based traveling humanities program called Chautauqua.

He was a cheerful, hard-working young man with a world-class smile that melted young women's resolve, but he did not at first seem particularly thoughtful to me, and his tastes were so far different from mine that I barely noticed him. My work life then involved daily encounters with half a dozen high-maintenance scholar-performers. Mike's quiet self-sufficiency seldom attracted notice. He worked out every day, without fail, and took great care over his diet, which ran to salads mostly, and after the day's labors were over he tended to meander the bar scene, not often to get drunk, but quite frequently to establish temporary recreational intimacies with local women. We were the circus and Mike was our dashing strong man. As the summer wore on I found that I liked him more and more, partly because of his work ethic, but mostly because he had a good wit, a rich sense of humor, and a healthy outlook on our professional activities.

Once in the early days of Chautauqua Mike and his brother Mark Waldera (we called them the Wally brothers) were roustabouts for the greatest of all tentmasters Ed Sahlstrom. To understand Ed Sahlstrom you must picture a man of unlimited theatrical talent, with one of the most expressive, mobile, and hilarious (not to mention massive) faces you have ever encountered, a man who could induce John Calvin or Savaronola to grin—all this trapped in the life of a high school speech coach. The Wally brothers were his apprentices and Ed supervised them as if erecting a canvas circus tent were a Mystery as rich and elusive as Alchemy or the cabala. He leaned on the ropes and lectured the boys with a glorious pedantry about knots, wind profiles, unplugged oratory, the ideal angle for quarter poles, and famous circus accidents that might easily have been avoided.

The Wallys were ideal students: that is, they let it all go in one ear and out the other, but when they swung their thirteen-pound mauls at the four by 38-inch wooden stakes, it felt like the third chapter of an Ayn Rand novel. You could trust the future of civilization—though not perhaps your daughter—to these doughty lads, who shrugged off their cuts and bruises like professional wrestlers, and who grinned the wider when the ground was hard as cement. Massive, work-hardened farmers used to gaze at them with wonder, and throw their backs out trying to keep up with the puissance of the celebrated Wally brothers. Ed Sahlstrom stood by with helpful hints about ideal weight displacement. Let the maul do the work, he barked at farmers who had squeezed profits out of a hardscrabble land for forty years.

We were in Epping, North Dakota, a village of 125 or so. There was no motel in Epping, so the Chautauqua "talent" were staying in Williston about 25 miles away. In those modest days the roustabout camp was a Coleman pop-up trailer that slouched next to the big tent. It was late in the evening. The program was over and the scholars had all rushed back to the Best Western in Williston to avoid the risk of experience. Ed stayed behind, as did I, as did the Wally's gorgeous mother Jean Waldera, a college professor, actress, elocutionist, Chautauquan, and a woman of stunning carriage and beauty. A thunderstorm had been predicted. So we stayed in Epping to keep the Wallys company, to help in case things got out of hand. Besides, Ed Sahlstrom loved a storm. Indeed, Ed loved a disaster of any sort. Without an admixture of chaos in his life, Ed was unable to thrive. He was a moth in search of a candle.

It was one of the greatest thunderstorms I had ever seen. It came on like a convoy of freight trains on parallel tracks. The lightning lashed the northern Great Plains without mercy. The whole sky was pandemonium. Anyone who disbelieves the Gaea principle, that the earth is a living being, has never experienced a thunderstorm in the empty quarter. Every time it thundered, the universe split slowly along its seams, like an over-ripe watermelon. The flashes of lightning revealed sheets of water cascading down the slick brown canvas of the tent, pools of water accumulating around the stakes, and—in those microseconds—we saw in each other's faces a mix of wonder and terror, joy and total presence. I knew beyond a glimmer of a doubt that everyone except Jean, who had no choice but to play the mother, was thinking, "it doesn't get any better than this!" It was also clear that those walls of the tent that were not secure were being shredded by the wind, and that the tent could not take much more buffeting without being destroyed altogether. On the next bolt of lightning I looked over at Ed, who wore the maniac countenance of Ahab as he sipped his pint bottle of Shenley's whiskey. He seemed to be trying to decide which would provide more pleasure, watching the tent blow into Minnesota or killing us all in an heroic attempt to save it from sheer destruction.

At the top of my lungs I shouted, "Ed, I think we need to try to strike the tent."

He looked at me with pity, as at a man who was not quite equal to the game of life, a man who might read Jack London's novels or even portray him in a Chautauqua, but never actually be him. It was clear that I did not have the right stuff.

On the next flash of lightning he shrugged his shoulders in his usual exaggerated way, glared at me, and shouted out, "Let's do it."

For the next fifteen minutes we scrambled about the sodden tentsite preparing to strike. This involved a series of maneuvers that are not particularly difficult in daylight and dry weather, but which were virtually impossible in such besotted circumstances. Every stroke of lightning revealed the whole world in freeze frame. It was as if the sky were a vast strobe light. Every flash trapped us in a posture of grotesquery, featherless bipeds scattered along the corners of the tent, leaning over wet recalcitrant ropes, waiting for the instant when the mass of the tent shifted our way and it might be possible to loosen the ropes before they snapped taut again. Everyone was drenched, everyone was in strain, and everyone was having the time of his life.

But we could not bring the tent down. The whole structure was held up by three giant center poles, made of very heavy iron, and forty feet high. With such a tent, the poles are erected first. They stand like a trio of evenly-spaced radio towers, the tallest in the middle. The canvas body of the tent is laced up around these poles on the ground and then drawn up and down like a 3-D Venetian blind by a series of ropes and pulleys. In good weather it is a fairly simple thing to loosen those ropes and lower the tent walls to the ground. Unfortunately, the wind had twisted the canvas so capriciously that the metal o-ring (it is always an o-ring) that was meant to slide up and down the center pole was stuck on something at the very top of the tent. Our urgent ministrations had only managed to make things worse. By loosening the guy ropes, we had given the winds more canvas to whip without being able to lower it out of the storm's reach. Now we were not only going to lose the tent, but there was also a fair chance that one of the wind-snaking canvas shreds would kill or maim one of us as we darted around the scene.

Now Ed Sahlstrom, the man with a thousand faces, assumed a look of deep lugubriousness: "It's all over," he said. "We're going to lose her. Tonight, my friends, you have seen the last of the modern Chautauqua movement. I figured we would lose our funding, sooner or later, but now it seems certain that by this time tomorrow we'll all be heading home for the summer."

The storm raged on.

I said, "Ed, you're the Tentmaster. Is there nothing we can do to get it down?"

He looked around like the last Marine on the beach at Iwo Jima. It wasn't clear whether he was grinning or grimacing. "There's only one remedy, and I cannot recommend it. If we could get to the top of that center pole, it's just possible that we could ease that o-ring past the obstruction."

Mike Waldera had already begun to strip off his coat. His mother, Jean, like Hecuba before the walls of Troy, forbade, rebuked, cajoled, begged, bribed, all but bared her breast to the storm—all, of course, in vain. The greatest of the Wallys, like Hector, had chosen his destiny. If he had prayed to the skygod Apollo for aid in the ordeal to come it would not have surprised me, but, of course, Ed was already performing that rite for him while lifting his Shenley's high over his lips. The time lag between lightning strikes and their attendant thunder was virtually nil. Every three or four seconds there was a streak of lightning the size of the Nile. At times we actually screamed in involuntary response.

The pure joy of the thing had clearly driven Ed Sahlstrom mad. As Mike worked his way up the center pole Ed had wandered off into a clear space and begun to channel King Lear. Through the locomotive sound of thunder and wind we could hear him shrieking,

> Blow, winds, and crack your cheeks. Rage, blow.
> You cataracts and hurricanoes, spout
> Till you have drenched our steeples, drowned the cocks.
> You sulph'rous and thought-executing fires,
> Vaunt-couriers of oak-cleaving thunderbolts,
> Singe my white head. And thou, all-shaking thunder,
> Strike flat the thick rotundity o' the world,
> Crack Nature's moulds, all germains spill at once,
> That makes ingrateful man.[†]

These words Ed actually recited in the pelting storm. When possible, always travel the West with a Thespian.

Jean Waldera retired to the pop-up camper to have her nervous breakdown alone. Mark Waldera was cursing his hesitation, which had cost him heroism and death. By the time I started in with, "Michael, there is no tent in the universe worth. . . ," he had shinnied up fifteen feet of the center pole, gripping it with his wrestler's thighs. He exhibited the concentration of a chess master. After infinite struggle Mike reached the top. We were all under the tent now and the staccato lightning illuminated our fetid ozone world like a bloat firefly. He found the obstruction. He found a way to wedge his body against the center pole and lift the o-ring up over a bolt with the strength of his legs. Then he gave us a

---

[†] *King Lear* III.ii.1-9.

Rodney Dangerfield A-Okay signal in the night, and we managed to lower the canvas—now ten times as heavy as when dry—to the ground. Mike rode down with the tent bestriding the o-ring like a Colossus, waving his right arm like the boldest rodeo rider in the world. The lightning was making a crosshatch of the sky. Mike's grin was the size of a rainbow. If lightning had struck the pole we would have had to scrape him into his body bag with a spatula. He had taken a staggeringly foolhardy risk. On the Great Plains a Webber grill is a tall object. Our 40-foot center pole was not only a skyscraper in such a landscape, but a lightning rod begging to be touched by the gods. But on that pandemonic night, the lightning did not seek out the center pole, did not make melba of Mike Waldera. Now he was everyone's hero, and, as he jumped from the soggy canvas to the ground, he had the wide-eyed look of the man who has wrestled with Death and survived.

Jean recovered her famous equanimity. Mike changed clothes and we all toweled off in the camper. The rain and wind had more or less stopped by now and what was left of the storm was nothing but pyrotechnics. From under one of the benches someone turned up a couple of cans of Beenie Weenies. We heated them over the Coleman cook stove, and shared out three beers. Jean claimed she had never really been worried about Mike's safety. Mark was magnanimous in his praise of his brother. Ed reeled in, a poor bare forked animal, and sat in the corner looking as if he had been with Paul at Damascus.

I never doubted the Wally brothers again.

———

ONE NIGHT, A FEW YEARS LATER, when we were in Sidney, Nebraska, way out in the western barrens of the state, Mike and I went out to have a beer and play a bit of pool: a typical night for Mike, a rare one for me. In each of these activities I resembled a young person lighting up a cigarette with the kind of self-conscious nonchalance that proves that smoking is a rare and even daring act. We went to a place on the main street of Sidney—it was called Stockman's or something equally creative. I had suggested the venue. I had actually been in that bar on a number of previous occasions, including during the 1987 Chautauqua tour, when we spent the Fourth of July in Sidney, and when—for professional reasons now hard to explain—I had a pony tail. Then, more slender than I have since become, sitting alone, slightly buzzed, at the mahogany bar at Stockman's, minding my own business and licking my wounds and meditating a Kansas farm woman who was causing me fits, perhaps the only man in Nebraska who was not among friends and charcoal on that summer holiday, and a Jefferson scholar to boot (alone on Jefferson's big day!), I felt someone tug my pony tail from behind, and say, "Wanna have some fun, honey?"

I turned around in my chair.

It was a beefy Marine who had come in with a group of his friends half an hour earlier, in a fairly advanced state of intoxication (he was, after all, celebrating his independence), who had not apparently studied me closely enough to determine that I was not a woman. All seemed vanity that day as I moped alone at Stockman's, in a pissy mood, so I turned around and looked my Marine square in the face and said sweetly, "What do you have in mind?"

He should simply have killed me on the spot and left me in the dumpster, but instead he burst out of the room with as much haste as if a rabid and frenzied bat were fluttering in his face. Within minutes the pub was mine alone. Homophobia, like everything else in the West, is limitless.

Stockman's had a long beautiful maroon bar on its west flank, with a giant mirror behind it, presided over by cow horns that were doubling as baseball hat racks. There were posters of siliconic women wearing very little, pursing their lips and leaning back as if to say, "Buy Coors and a woman just like me will sleep with you tonight!" There were plaques that said things like, "Insured by Smith and Wesson," and "Employ a Spotted Owl Today!" There were hundreds of bottles of alcohol so colorful that it looked more like a barber shop than a bar. Death had come to Stockmans disguised as the elixir. There were trophies from *Iliadic* triumphs on the local softball fields. From the counter you could buy pickled eggs, pickled pigs feet, or fat gherkins.

Above the booths on the east wall there were busts of famous Nebraska bulls—I love a bar protected by Minotaurs—and each booth was sufficiently enclosed with dark plywood partitions to provide cover for gropings or drug deals. Each had its own light fixture, most of which were switched off or burned out. Over on one side there was a big old classic juke box with a preponderance of Hank and Willie and Waylon and the boys. Mamas, don't let your babies grow up to be cowboys. Drop kick me Jesus through the goal posts of life. You picked a fine time to leave me, Lucille. And, by the way, take this job and shove it. In the back, three pool tables glowed in the smoky gloom, each with a green beer distributor light fixture hovering over it. A rack full of indifferent cues and some mottled old chalks was affixed to the wall. On the periphery were nickel-legged Formica tables with small Grainbelt drink glasses strewn over them, and a few red plastic trays with the husks of onion rings, fries, and over-salted popcorn. Service at the Stockman's was minimal.

The back walls were painted a deep whorehouse red, and by the men's and women's bathrooms—filthy, fetid, and in the men's a novelty condom machine with dayglow tickler items the purpose of which I could not quite make out in my vigils at the urinal— were crude black silhouettes to signify the intended visitors, over one door a classic bestriding man icon, with a penis penciled in by an inspired local tagger, and, for women, the spray paint equivalent of the silver-titted woman on the mudflaps of every gen-u-wine redneck trucker in America.

The three pinball machines featured display graphics of breasty women in impossibly revealing thongs looking as if they dreamed of nothing in the universe so much as fellating the Ramboesque men they stood beside. Rambo, meanwhile, seemed solely interested in carnage not carnality.

I called it **"The House of Id,"** a place where all one's shadow urges were offered satisfaction. So far as one could tell, you could count on getting drunk, getting high, getting laid, or getting beaten up at the Stockman's, perhaps all in one night, and I had no doubt murders had either occurred there in its seedy history or been planned in the booths. Stockman's plainly acknowledged that man is a creature of appetites, and that those appetites have a right to be met without any matrix of judgment, after the shortest possible train of preliminaries. This was not the kind of bar that permitted wives and girlfriends and achy-breaky husbands to call by phone looking for their straying mates. You come to the Stockman's, you hang up your conscience by the door. If you don't like that arrangement, well there's the VFW next door, the Shamrock down the street, or the Ramada lounge out on the edge of town.

I felt sexy and a bit besmirched just being in such a place, but on the whole it felt very good indeed. It was the kind of bar where you didn't dare make eye contact with anybody you weren't prepared to spend the night with. All the women looked like they had a lot of miles on them and the men appeared to have made it their life's purpose to concentrate all the possibilities of their souls into the crotch and the throat. Think about it: it's quite an achievement. Hamlet perhaps would not have felt entirely at home: "What is a man," he asks,

If his chief good and market of his time
Be but to sleep and feed? A beast no more.
Surely he that made us with such large discourse
Looking before and after, gave us not
That capability and godlike reason
To fust in us unused.[†]

Fusting is a way of life in Sidney, Nebraska.

Mike was famous for his effortless sexual conquests, and yet there was nothing of the braggart soldier in him. When we were out and about in America, he could have a different woman every night, certainly a different woman in every town. Often when I rose early at the motels we frequented, and went out at sunrise for a run, I'd see a lithe beauty slip out of Mike's room and into her car, buttoning all the way, casting a nervous glance about her and avoiding eye contact. Later I'd walk up close to him as he performed his work and say, "I trust you had a restful night of sleep," and he'd look at me for a second and relax and smile a vast shy smile and say, "I have never felt more completely rested, thank you."

So as we walked into the bar, two thirsty young men at the end of a day of good labor out in the heartland, I turned to him and said, "Show me how it works." Mike did not need any exegesis of this request.

We sauntered in, surveyed the room, John Wayned it up to the bar, ordered a couple of beers and a couple of shots, slapped down some money, strode back to the pool tables, settled into a couple of off-balance chromium chairs, toasted each other silently, smiled the smiles of a couple of guys out for a beer with nowhere they had to be, put down our drinks, put a quarter into the pool table, heard the thunder of the balls dropping, racked them, selected sticks and powdered them, encouraged each other to break in the

---

[†]*Hamlet* IV.iv.34-40.

elaborate ritual of male-bonding protocol, and settled into our first desultory game of the night. A few minutes later I was concentrating on a (for me, impossible) bank shot when I felt Mike's smile from across the table. I looked up. His eyes were dancing. He twitched his famous moustache and turned his eyes towards the middle of the room, and said,

"That one."

She was pretty, fit, young, and well-dressed. She looked like a slightly fuller version of Debra Winger from *Urban Cowboy*. She had buttoned one too few of the buttons of her blouse, as if to say, "and then there were three." She was standing with two other women at the near edge of the bar. I believe the correct local phrase is, "I wouldn't kick her out of bed for smoking!" As if any one in the region had ever kicked any woman out of bed for any reason whatsoever.

And sure enough, two hours later, Mike and his date left the bar together for another night of perfectly restful sleep. Me, I read forty minutes of Stephen Ambrose's *Crazy Horse and Custer* before I turned out the light.

———◆———

THAT SAME SUMMER WE WERE IN MARMARTH a day or two ahead of the rest. We had nothing to do so we decided to drive up North Dakota 16 to look at the Little Missouri River. The only vehicle we had with us for the moment was a little Mazda pickup—a toy in these parts. Any number of people would have lent us a serious four wheel drive vehicle, but we were treasuring a rare moment of uncomplicated quiet, so we decided to settle for the Mazda, even though it wasn't big or tough enough for ND 16. Mike drove. ND 16 is not much of a road unless you love improbable things. None of it is paved and most of it is only minimally graded.

In a rain it turns to bentonite gumbo and throws almost anything you've got into the ditch. There are, in addition, not one but two washes that are always filled with a little and sometimes a great deal of muddy water. A big pickup slogs through without a qualm, but anything else is a crapshoot. If you hit the wash basin wrong any number of unpleasant laws of physics can take over. I've never gotten stuck in the ND 16 washes, but more than once my heart has dropped to the floor mats of whatever vehicle I happened to be driving.

This section of North Dakota isn't called Dinosaur Alley for nothing. At every turn we half-expected to see a Triceratops lumber across the road, and if ever there were a place where such an event would not be flabbergasting, this was it. General Alfred Sully called the badlands of Dakota, "hell with the fires put out." The breaks, the gullied hills, the striated bluffs, the severe cuts made by the river and its pathetic tributaries, the alkali scourings, the sorry looking fences, the twistifications of the windblasted cottonwoods, the pine ridges, the heartbreaking faraway buttes, the abruptness and the misshapenness of the countryside, all made it feel like God's back room where the materials of creation had been assembled, with some bits never used and some things brought home for further consideration, and the mess of the eighth day never quite cleaned up. If we were not a nation of beefeaters and if there were not thick crude oil at 9,000 feet, such a landscape would be utterly deserted. As it is, only the marginal live here: marginal members of the mineral extraction industry, marginal members of the food production system, marginal members of the social structure. And coyotes.

We drove along gabbing and nursing cold beers, listening to each other in a way that new friends do, before they think they have heard it all and shut down all curiosity. It was the kind of loafing that you dream about all of your life, pointlessly joyful, an evening without responsibilities of any sort except to get that Mazda back to Marmarth in one piece. There were long stretches of silence, punctuated by bursts of talk, mostly about what was passing along the road. Among the things we shared was a sense of the absurdity of our official summer labors. We got some of that out of the way first, debriefing each other about the little crises of little enterprises. In open places you have to work off the noise first before your mind can begin to flow outward.

Our basic orientations were different. We were both enamored of the outback of the Great Plains, but Mike came to the countryside as a hunter, I as a camper and student of the wilderness. We had plenty of respect for each other, but each of us felt slightly judgmental about the other's avocation. Without having planned this excursion in any way, there seemed to be a tacit agreement that we would try to explain ourselves to each other before we turned back to town. Neither one of us was willing to risk the full argument so early in the evening, so we were still swapping funny anecdotes when we approached the first wash in the road. By now Mike was driving pretty fast.

I said, "This wash can be tricky. Careful."

Mike said, "Hey, no-ooo problema."

We hit the wash at about 30 miles per hour. As we cleared the last swell before the wash itself, we realized we were in trouble. Although the countryside was bone dry in every direction, the wash was running much fuller than usual. We had been expecting a trickle. I had seen worse in my many forays up ND 16, but on those occasions I had always expected worse. There must have been a localized rainstorm to the West a day or two before our adventure. Now we were about to crash into 18 or 20 inches of muddy water in a toy pickup moving at least triple the safe speed.

We turned to each other in a slow-motion exchange of delight and terror and at the same instant shouted,

"Oh, shit!!!!!!!!"

Our crossing was inelegant in the extreme. We sashayed through the wash, beers and caps flying to the top of the cab, slammed into the opposite bank with a thud, rocked back and forth in a nauseating way, spun our wheels for a few seconds, then dug up and out and onto the bonedry road again. We turned to grin at each other.

"Oh, man," Mike said, "that could have come out in any number of ways."

"Thank you, Great Goddess Serendip," I said. "This creek eats pickups like this one for breakfast."

A mile or two down the road we pulled over to inspect the front of the truck. It was covered with mud and grit as old as Tyrannosaurus Rex all the way to the bed, but there was no apparent structural damage to the pickup. The Mazda looked like a wreck but wasn't one.

"Let's take a break and walk over to the river," Mike said with a wry smile. "It cannot be more than half a mile to the east."

So we walked.

I told Mike about the year I hiked the entire course of the Little Missouri River. It had been brewing in my mind for a decade, since my friend Douglas and I were sauntering on the Adriatic near Split, Yugoslavia, on Easter Sunday, 1979. We were spending the Oxford spring vacation hiking and camping in the Kamnik Alps of northern Yugoslavia. We were about to be arrested as Yankee Dog Capitalist Imperialist Spies by the Yugoslav secret police, but that is a story from another journey. As we paced in perfect rhythm along the strand of the Adriatic, it came to me like a vision that I should find out the source of the hapless Little

Missouri, somewhere near Devil's Tower in Wyoming, then hike along its whole course to the point where it empties into the Missouri River proper in North Dakota. I had read in Lewis and Clark that one of the Frenchmen they hired in 1805, Baptiste LePage, had descended the river from the "Black Hills," which then meant something like greater Wyoming, to the Mandan villages in Dakota, where Lewis and Clark first encountered him. So I'd be the second man to make the journey. Nobody would have been nitwit enough to have done so in the interim. It had turned out to be the greatest adventure of my life, and I kept Mike laughing as I recalled the innumerable mishaps of an over-civilized man alone in the starkest ice-free landscape on earth. It was a six week adventure and there had been brushes with death—and God.

To Mike, the whole thing sounded like a pointless absurdity of the most satisfactory sort, which, of course, is precisely what it was. Now we were on the banks of that same river, at a place I had passed on a blistering September afternoon in another life. We stood silently on the edge of the river together. It was a perfect evening. The waning light had a pinkish orange cast to it. All the contours of the earth stood out in sweet relief. The cottonwoods soughed and shook off the day's heat. It felt like African Savannah—a far country minding its own business from time immemorial with a sluggish river running through it. If man was a part of the scene, he was, so far, living lightly on the land.

Mike said, "So what's this theory you've been working on about stages of wilderness consciousness?"

"I've been thinking about it all summer," I said. "Last year I took my friends from UND camping at Buffalo Gap. . ."

"That's like camping in a Holiday Inn parking lot."

"I know, but they are not really camping types, and I was just grateful that they were willing to try. Well, it rained a bit in the night—about a sixteenth of an inch. I have a priceless photograph from the morning after our one night out—all in good, watertight tents—and you should see their faces. They look like Noah's third cousins, unfortunately removed, or Afghani refuges whose village has just been destroyed by a Soviet air raid. Their frowns are only limited by the boundaries of facial musculature. You can see on their faces that they would sell their grandmothers into white slavery for a hot shower. I'm sure if they were honest they would have admitted that it was the most miserable night of their entire lives. In their frowns I could see a lively mix of sulkiness, misery, and open hostility against the "friend" who had talked them into so dangerous a project."

"I'm guessing that this represents a relatively low stage in your wilderness consciousness scale."

"Indeed," I said, "but unfortunately not the lowest. You have to wake up pretty early in the morning to get more bourgeois than that, but it is possible."

"Stage One of wilderness consciousness is total aversion. My father would not camp out under any circumstances. It is not merely a matter of comfort. Assuming the comfort problem could be solved, he would still regard a campout as a piece of colossal nonsense. Why would a civilized man renounce a millennium of promethean progress to squat on his haunches around a smoky fire, eat third-rate food and pronounce it delicious, and then sleep on the ground in the middle of nowhere? Who ever got a good night of sleep camping? My father's idea of paradise is a short day of work, followed by drinks and dinner at the Elks with literate friends, then a few "nightcaps" and cigarettes in his chair with a good piece of nonfiction and *Crossfire* before bed. When I hiked the Little Missouri River, he said, 'Why not just drive along the river roads instead, and get out of the car from time to time to take a look?' He was serious."

Mike said, "That's pretty pathetic, but most people I know feel that way. How'd you ever overcome such a beginning?"

"Long story. Short answer. First, my mother is a romantic and an adventurer at heart. She wants me to be John Colter. Second, my mentor Mike Jacobs, you know the journalist, taught me how to be a true North Dakotan."

"So if that's Stage One, what do the rest look like? It can only improve."

"I've given you an example of Stage Two, or maybe that was 1.5. A couple of nights in the tent, some hiking, with ritual expostulations about how refreshing it has been, but the essential experience is of discomfort, and the whole thing is a low-level ordeal. Stage Twoers bring a fair amount of good faith to the enterprise, but after a couple of mostly sleepless nights and a sloppy attempt to make love in the wilderness, they are desperate for a hot shower and a Big Mac. The experience is endured more than enjoyed, but even the miserable realize, at least in retrospect, that it was worth the trouble. They feel renewed somehow, and proud of their ability to survive in the wild—if you realize that they "survived" thanks to the world's finest high-tech equipment, plenty of food, no predators, a set of car keys in their pocket, and an escape vehicle within 100 yards of the tent, and that they were in "the wild" only in the sense that it was in some vague way an outdoor experience. My sister, for example, one of the most delightfully sarcastic people I have ever known, goes into a camping experience kicking and screaming, takes way too much stuff, whines the entire time, makes Jiffy Pop in the wilderness and of course sings the Jiffy Pop jingle to boot, rushes home to her comforts, and then boasts of her wilderness prowess for months afterwards.[†] Thus Stage Two."

[†] Update: My sister has since divorced her first husband, a man sendentary like my father, and married an outdoorsman, a hunter, a man who has taught her how to do it in the road.

Mike said, "I agree with your description. That would be my mother, I think. It's not total aversion like your father's, but it is not exactly a picture of a happy camper either. But let me ask you, doesn't everyone want a shower at the end of a camping trip?"

"Yes of course," I said. "The question is how much one dwells on it throughout the experience.

"Stage Three is much more interesting. I don't know you well enough to judge, but I'm guessing that you and I are essentially Stage Threers in most moods. In Stage Three you spend more rather than less time in the wild, and you get farther from the Grid. These trips can be undertaken with others, but they are more often experienced alone. Three important things happen in Stage Three. First, at some point you stop wishing you were home. The initial shock of discomfort ends, and you actually get into the rhythm of simple living. It is not that the discomforts disappear, but they cease to be paramount, they cease to plague you.

"Second, at some point the junk that normally clutters up the mind slips out of your consciousness and into the empty landscape. For the first couple of days of any camping trip, you think about insurance and work duties and calls you ought to make, fights you had with your girlfriend or your brother, all the unfinished business of your life. On about the third day you begin to shed all that nonsense like old snake skins. Your mind opens up, and a new kind of clarity begins to assert itself. Mostly this comes from a deliberate slowing of the pace of life, and the perspective that a wide empty place brings to petty anxieties over tax returns. It could probably happen in yoga or serious meditation, but it always happens in the wilderness. It's one of the gifts wilderness gives to you.

"Third, at the end of the trip, although you are ready enough for a shower and a cup of good coffee and a soft bed, you realize that you could have carried on in the wilderness longer, possibly even indefinitely. In fact, you feel a pang of regret when you move back toward civilization. In a sense you have begun to see right through the illusion of civilization, and though the new clarity is slightly frightening, it is also empowering and potentially revolutionary. You go back to town, because you must, but you are not quite the same when you get back. And when you take that hot shower you feel like a pussy."

Mike said, "I love that feeling—not the part about feeling like a pussy, of course. When I start for home at the end of a long hunting trip I always drive very slowly at first, a little bewildered, and I'm annoyed by the impatience and the pace of the other travelers I meet."

"Exactly," I said, "and you realize that you are leaving behind some of the best parts of yourself in the wilderness. You think, civilization is not an unmixed blessing. Civilization is more efficient than fulfilling."

"Ok, I think I'm ready now for Stage Four. I'm assuming that this one is pretty hard to achieve."

"Indeed. I need to start by admitting that I have only experienced Stage Four once or twice in my whole life, and then for very brief moments. This is for two reasons. First, I am hopelessly bourgeois at heart, whatever I might wish to believe about myself. Second, Stage Four is really a spiritual awakening and which of us, really, is capable of that for more than a few seconds in a long organic life?

"Stage Four requires time. You have to stay out long enough to get over what Robert Pirsig in *Zen and the Art of Motorcycle Maintenance* calls "gumption traps." These include physical discomfort, belief that you have urgent duties elsewhere, diurnal concerns like bills and Mother's Day, and of course the myth of indispensability, which is what the poet Milton might call that "last infirmity of noble mind." I don't think you can achieve this in less than five days. Your sleep patterns need to re-center, and your digestive tract, and you need to work out the kinks in your muscles and the blockages in your heart, your chakras, and your mind."

Mike asked, "Can this stage be reached in the company of someone else?"

"Maybe, but I doubt it. My feeling is that unless the other person is a very special kind of friend, he or she will only get in the way. I know this much. Most people chatter way too much in the wilderness. When you find yourself reminding each other of old episodes of the *Andy Griffith Show* or *Star Trek*, you're doomed. Stage Four requires long stretches of absolute silence. And I don't think it can be achieved in the presence of someone you are sleeping with. There is too much baggage whenever sex is involved. Intimacy is fatal to wilderness consciousness.

"In Stage Four a couple of really important things happen. Most important, at some point as you are walking along, you realize, all of a sudden, that the veil has been lifted and that you are beginning to see the world in some primordial fashion again. The dross—or the toxicity—of urban industrial civilization has dissipated and you start to see life with young eyes again. All the colors are more vivid. Every meadowlark sounds like the voice of God. The pack on your back has ceased to be a burden. It feels like a natural extension of your bones and muscles. You feel monstrously alive. When I finished my six weeks on the Little Missouri River I was, for the only time in my life, totally in tune with my body. Normally I am nothing more than a head-delivery-system, ill at ease with carnality in all of its forms, averse to sleep, averse to relaxation, a creature without integration in any significant sense. But when I finished my 650-mile hike, and my parents came up to collect me in the north unit of Theodore Roosevelt National Park, I knew that if I had world enough and time I could stride to the North Pole and beyond. I was sorry to come in. I was almost a Wally!

"In Stage Four you not only are totally in tune with the wilderness but you feel, no *you know*, that you are actually your best self there, more authentic, more of what God and destiny and Gaea had in mind for you. You know that your return to civilization is in many ways a tragic decision and that you will necessarily be shrunken there. You realize that your dream of yourself involves a wild place under the stars where you are at home and enormously competent, not a boardroom or the library or the bank. You feel that you have rediscovered your true self after a long period in the Inferno. When you return to civilization, you feel like the man in Plato's cave, coming up reluctant and bewildered into the tedious world of appearances after having experienced the Forms in their full majesty.

"And at its very best, Stage Four opens the doors of perception just a crack and you find yourself in tune with the cosmos in a way that you never thought possible. I can remember sitting at the end of the day in the Little Missouri River, loafing, completely without an agenda of any sort, just absorbing the molecules of the universe in a way that was totally accepting yet totally present. There were moments when I understood that the molecules in my calves and those in the river or in the carp in the river, were as one, that they were commingling, that the cosmos is a vast slow motion flux of materials effervescing in every possible form. It is metaphysics at the quantum level. The cottonwoods, the incredible cerulean blue of the sky, the patterns and the playfulness of the breezes, the sound of the lark and the cricket, the massage of flowing water, the distant undulating ridges, it all felt like a Jungian archetype of Genesis. The world before we did the terrible thing we have done to it. Atlantis. Eden before the wound. On several occasions just for an instant I felt that there was no real boundary between my body and the river and the earth and the sky and the things of the spirit, and that the problem of existence was to overcome the ego-insecurity of being a guy with a job, a Social Security number, a name, and a prickly sense of human dignity. For a moment the door would open and I would see something elemental and paradisiacal on the other side. And I was in it! And then the door would swing shut again and I would be aware of myself as an identity and get up to pee or make dinner.

"It's implicit, I think, in the title of Norman MacLean's book, *A River Runs Through It*. Without any doubt whatsoever, I consider life best when I am in a wild place alone or nearly alone, looking around with that light and intoxicated feeling of being alive again after a long period of slumber, standing in wonder like Adam and trying to drink in the landscape and all of its creatures, standing at the center of the universe in a circle of land and sky that has no impediments in any direction except the curve of the good earth, and seeing a lazy untapped river slide through on its way to the gulf. Eden.

"You cannot experience the grace and the divinity of that moment from a car or a train, or even by getting out of the car and standing in that same place. If there are keys in your pocket, you cannot know the West. Everything sacred has to be earned in the old fashioned way, by a migratory biped on his stout legs, walking with the soulfulness that Thoreau describes in one of the greatest essays in American history, 'Walking'. 'We would fain take that walk', the righteous brooding naturalist writes, 'never yet taken by us through this actual world, which is perfectly symbolical of the path which we love to travel in the interior and ideal world; and sometimes, no doubt, we find it difficult to choose our direction, because it does not yet exist distinctly in our idea'.

"You cannot open those doors of perception with drugs or sex or drink or even disciplined yoga. Somehow it has to be a human being in a landscape that has not been messed with. There is nothing like it in the world. And once you have had it, nothing else will ever be quite adequate.

"The problem, of course, is that it takes time to reach that moment, and a good deal of exertion, and not a little bodily pain; and just about the time you achieve it, you need to turn back because there is a warm body waiting for you in a bed somewhere, or a vocation or an important appointment."

I stopped talking. The universe swallowed up my puny gusts of utterance—effortlessly. We stood for a long time gazing at the sluggish river bathed in autumnal light. We were silent mostly. The bare flesh of our forearms recorded the drop in temperature one degree at a time. Summer afternoons in this country are unrelenting, all bleach and bluff and oven-heat, but in the rosy evening the universe was collapsing in on us in slow motion, and we suddenly became aware, both at the same instant, of the immense silence of the West. The heat relaxed. The gusts of wind relaxed. The cottonwood leaves relaxed. The quality of light relaxed. The meadowlarks relaxed. The sky relaxed. Even the river relaxed. And so did we. Only the crickets seemed to be stirred up. There are few other experiences that please one's thirst for the sensuous quite so fully as the moment when one becomes aware of dusk in the middle of the Great Plains. One of them is rediscovering the morning star, Venus, at daybreak, when you have been up all night. What a pity the Cheyenne gave that vile man Custer the greatest of Indian names: "Son of the Morning Star." Such an epithet, even if it accurately describes Custer's propensity for dawn attack, is too poetic for such a butcher and such a buffoon.

After a time, Mike turned to me and said, "That was some analysis. I was expecting a comic progression, but by the time you finished I was reliving all the greatest experiences of my life. I've knocked on the door of Stage Four a time or two, but not often enough, and not recently."

I said, "Amen on recently. I haven't done the subject justice, Mike. Language is so inadequate, or rather I am so inadequate a user of language. But, as Hamlet says, 'something too much of this.' You get the picture. So tell me, my friend, what is it about hunting that you find so attractive?" He could tell from the tone of my voice that I meant it, that my mind was open, that I would not argue with him, that I was prepared to be convinced by whatever he had to say.

Mike said, "Let me tell you the story that means more to me than any story I know.

"A few years ago I decided to go hunting alone in the badlands. If you think that hunting is ten fat middle aged men drinking beers and waddling through the countryside side by side, banging away recklessly at whatever moves, you'd be right in general, but I do not consider that hunting, any more than you would consider someone with a Harlequin Romance as reading. The only people I hunt with are my brothers, my father, and a few friends whom I've learned to trust over the years.

"The killing is not the point, though without the eventual killing there would be no point. My rule for myself is never to shoot unless I have a killing shot. Nothing upsets me more than to see a dead deer that has been wounded, but not killed, by a lousy hunter, who then left it to bleed to death in the woods.

"If my brothers and dad are not available, I'm happy to go hunting alone. Sometimes I prefer it. There is something special about being out all alone in an empty place, with a purpose, and kind of listening to yourself concentrate in complete silence. I cannot explain it, but it is to me much more satisfying than just hiking in the hills. Just holding a gun on your shoulder and walking with special caution is one of happiest feelings I ever have.

"I try never to hunt cold. I try always to scope out a place before I take my gun into it. I had found this valley over near the Burning Coal Vein. It was way off the road. It takes an hour of hard walking just to reach it. I figured there must be a herd of deer in there somewhere and I knew most hunters are too lazy to get that far away from their vehicles. So I drove out a couple of times in the early fall to check it out. Sure enough, on the second visit I scared up an incredible buck. He looked like the king of the forest. I decided right then to come back to get him once the season started. He was old enough to have eluded a lot of hunters in his time.

"For weeks I dreamed of that buck. I mean literally. I worried that someone else would find him too. I found myself sitting around thinking about his habits—where he slept, how fast he ran, where he hid himself, how many does in his harem, whether he had ever been shot at. I know it sounds silly, but I even tried to imagine how he thought, even what he thought about.

"I don't know if you ever saw the movie, the *Deer Hunter*. It's one of the greatest movies I have ever seen. There is a character in the movie played by Robert De Niro, a hunter. He's kind of arrogant, but he has great discipline, and his philosophy is never to have to take more than one shot at any deer. It's his commitment to excellence, and his discipline, that enable him to survive a time in Viet Cong prison camps and to survive even a kind of Russian roulette torture that the Communists force their prisoners of war to play. If you haven't seen the movie, you've got to do so."

"I saw it in London with my friend Douglas," I said. "We left the theater and walked in silence for more than hour through the streets of Notting Hill Gate. This was 1978, not so long after the war ended. When the survivors sing "God Bless America" at the end of the movie, Douglas and I sat with tears streaming down our cheeks. At any rate, go on."

"I'm glad you liked the movie. In a way, it explains everything I'm trying to say about hunting. It's not a weekend sport. At its best it is a kind of artistry. It might even be called a Way in the eastern sense. I don't pretend to have mastered it, but I always go out with the intention of bringing the best of myself to the hunt, with the intention of mastering it just the way you might master a Bach concerto.

"When the day finally came, I got up really early, long before dawn, and ate a piece of toast, and kissed my mother good-bye. She was up, the way she always is when we're going hunting. She had made coffee. She wanted to cook me a full breakfast, but it was like four in the morning and I wasn't that hungry. As I was leaving the house, she said, 'Mike, have a good time. Make good choices.' I don't think I've ever gone hunting when she didn't send me off that way. I drove in a morning fog to the trailhead.

"It was still dark when I parked the rig. All this happened a couple of years ago, but I can still remember loading the gun, strapping on my ammunition belt, making sure I had my knife, lacing up my boots in the headlights in front of my pickup. I took a last sip from my thermos and I peed into a sagebrush. The stars were amazing. The morning star was quivering on the eastern horizon, and you could see just a streak of dawn. It was cold. I could see my breath. As I stood there alone in the dark, I suddenly did not feel so confident. It seemed that the buck had all the advantages: home court, great speed, endless space, camouflage, a lifetime to learn the contours of his habitat.

"There wasn't anything to do but start out down the valley and wait for first light. I tried to walk as quietly as I could. I remember thinking, 'Thank God I live in North Dakota.' I wouldn't want to live anywhere else, ever. Dickinson is no culture capital and there are plenty of things that we cannot get out here, but most of what one really needs is available in the local shops. As long as gas is cheap I'm happy to drive elsewhere to get what we don't have, but you cannot buy the sparse population, the openness of the countryside, the clean air, the brightness of the stars. It's totally amazing to me that we can live at the end of the twentieth century in the most industrial civilization in history, and yet there are places within an hour's drive of my house where you can return to the landscape of Lewis and Clark, hell, to the landscape of Moses. There's nothing I would rather do than camp around an open fire, sleep under the stars, and go hunting at dawn."

I was laughing now.

"And that includes sex," he said. "I love sex, but sex is easy, hunting is hard. There is really no comparison."

"Sorry," I said. "Go on."

"Even though I was being as quiet as possible, I knew that buck already knew exactly where I was. After a while I was way down the trail, farther than I had been when I first saw the buck months before. It was as if he was leading me deeper and deeper into the valley, farther and farther away from my truck.

"It was a perfect fall day: cold and sunny with that weak, really yellow sun that you see in the winter in North Dakota. Everything on the land stood out—the cottonwoods, the sagebrush, the scoria, the look and the sound of the birds. It seemed to be getting colder as I walked, but I was sweating in my hunting overalls and I felt as alive as I have ever felt. I was determined not to come back without that buck.

"It must have been around 9:30 or 10 a.m. when I came around a bend in the draw and finally saw it, nosing in a willow thicket a little more than a quarter of a mile away. I didn't dare move. I knew if I shifted even slightly he would see me and bolt away and that would be the end of the game. My only hope was that I could get off a good shot before he sauntered away. I got down on one knee and brought my rifle up to eye level.

"He was browsing in a kind of aimless way, but lifting his head up every few seconds to see what was on the wind. God, he was magnificent. From where I was crouching it was going to be a very difficult shot, and I wasn't going to press the trigger unless I thought I could hit him in the front shoulder. I waited thirty seconds, a minute, then two minutes. He was partly obscured by the willows. The gun was getting heavy. I could feel my right leg starting to go to sleep, but I didn't dare shift my position.

"Just then he looked up at me. I remember the rest of what happened as if it were the Zapruder film. It felt for an instant as if we actually had made eye contact, and then without even thinking about it I squeezed the trigger, and the gun kicked, and I staggered to my feet, and I can remember thinking I was going to fall over from the numbness of my right leg, and suddenly I heard a plane droning far away overhead, and it was as if the cottonwood trees were alive in a way that I had never noticed before, and the buck was starting to move off up the draw, and then it jumped about two inches where it stood, and there was a snort and the grunt of death, and I started to limp forward on my leg, and the gun felt very heavy all of a sudden, and the deer staggered a few feet into the open grass, and tumbled down onto its side, and I felt a huge wave of triumph and sadness—simultaneously—and it struggled up onto its feet and dragged itself a few more feet into the clearing. Then it fell for the last time.

"As I came up upon him, I knew that he was dead. I leaned my gun up against a tree trunk. I took off my cap and set it on the ground. In the place where the brim of the hat had been gripping my head, I was sweating and it suddenly felt cool. I looked down at the deer. There lay one of God's great creatures. A moment ago it had been alive with a vitality and presence that humans can never achieve in their less intense lives. There wasn't an ounce of fat on him. The rack was like a symbol of virility. Eight points. A moment ago he had been the most magnificent creature in North Dakota. Now he was venison. And I had killed him. It's true that the gun had brought death into the picture, but in the hands of what you usually think of when you think of "hunter," it would never have happened. The buck was too smart, and it was way too deep into the badlands. That's no doubt why it had lived so long. It's hard to explain, but it's almost as if the gun was an extension of my will. I try to be a very disciplined hunter. I never kill wantonly and I never celebrate the kill. Nor have I ever left anything behind.

"I knelt down next to it and put my hand on the flank just behind the right front leg. It was still warm. God, that's a sensuous feeling, the mammalian warmth of a creature that has just died. It is every bit as pleasurable as stroking the thigh of a lean woman on the first night you ever sleep with her.

"Well, then I took the knife out of my sheath and slit its throat. I bled it out until there was nothing left. I turned it on its back and eviscerated it, being careful to draw out the gall carefully in the way my dad had taught me when I was just a boy. I cut out the internal organs and put them in a neat little pile next to a rock at the edge of the willows. Food for the coyotes. There's some kind of Sioux tradition about that. I put the heart in a little plastic grocery bag I had stuffed into my pocket at dawn. The carcass was cool now, and hollow.

"It was the biggest deer I ever killed. It took probably half an hour to dress it and I suddenly felt pretty hungry. All I had was a power bar in the breast pocket of my overalls. I tore the wrapper off with my front teeth and ate it in two or three gulps. I remember thinking, 'It doesn't bother me a bit to hold this bar in my bloody and stiff fingers out here (and the blood's not even mine), but if I were home and I had pricked my finger on a needle or something, I'd be in the bathroom washing it off before I would ever think of touching food.'

"When I finally stood up and wiped my knife on my pants leg and put it back into the sheath, I suddenly became aware of two things. First, I was a helluva long way from my truck. Second, a kind of front had moved in while I was squatting beside that deer and now the sun was gone, the sky was all clouded over, and the wind had come up. It wasn't a blizzard, but it seemed as if a blizzard might be moving in. I suddenly felt a very long way from home.

"I was at least four miles from the truck and, even eviscerated, the deer carcass must have weighed more than 150 pounds. Plus I had my gun. I'd been up for eight hours already with not much to eat during that whole time (should have listened to my mother), and now I had no choice but to carry that buck all the way back to the pickup. So I slung it over my shoulders and tucked the gun under the hind flank and started for the truck.

"The weather was steadily worsening. The wind was beginning to be a factor. I was beginning to feel cold. The deer was very heavy. I had not brought gloves. My fingers were getting numb and there was nothing I could do about it without putting the carcass down and I wasn't about to do that. By the time I had walked two miles—maybe a little less than halfway—I was really exhausted. I sat down and rummaged through my pockets. I found an old two-pack of saltine crackers that I had picked up at a salad bar somewhere. They were crushed mostly, but I sucked them down in an instant. I took a sip from my canteen. The weather was really bad by now and I would have been a little worried even if there had been no deer to worry about. I knew my mother must be worrying too.

"As I sat there, I tried to think clearly about what I should do. My options were to abandon the deer altogether—something I would never ever do—or leave part of it behind, or hang it in a tree and come back for it later, or cut it up and carry it in shifts to the pickup. I was amazingly tired and also emotionally drained from a long day of concentration and tension.

"As I sat there in the badlands I suddenly started to cry. What just an hour before had seemed like a triumph was now becoming an ordeal. I was still at least an hour from the truck and I didn't know where the energy was supposed to come from. I knew it would be a sacrilege to take the life of that great buck and not treat its carcass with respect. But I needed help and I didn't have any. I felt like that character, the fisherman, from Hemingway's *The Old Man and the Sea*, who caught the great fish but then couldn't get it back to shore. I never carry a portable radio transmitter and even if I had one, who would be within range? I was really out in the middle of nowhere. Besides, I felt responsible for the whole experience and I didn't want to shirk my duty. Nothing bothers me more than a hunter who abandons his kill. I kept thinking, what would my father do in this situation? What would Dad do?

"I fought back my tears with the sleeves of my jacket and I said to myself, 'I have no choice but to suck it up and finish carrying that buck back to the truck. I'll go as fast as I can while still pacing myself enough to be able to make it.' It was snowing now.

"So I took a deep breath and lifted the carcass back onto my back and started slowly off. I began to recite everything I had ever learned by heart: the Lord's prayer, some nursery rhymes I still remembered, and Walt Whitman's "Oh Captain, My Captain." OK, it's a lousy poem, but it was the only one I could think of. Visibility was dropping fast. It felt like dusk even though I knew it couldn't be much later than two p.m. But I got into a kind of rhythm and I managed to make pretty good progress. I had to stop three times to rest. I'd sit on a log and look at that deer as if he were my enemy, or the karmic response of the universe for having killed one of its most amazing creatures. But it also seemed like my brother in some important way. At one point I was almost drifting into unconsciousness as I sat in the cold moist gray air. I remember thinking, 'I'll never kill in quite the same way again. It's not that I'm sorry I killed this buck, but carrying it out all this way has made me aware of the burden of killing it. In all the hunting I ever do from now on forward, I'll never waste a shot and I'll never make light of the fact of killing. When I cut this critter up for meat, I'm going to do it alone, in silence, and I'm not going to waste even a sliver of the meat. And I'm not making ground venison out of it for tacos. I'm going to eat this one like steak.'

"Well, at last I saw my pickup in the distance and I picked up my pace. You can say what you want about your stages of wilderness consciousness, but there are times when the industrial paradigm is the only thing that will serve. I cannot tell you how glad I was to see that truck. When I finally staggered up to it, I lowered the carcass into the bed of the truck as gently as I could, and put an old blanket over it, and tied it down for the ride home. I was a mess. My clothes were bloody. My lips and hands were chapped. I was bone weary right to the core. I was so hungry I could have roasted that deer right there next to my truck. I was cold and emotionally on edge. It was getting dark. I suddenly felt panic about my keys: what if I lost them out there somewhere, but of course they were right where I had put them in the zipped compartment of my overalls. The pickup started right up and KFYR was blaring on the radio. It seemed obscene now—all that over-hyped advertising for used cars and cell phones, and the false good cheer of the disk jockeys so I snapped it off and put the truck into gear and moved slowly off up the trail to the road.

My mind was numb all the way home. I don't remember anything about the drive except rediscovering the caked blood on my fingers from time to time.

"My mother chided me a little when I got home, but I could see that she had not been really worried. I hung up the carcass in the back yard and two days later butchered it as if it were the last mastodon ever hunted on the northern plains. I didn't serve that meat with the same kind of bravado I had shown from previous hunts—I ate some with my girlfriend, and with my parents, but I did not serve it for groups of friends. And every time I took a bite of it I remembered bursting into tears out in the middle of that draw, tired and frustrated and not certain that I had done the right thing.

"The strange thing is that I finally became a true hunter that day in the badlands of North Dakota. I finally learned to understand what hunting is. I've killed probably a half dozen deer and a hundred ducks and pheasants since then, but I have never looked on the sport in quite the same way. Some part of the boyish exuberance of hunting left me that afternoon. It reminds me a bit of St. Paul's "when I was a boy I did childish things," speech.[†] In those few hours, I crossed over some indescribable line in my life. Ever since that day, hunting's become a sacrament and like all sacraments it's much deeper and more important, but it's also less fun."

When Michael finished his story it was almost dark along the Little Missouri. We could have been two bushmen of the Kalahari. He began to kick pebbles around the embankment—embarrassed perhaps. I moved next to him and hugged him by the shoulder for a second—no more—and said, "Michael, that's one of the greatest stories I've ever heard. Thank you."

[†]"When I was a child, I spake as a child, I understood as a child, I thought as a child: but when I became a man, I put away childish things." I Corinthians 13:11.

We stayed out another half hour hoping to hear the wail of the coyotes and we did hear a few in the distance, as well as a freight train whistling its way to the Pacific at some infinite distance from the river. Then we drove back and went our separate ways.

The next morning, when we met for coffee, I said, without having planned to say anything, "Mike, would you be willing to take me hunting with you sometime? I believe I would like to try to shoot a deer once in my life, and if I did so, I want you to be my guide." In the night I had recalled that great passage from Thoreau: "There is a period in the history of the individual," he wrote, "as of the race, when the hunters are the 'best men,' as the Algonquins called them. We cannot but pity the boy who has never fired a gun; he is no more humane, while his education has been sadly neglected." This is precisely how I felt in the morning after Mike's riverside narrative. I felt that he was a truer child of the plains than I. I felt that my own claim to be a citizen of this landscape was suddenly thin. Mike agreed to take me hunting whenever I wished it.

A part of me lives for that distant day, when in the doldrums of middle life, when everything has turned to sand, and we are both at loose ends at the same moment, and we somehow find each other across the years of the inevitable drift, when we agree to meet in an improbable place that nobody else loves—with the spanking new equipment of middle-age and prosperity—and spend ten days together learning the art of life again. In the back of my mind I hear, faintly, and at a great distance, the mingled strains of "Dueling Banjos," the Hemingwayesque laugh of the Wally Brothers, and the music of the spheres. And the death call of that buck when he took a bullet perfectly cast into his majestic shoulder out near the Burning Coal Vein.

Nausicaa

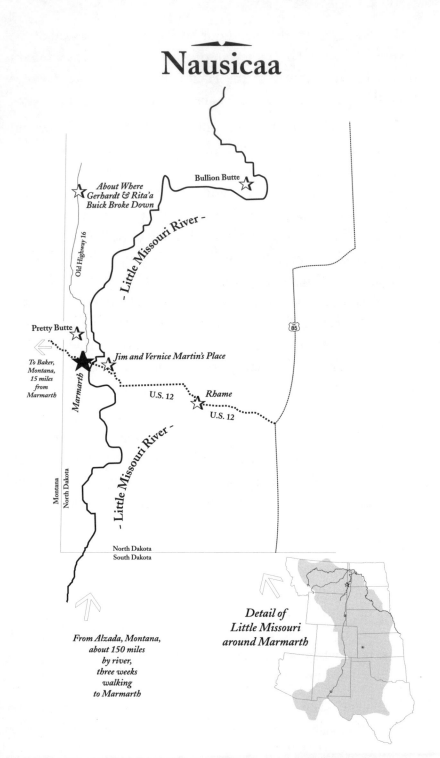

About Where
Gerhardt & Rita'a
Buick Broke Down

Bullion Butte

Old Highway 16

- Little Missouri River -

Pretty Butte

To Baker,
Montana,
15 miles
from
Marmarth

Marmarth

Jim and Vernice Martin's Place

U.S. 12

Rhame

U.S. 12

Montana
North Dakota

- Little Missouri River -

North Dakota
South Dakota

From Alzada, Montana,
about 150 miles
by river,
three weeks
walking
to Marmarth

Detail of
Little Missouri
around Marmarth

Nausicaa

PATTI PERRY, THE SOMETIME MAYOR OF MARMARTH, is not the kind of woman whose photograph appears on the pages of *Cosmopolitan* magazine. She is stout, unsculpted, permanently disheveled, and unmade-up. Her hair, though permed, is seldom orderly. By the artificial standards of what passes for urbane civilization in America, her speech is coarse, blunt, and unpoetic. You'd sooner see her in Roller Derby than on a fashion runway. She is, in many ways, militantly attached to her persona. Like everyone else, she has a set of character armor. She does not believe in second hand smoke and she is not convinced that smoking while pregnant is particularly unhealthful. She is a deeply skeptical woman, and she is openly derisive about faddish, New Age, environmentalist, and politically correct notions. If you are looking for Thomas Jefferson's "softness of disposition that is the ornament of her sex and the charm of ours," don't slow down in Marmarth.

II

IN THE TWENTIETH YEAR, WHEN THE GODS FINALLY AGREE to release Odysseus from the sexual snare of the goddess Calypso, and at last he is permitted to go home to his faithful, long-suffering wife Penelope, he constructs a raft and sets out alone on his last great journey. The god of the sea, Poseidon, who has reason to hate Odysseus, thwarts the hero one last time by stirring up a massive storm and shattering his raft. Odysseus nearly drowns. At last he washes up, more dead than alive, on the shore of a strange island. Exhausted and disoriented, and close to death, Odysseus buries himself under an olive tree near the shore, covers himself with leaves, and falls into a deathlike sleep.

Ah, but there is nothing like a good night of sleep.

Odysseus is discovered the next day by an inspired young virgin named Nausicaa. Her blood is royal. She is the daughter of the king and queen of Scheria, home of the remarkable Phaiakians. After being visited in the night by Odysseus' guardian god Athena, Nausicaa borrows her father's best wagon and takes the family's laundry—and a number of her girlfriends—to the seashore. It is easily the most erotic clothes-washing scene in western literature.

> . . . they unyoked the mules and set them free from the wagon,
> and chased them out along the bank of the swirling river
> to graze on the sweet river grass, while they from the wagon
> lifted the wash in their hands and carried it to the black water,
> and stamped on it in the basins, making a race and game of it
> until they had washed and rinsed all dirt away, then spread it
> out in line along the beach of the sea, where the water
> of the sea had washed the most big pebbles up on the dry shore.[†]

Their duties complete, the nymphs bathe in the river, oil their nubile bodies, have a picnic, and toss a ball to each other in the surf.

The shipwrecked Odysseus is awakened by the playful volubility of the nymphs.

He climbs out of the pit where he slept, a broken, exhausted, briny wreck of a man, covers the worst of his nakedness with a tree limb, and delivers to Nausicaa a supplication speech of stunning subtlety:

I am at your knees, O queen. But are you mortal or goddess?

[†]from Richmond Lattimore's magnificent translation, vi. 88-95.

If indeed you are one of the gods who hold wide heaven,
then I must find in you the nearest likeness to Artemis[1]
the daughter of Zeus, for beauty, figure, and stature.
But if you are one among those mortals who live in this country,
three times blessed are your father and the lady your mother,[2]
and three times blessed your brothers too, and I know their spirits
are warmed forever with happiness at the thought of you, seeing
such a slip of beauty taking her place in the chorus of dancers;[3]
but blessed at the heart, even beyond these others, is that one
who, after loading you down with gifts, leads you as his bride[4]
home. I have never with these eyes seen anything like you,
neither man nor woman. Wonder takes me as I look on you.
Yet in Delos once I saw such a thing, by Apollo's altar.[5]
I saw the stalk of a young palm shooting up.[6] I had gone there
once, and with a following of a great many people,[7]
on that journey which was to mean hard suffering for me.[8]
And as, when I looked upon that tree, my heart admired it
long, since such a tree had never yet sprung from the earth, so
now, lady, I admire you and wonder, and am terribly
afraid to clasp you by the knees. The hard sorrow is on me.
Yesterday on the twentieth day I escaped the wine-blue
sea; until then the current and the tearing winds had swept me
along from the island of Ogygia, and my fate has landed me
here; here too I must have evil to suffer; I do not
think it will stop; before then the gods have much to give me.
Then have pity, O queen. You are the first I have come to
after much suffering, there is no one else that I know of
here among the people who hold this land and city.[9]
Show me the way to town and give me some rag to wrap me
in, if you had any kind of piece of cloth when you came here,[10]
and then may the gods give you everything that your heart longs for;[11]
in all things, for nothing is better than this, more steadfast
than when two people, a man and his wife, keep a harmonious
household; a thing that brings much distress to the people who hate them
and pleasure to their well-wishers, and for them the best reputation.[12]

No wonder they called him a survivor! In the course of this
magnificent speech, Odysseus manages to inform Nausicaa—upon
whom his homecoming and perhaps even his life depend—that
he worships the official gods of the Greek world, Artemis[1] and
Apollo,[5] that he looks upon her not as a defenseless girl but as
someone with a family, with parents and brothers,[2] that he is a

---

†from Lattimore, vi. 149-185

cultured man and not merely a pirate,[3] that he is a man who respects and observes religious rituals,[5] that the imagery he associates with her is innocent and organic, not sexual,[6] that he is a leader of men,[7] that he has suffered much,[8] that he is depending upon her assistance,[9] that he is ashamed of his nakedness,[10] that he is solicitous for her happiness, and that he is as concerned as she is about matters of reputation.[2] Odysseus also notices not once but twice that she is of marriageable age, and he hints carefully at his own potential availability.[4 & 11] If ever a speech delivered by a desperate man was laced with information designed to disarm his listener's fears or hostility, this is it. By the time he has finished, Nausicaa can only conclude that he is a respectable, even an important, man worthy of her hospitality. And indeed, it is Nausicaa who smoothes the way for Odysseus at the Phaiakian court. The princess saves his life.

Nausicaa proves to be the last of Odysseus' temptations. He has, in the course of his twenty-year absence from Ithaka, been tested in every possible way—by hunger, by greed, by one-eyed monsters, by pride, by his own Faustian curiosity, by his rage for experience, by angry gods, by the outmoded codes of the Mycenaean warrior hero cult, and indeed by minor but powerful goddesses who want him to share their beds forever. But the last temptation of Odysseus, like the last temptation of Kazantzakis's Christ, is the promise of a new life with a young mortal woman. The King of the Phaiakians offers Odysseus his daughter and eventual dominion over his wealthy and fertile kingdom, vastly more Edenic than rocky Ithaka. Nausicaa makes it clear that she is willing to wed the charismatic stranger. Odysseus need only say yes and he will live out the mid-life fantasy of virtually every man in human history: the new young (impressionable and unfinished) trophy wife, plus early retirement. He is being offered what every man most desires, and the price is merely acquiescence.

But many-minded Odysseus decides to go home instead, to his wife Penelope, to his son Telamachos, and to hardscrabble Ithaka. He cannot know, when he makes this dread choice, whether his long-suffering wife is even alive. He has been warned repeatedly that he should not count on Penelope's having remained faithful to him across such a gulf of time. He has been informed, more than once, that his commander Agamemnon's wife Clytaemnestra not only took up with a lesser man in his absence, but she murdered her husband, the leader of the Achaeans (Greeks), on the day he returned from his ten-year ordeal in Troy. Nor can Odysseus assume that he can simply resume lordship over the people of Ithaka; perhaps his enemies have seized power in his absence, perhaps he has merely been forgotten. At the moment of his decision, Ithaka represents risk, uncertainty, danger, old routines, and a middle-aged wife. Odysseus opts for home with no guarantee that there is a home to go home to.

Odysseus can start his life over again with a fresh young wife in a fresh land—who could blame him?—but he decides instead to take the risk of homecoming. In one of the most delicate moments in all of literature, Odysseus says farewell to the lovely princess, and turns for home. Odysseus makes the right choice. Telemachos is a bold, virtuous lad on the cusp of manhood, and he has not for a moment forgotten his father. Penelope, it turns out, was faithful after all. And, before their reunion, Athena gives her the Homeric equivalent of a round of plastic surgery so that Odysseus will not be disappointed by his choice.

Resourceful, many-minded Odysseus, the man who was never at a loss, possessed what I am calling spirit of place. Ithaka was not paradise, but it was home. It meant father and mother, wife and child, faithful dog (Argos), flocks, vineyards, orchards, olive groves, a community of men and women who were familiar but far from perfect, a view from the kitchen window, above all a bed that he had made himself and rooted firmly in the good earth. If ever there was a poem about "family values," it is Homer's *Odyssey*. Thomas Jefferson was right. It is worth learning Greek to read Homer in the original.

III

I AM NOW GOING TO ARTICULATE one of the key insights about life. Nausicaa is not always a nubile nymph.

IV

I HAD BEEN HIKING ON THE LITTLE MISSOURI RIVER for more than three weeks. I had been carrying more than half my body weight in the pack on my back a distance of more than 150 miles. It was the most literal odyssey of my life. When my mother had dropped me off at my entry point at Alzada, Montana, anxious for my safety in the way of all mothers, she had sat in her Honda Accord by the side of the dirt road as I shouldered my ludicrous burden and lumbered off on a northwest tangent towards the river. Later she said that the image of me lurching over the sage meadow towards the river, nearly doubled over by my bright red pack, wincing all the way, was as pathetic a thing as she had ever seen. She was half-convinced that she would never see me again. But in spite of her misgivings, in the way of mothers, she eased her car back onto the gravel roadway and drove the entire course of the Little Missouri River in a single afternoon.

My pace was decidedly more modest. I hiked with a kind of grim determination for slightly more than an hour before I stopped for a drink. On a grassy knoll graced by a wind blasted cottonwood tree or two, an oasis in this godforsaken place, I offloaded my pack, and pulled out a plastic flask of water. A few horses nosed around the periphery, curious, skittish. There was a light wind that made the place seem even more desolate than it was. A few dozen billowy cumulous clouds migrated eastward like a convoy of stately tanker ships. A meadowlark piped its liquid note. I decided to lay my head back on the turf for a few seconds of meditation. I fell instantly asleep ("fell" does not begin to do justice to my collapse), the profound sleep that the body insists upon when it has the most critical recovery work to perform. When I woke up, bewildered, an hour or two later, I could barely stand. It was the beginning of a long day that ended with the most terrifying lightning storm I ever witnessed.

And that was Day One.

The next morning I buried three books in the sandy soil under a clump of cottonwood trees, mentally marking the spot in case I ever wanted to return to reclaim my treasure. I also burned a shirt, a pair of pants, and shorts in my campfire. I poured out two bottles of water and I tore my journal in half and left the blank pages in a hollow. Perhaps I had lightened my load by eight pounds, perhaps less. It had become clear to me that every ounce was going to count.

By the time I staggered, three weeks later, into Marmarth, the first town on the Little Missouri River in North Dakota, I was a wreck. My body had absorbed too many strains in too short a time. I had used muscles that had lain dormant for years. I was badly in need of a couple of rest days, packless days, bootless days, barefoot days, but out on the river trail I had been unwilling to hole up or even slacken my pace. There was nothing wrong with me that time and sleep would not repair, except possibly the sore in the small of my back. My pack had a pliable aluminum internal frame, which had somehow chafed and then dug into the soft spot on my back just above my right kidney. Every day I had fidgeted endlessly with the pack to take pressure off that spot, but nothing had helped, not moleskin, not strap adjustments worthy of a nervous boy scout, not a continual reshuffling of the weightiest items in my kit. I knew there was serious pain around the trouble zone, and even some bloody discharge, but I did not then know that I was in possession of a deep open sore that was digging its way rapidly to my rib bone. I was going to have to do something about that wound, or I would not be able to continue my trek. Still, I was having the time of my life.

Marmarth was never so like an oasis as it was at the moment I spotted its water tower and cottonwood streets off on the northern horizon on a blousy September afternoon. A couple of hours later I tramped up the dirt streets of Marmarth and found my way up to the Perry residence, a refugee of the river wars, dropped my pack to the ground, and opened the screen door. Patti was in the kitchen doing something heroic.

"Well, I bet you won't ask me today where I'd choose to live if it weren't Marmarth," she said as she carefully shaped dinner rolls and notched them precisely in a bread pan. "Looks as if you lived to tell your story."

"That's far from clear," I said. "I've got at least three hundred miles to go, and I'm just starting to move into badlands country."

"Why anyone would want to walk that poor excuse for a river I don't know. Have you ever heard of the horse?"

I sat down and let her start pouring me endless cups of coffee. She rustled up some lunch.

An hour or so later, when it could no longer seem that I was whining or dwelling on my troubles, I asked her if she would take a look at the sore on my back. I lifted my shirt and bent over slightly to give her easy access to the wound. "Jesus, this is a serious problem," she said. "This is the kind of thing a guy like you would probably see a doctor over." I asked her what she would recommend. "Well, I'd keep your damned pack off your back for a couple of days, that's for sure. Maybe haul a few less books." She laughed wickedly for a while. "There's a pretty good discharge and I think probably quite a bit of infection. At least there aren't any maggots vacationing in there yet that I can see. I'll find some disinfectant, and when we go to milk, I'll get some goat balm to spread over the sore."

I took one of the longest and most satisfying showers of my life. The Perry's bathroom is a bit quirky. Above the toilet paper dispenser, for example, is a red plastic embossed label that says, "Warning. Do not exceed 250 rpms." I shaved off my month-old beard, changed into fresh clothes that I had weeks earlier cached with the Perrys, called my mother and my girlfriend, and returned to the kitchen. Patti sat me down and dressed my wound. I tried not to grimace. She had, while I was showering, driven up to the barn to get the goat balm. She covered the whole business with a loose bandage, not wanting to keep the healing oxygen from the wound. She was surprisingly tender for a tough woman.

"Where's Gary?" I asked.

Patti told me that he was in western Montana hauling gravel for a big road-widening project not so far from Yellowstone National Park. He had taken their daughter Heidi with him, and a small pickup camper, and he was going to be gone for six more weeks, at least. It was a good steady job. The Perrys needed the money. I have never really understood where their cash comes from—Patti buys and sells goats, sells goat milk, and takes in a bit of cash in her roles as Mayor of Marmarth, ambulance driver, EMT, CPR leader and instructor, and who knows what else. Gary drives truck, fixes giant engines, digs stock dams and embeds cattle guards for ranchers in the district. There is nothing mechanical that he cannot do with mastery. So far as I can tell, they live mostly outside of the money economy. They butcher their own critters. They grow much of their own food. They cook their meals at the raw rather than the highly processed end of the spectrum. They do all their own cleaning, plumbing, snow removal, furniture repair, carpentry, wiring, vehicle service, welding, home decoration, etc.

When all the grids go down, and the shelves in all the stores of America are empty, when the rest of us are screaming for relief and clawing each other's throats for the last bag of corn chips, the Perrys will quietly go about their business and indeed share what they have with a range of grasshopper people like me, some of them complete strangers. They are together the most self-reliant people I have ever known, and that includes my grandparents of Minnesota, dairy farmers who, unlike the Perrys, lived through the Depression, whose peak income in the flush 1970s was between twelve and fifteen thousand dollars per year. I'm sure Patti and Gary could live a year or more without any help from the economy. Or rather they remind us that the Greek word *oikonomos* means household management. It's an achievement that we slickers cannot understand or appreciate. But when you are tempted to be amused by Patti's unpolished appearance and blunt English, just imagine her delivering a baby by the side of a road in a blizzard one day and then welding a trailer frame in the shop the next, and never calling attention to either except to declare that the woman was a damned fool for starting out in an ice storm and that Gary was supposed to have laid in a supply of No. 6 rod last time he went to Rapid City. When the universe turns to shit, you want Patti or Gary Perry, and not a Nobel Laureate, in your camp. Patti Perry is equal to anything.

For the next five days I followed Patti around her world. We milked 50 goats twice a day, and fed her bizarre menagerie. We bused school children over back roads to school and got them home again. Patti threatened to cuff a couple of the older boys when they got rowdy, and they got quiet quick. We worked in her garden. We fed bum lambs. We ran errands in faraway Bowman (32 miles) and nearby Baker (15) and we had dinner twice in Rhame (12). We made two batches of goat cheese in her kitchen. She taught me not only the chemistry of cheese making, but the technique, start to finish. We took care of some mayoral duties, which included delicate negotiations with representatives of several law and order jurisdictions, and the husband of a former town officer who had embezzled about two-thirds of Marmarth's annual budget, lied, got caught, confessed, and had now made herself pregnant in hopes of avoiding a jail sentence. We met with the Marmarth Historical Society. We scrounged for and examined historical photographs. We met with a local woman who owns some important early film footage of rodeo, but who suspects that someone is trying to dispossess her of her treasure, and consequently trusts no one. Paranoia is the official civic philosophy of Marmarth. Every night we went to the Pastime to meet fellow Marmarthians, and whoever else drifted in from the West. We drove to the Pastime, of course, even though the Perrys live only four blocks away. We had endless conversations about everything, from the river to the oil fields to the economics of goat dairies to the purposes of education to one of Patti's ne'er-do-well sons-in-law who was either just into or just back from the pen and who had way too many guns, and a violence streak the size of Alberta.

Patti was no gossip, but she could tell stories about everyone we met that would make your hair curl.

One night two of the young bucks in the bar got into a fistfight. They were both drunk. There was ancient bad blood between them, Patti said. The grudge involved a woman or something, and from time to time it broke out into violence. "If they don't loosen each other's teeth once every couple of months, they get restless," she explained. They had been circling each other verbally for hours from opposite ends of the bar. Finally, one of the boys called the other out and they shouted at each other for a while like a couple of braggart characters out of a Mark Twain novel, and then strode out into the rain and beat the living Jesus out each other. There were two types of people in the bar that night, those who ran out to watch, and those who stayed in the bar pretending that the whole business was infantile and waited instead to interrogate the heralds of the brawl. It was all over in less than ten minutes. The combatants returned to the bar with their shirts torn and their faces bruised. One had a bloody—possibly broken—nose. Their knuckles were scuffed and torn. Their eyes were big and supremely alert. They took turns using the phone to call home. Patti told each one he was a damned fool and that if Gary had been around he would have given them both plenty to think about, and each one of them listened to her with the respect that comes from hard experience. Patti Perry was easily the most sensible and intelligent citizen of Marmarth, and everything she said commanded immediate respect. Plus, she could whup both of them herself if she had to.

Then an amazing thing happened. As the conflict developed and spilled out onto the street in a kind of helpless slow motion, I felt like the boy in *Shane*, witnessing something that never occurs in the world in which I travel. Now the door of the Pastime opened and two women walked in, talking to each other in a friendly way and even laughing a bit. Each one found her man. One made a fuss over the man who lost the fight, cleaned up his bloody nose, and investigated the shirt to see whether it could be rehabilitated. She kissed him carefully on the cheek and sipped a beer as he brooded into the bar mirror, probing his wounds with his fingertip, and (typical man) stiffing her for her generosity of spirit. The other woman strode up to *her* man, the conquistador, called him an f-ing moron in a voice that was somehow at once affectionate and deeply sexualized, and then she kissed him passionately on the mouth while running the knuckles of her delicate right hand over his exposed sweaty belly and—indeed—on down to the bulge in his trousers. It was the starkest public expression of sexual desire I have ever seen. I wanted to get into a brawl in the bar just to test the theory! I longed to have such a woman in my life, a lover who would stroke me for my deepest stupidities. I turned wide-eyed to Patti. She could only muster, "Whatever floats your boat, I guess."

The happy couple soon left the Pastime for more agreeable violence, but not before the victor slapped a five dollar beer on the bar and said, "Dude,[†] buy my friend here a couple of drinks." He clapped his bloody antagonist half-affectionately on the shoulder and walked (there was higher primate in his gait) out the door. His woman, meanwhile, said, "Good-bye, Karen," to the other, as if they were leaving a church circle or a bridal shower.

The contest over, the bar settled down to serious drinking.

Later Patti told me that she would have broken up the fight—had done so in other years—but one of the couples was involved in the embezzlement scandal and she didn't want to muddle the legal issues at this stage in the deliberations. Don't you wish you lived in a world where the bankruptcy of New York City or Orange County ended in a barroom brawl? Shane, come back! Come back. Shane. Come back.

In a few days my back healed, after a fashion, and by now I had gotten a pretty full dose of Pastime culture. One night I had driven out, very late, with the most successful young rancher in the district, to call coyotes with a dying rabbit call he had purchased. We drove with a six-pack of beer fifteen miles north of Marmarth on lovely, lonely ND 16, called a half dozen coyotes within a hundred yards or so, talked the issues, and then decided to call it

---

[†]That was the name of the bar owner, a woman straight out of a *Gunsmoke* rerun.

a night. But when we fired up Scott's massive ranch pickup, the differential fell out onto the ground just like that, and it could not be fixed with what he had in the back of the truck. So we had to walk back to town on ND 16 on the darkest night I have ever spent in the Little Missouri valley, more fatigued and more sober with each mile. It was almost impossible even to see the gravel road that night. So we stumbled our way home observing the majesty of the stars and shivering against the chill. Patti was waiting up when I returned about 4 a.m. "You may as well stay up and come milk the goats," she said. "There are two types of stupid. Those stupid enough to close the bar and go out coyote calling. And those who have to walk back to town. You make me craaazy." She made a giant pot of coffee, and started hauling cartons of eggs and packages of goat sausage out of the refrigerator.

By and by (to use Twain's wonderful phrase), a companion— late as always—finally showed up to join me for a few days on the river. Patti made sure we had plenty of her homemade lamb jerky, and sugarless Koolade packets to make the waters of the Little Missouri palatable, and freshly washed and folded clothes, and new batteries for my flashlight. She had poured enough coffee down my throat to get me to the North Pole. She had fashioned a patch-pad to protect the sore place in my back and she had done some assault and battery on the aluminum frame of my backpack. She drove us over to the river, called us damned fools, gave us bear hugs, and made me promise to stop back in at the end of the journey.

Beneath the gruff, tough, you bet your sweet ass surface, Patti Perry is as tender a woman as I have ever met. Twice a day for most of a week she had coaxed goat balm into my wound. She cooked me exquisite meals and hauled me around to see the glories of the district. She taught me a range of practical arts that are, in Thomas Jefferson's phrase, worth a century of book learning. She introduced me to her friends and told me their stories, even their dark Marmarthian secrets. She stood by patiently as I learned to milk her goats with modest facility. She laughed at me a score of times each day, but there was an affection in her mirth that even she could not deny. By the end of our time together I had come to depend on her chorus line: "You make me craaaazy!" as the deepest assurance I would ever have of the essential rightness of things. If Sacagawea had been like Patti Perry, *she* would have led the Lewis and Clark Expedition, and Meriwether Lewis would have cheered up and written in his journal every day per the President's instructions.

Patti was a wonderful woman married to a wonderful man,[†] and over the course of the years they have done for me more than anyone could ever deserve. Before I shouldered my pack and got back onto the river, I ordered for her a gleaming new goat cheese press (there is a catalogue for everything), and a few dozen packets of rennet (the chemical, taken from the stomach of the cow, that fixes whey into cheese), and some exotic cheese flavorings (which I'm sure she discarded), but these gifts—though by no means cheap—were pitiful recompense for her gifts to me. She had given me pearls without price.

So who do you want in your life, in your space, in your kitchen, in your bed? The lithe unmuscled liberal arts BA, who reads Jung and wears clothing from Nordstroms, whose fairy godmother is Martha Stewart, who takes all the quizzes in *Glamour*, searches *Cosmo* for tips on how to have an orgasm every time, and whose idea of a wilderness adventure is a week in a four star at Cabo San Lucas? Or someone who can weld a car chassis and maybe yours too?

Most men are errant fools—like Paul I am the chief of sinners— and though we know in our heart of hearts what is good and

---

†Unlike Homer's Nausicaa, Patti was not single and not available for romance.

what is bad for us, what social constructs are hollow at their core and what habits of the heart might actually enable us to thrive on earth, we repeat the tragedy of the Trojan prince Paris every time, and choose the woman for whom pulling a weed is an adventure and a beauty risk, for whom pulling a calf is beyond comprehension and beyond capability. We always choose feckless, self-indulgent, narcissistic, unreliable drop-dead Helen, the Queen of Thanatos, when we might have chosen Hera, the goddess of domestic life, or Hestia, the goddess of the hearth, or Athena, the goddess of life mastery. Ah, the abominable corruptions of patriarchy.

One of my wise friends, a California poet, said once, "If Jesus appeared on earth today, he would not, I think, come in a flowing robe, with shoulder-length hair and Aryan eyes. The divine, my young friend, comes in the least likely packages to test our authenticity." To understand this is to understand everything.

Patti Perry is more truly Nausicaa than all the lean and petite beauties I have known, all the boneless women of Cranach, all the exponents of postmodernism and contributors to PETA. Patti Perry's crust is all initial. With all the others, the envelope is gloriously alluring, and you don't wake up to the tectonics of the crust until it is far too late. This is the lesson of life. I am hoping to learn it one of these days.

V

ONCE DURING THE GOLDEN EARLY DAYS OF CHAUTAUQUA, Gerhardt and Rita Ludwig drove out to spend the week with me in Marmarth. They had had T-shirts made that said, "Chautauqua Trash and Proud of It," a parody of the then-ubiquitous "Oil Field Trash and Proud of it," shirts that provided a clue to one of the perennial social fissures of the American West. They drove out in their new car, a giant gold Buick sedan that had been handed down to them by Rita's parents, who were prosperous farmers in the sandy loam district of northeastern North Dakota. It was one of the biggest cars I had ever seen and it was, of course, in gleaming mint condition with about 40,000 miles on it. It burned a fair amount of gas, but hey. . . .

Gerhardt and Rita were new to this wild country. They decided to stay in a motel in Bowman, strategically located outside of the badlands country, and they were not then as willing (that is reckless) as they later became in the anarchic world of public humanities programs. We had a great week. The people of Marmarth love Chautauqua, though not always perhaps for the right reasons. They are glad to have a tent to put up on the rodeo grounds. They are delighted to have a reason to open up the chuck wagon and turn out beef burgers in gargantuan quantities. They are glad to have reason to gather in one place in the cool of the evening—there is no public meeting hall in Marmarth of any sort. And they are glad to have new friends to take into the Pastime after hours. After a week in Marmarth, you have to make a choice: either you go native and buy one of the hundred or so rundown bungalows that sit among the cottonwood trees in the Little Missouri River's one true oasis and start on your slow burn towards death, or you run away and check yourself into the Betty Ford clinic.

Fundraising for Chautauqua has always been irregular in Marmarth. One year Patti and Merle Clark simply handed me a wrinkled brown paper bag filled with $1500 in wadded-up small bills. On this occasion the Historical Society had sagely decided to recoup its investment by way of the Chicken Board and the Humanist Dunking Stool. Each evening, before the grave "humanities portion of the program," when 250 or 300 people were milling about the big blue and white tent, the local coordinators would take bets on squares of a ten by ten foot plywood board, painted white, gridded into a checkerboard, with squares numbered one to 64. Then, at the moment of maximum drama, when all the bets were in, Patti would release a huge white chicken in the center of the board. The chicken determined the lottery winner by, er, making a deposit on the square of its choice. The lucky winner took home about half of the purse and the Historical Society raised money for the humanities. This fundraising ritual—unique, may I say, to Marmarth, among the 100 or so host communities of Chautauqua—led my philosopher friend Gerhardt Ludwig to explain later in the Pastime Freud's insights about the psychic connection between money and excrement. The citizens of Marmarth universally denounced Freud's theory as "total bullshit" (Gerhardt found that amusing), and I listed their Chicken Board contributions to Chautauqua as "miscellaneous donations" in my final report to the National Endowment for the Humanities.

The Humanist Dunking Stool turned out to be infinitely more lucrative than the Chicken Board. The six participating humanities scholars—most of whom were not altogether happy to be spending the week in grungy godforsaken Marmarth—were invited to sit on a dunking stool, preferably in full costume, while the locals lined up with their dollars and an endless supply of baseballs. The locals were, on the whole, extremely adept at this sport, and more eager than one might have anticipated to drown a university scholar. Successful throws pitched the humanities scholar into an aluminum watering trough that had two unfortunate peculiarities. First, the trough was not very deep. Second, the water—straight from the river—was not very clean. Not all of our participating scholars welcomed the Humanist Dunking Stool in full measure. Several announced sore tailbones after the competition, and several let it be known that this would be their last season in Chautauqua. It always seemed to me that the dunking stool was harmless enough, and I do not think it can be denied that it fulfilled one of the prime directives of the National Endowment for the Humanities, viz., closing the gap between the academy and the wider American community. Everyone who had ever gotten a C- on a chemistry test, or failed calculus, got a little "closure" on the rodeo grounds of Marmarth, without having to bare all to a clinical psychologist. The rate was $1 per toss rather than $125 per session.

One afternoon when we had no evening program to prepare for, I decided to take Gerhardt and Rita on their first journey up ND 16, my favorite thoroughfare in the American West. They were reluctant to take their new car on an untried gravel road, and they would positively have vetoed the idea had I told them the truth about a few of its routine obstacles. We started out in good form with plenty of sodas, candy bars, and licorice, and smoke for Gerhardt. The scenery was sublime, the antelope were jumping, and the sky was magnificent.

It turned out to be a long day's journey into night.

As we were humming along without a care in the world twenty miles north of Marmarth, we heard the sickening sound of base metal colliding with base metal, with no room to negotiate, and the car lurched to a sudden stop. We got out and poked around until we determined that we had some kind of terrible "rear end problem." We hitched a ride to town—it was virtually a miracle that a rancher came along on his way to Marmarth to drop off a few hay bales for someone. We went immediately to Patti's.

Gerhardt explained—dancing on the lip of hysteria—that the car was marooned in the middle of nowhere, that we had barely made it back to town, that something terrible was wrong with the Buick, that it wasn't clear how they were going to get back to Grand Forks, that he wasn't even sure how they were going to get the car back to pavement, etc. Patti listened for a time and then said, "Well, for goodness sakes, let's start by getting the car back to town." She got out a fifth of whiskey and everyone began to drink.

So we drove out in one of Gary's pickups and dragged the stricken Buick back to Marmarth. Gary took a look at it and said all we probably needed was a new differential gear, and it would be easy enough to put it in and get us back in business. Gerhardt asked where the nearest auto parts store might be. Gary said Bowman, but it wasn't open at this time of night, and they probably didn't have that kind of part on hand anyway. Rita moaned, "What are we going to do?"

Now Patti took over. "We'd better go out to Jim Martin's." By now we had been joined by a couple of Chautauquans: tentmaster Ed Sahlstrom, arguably the funniest man ever to have lived in North Dakota, and Professor David Miller of Black Hills State College in Spearfish, South Dakota. They had been celebrating life in the Pastime with some vigor, so they were, by now, equal to any adventure. Ed Sahlstrom did not need to take on a historical character to be one. David Miller was portraying that summer a composite fictional character named Levi Davis, Buffalo Hunter. We had long since begun to caricature his dramatic monologue by imitating his weak Arkansas accent, and parroting two lines that jumped out of the sea of details about buffalo skinning, Indian policies, gun dimensions, the effect of the Civil War on the American West. One line that we all repeated endlessly—though not so often as David Miller, particularly when he had been celebrating—was "Life is hard in the wild, wild West." The other: "At the time, it seemed like a good idea" (pronunciation: "At the tiiiiiiime, it seemed like a GOOOD i-DEEEE-a"). It was this company, plus Patti's dwindling fifth of whiskey, that ventured out to the Martin spread, the Buick in tow.

Jim and Vernice Martin live in a gray doublewide east of Marmarth. Jim is an exuberant boy in an outsized man's body.

Vernice holds the family of four or five young children together by working part-time in Mert's Café. Jim can fix just about anything. We pulled the Buick over the pit he had dug out to enable his part-time auto repair service. He got under the car and pulled the differential plate while we drank and watched Ed's comic routines—mugging, mime, bits from sitcoms and old movies; circus, Toby Show, and Chautauqua war stories; a glorious blizzard of shtick that had us roaring with laughter and nearly peeing our pants. Levi Davis was descending rapidly into a stupor. Every four or five minutes he'd burst out with, "Life is hard in the wild, wild West," each iteration a bit weaker and a bit sadder. Patti made sure everyone's glass was filled. She laughed harder than anyone at Ed's gags. Vernice put on a pot of coffee for Rita, who had the lugubrious look of one who expected to spend the rest of her life with these folks. It was getting close to midnight. The Martin kids were worming in and out of the pit, in and out of the Buick, in and out of the house, up onto Vernice's lap and instantly down again, over the tops of all the vehicles in the yard, and there were many. They were a perpetual motion machine. Not one of them was more than eight years old. Gerhardt said, "I don't know why we had to drive up such an unreliable road on the last day of our stay here." Levi Davis perked up long enough to say, "At the time, it seemed like a good idea," and nodded off again.

Eventually Jim emerged from the pit heavily smudged with grease, the failed differential gear in hand, to announce that he could fix the Buick if only they could find a matching part somewhere. Patti said, "Jesus, Jim, you've got about a hundred junked cars out to the draw. I'm sure one of them has a similar differential." Jim agreed. "Yeah, you're right Patti. I think I even know where there is a Buick of about the same year, but I'll be switched if I'm going out into the draw at this time of night to find it. Hell, there are rattlesnakes all over out there, and skunks, and who knows what else. If you all come back in the morning, I'll find the right gear and get you back on the road."

Patti said, "Jim Martin, I believe I've known you twenty years and I didn't know until this moment that you were afraid of a few old snakes. If you tell me what I'm looking for, I'll go in and get your differential thingum."

Ed Sahlstrom rose up histrionically on his heels. He walked over and shook Levi Davis Buffalo Hunter awake. "No snake's gonna bite Levi here in the state he's in. Any bite would be fatal for the snake. Jim, I need two flashlights, a couple of old hubcaps, the necessary wrenches, and baseball caps for us both." Jim's kids sprinted off to fetch what Ed had asked for, while Levi Davis did a series of spastic jumping jacks to prepare for his ideal. He had a platinum leg from some dread parachuting accident that occurred long ago over the Khyber Pass on a mission he preferred not to talk about—such at least was his story. Each of them took one last swig straight from the bottle and they staggered off towards the junk yard arm in arm. As they disappeared from view I could hear Ed humming the theme song to *The Guns of Navarone* and Levi mumbling, "At the time, it seemed like a good thing to do."

They were gone for most of an hour. Every few minutes we heard screams and laughter and the steady beat of a wrench on one of the hubcaps. Everyone was wide awake now and in a new stage of intoxication that was, in its way, even more lucid than sobriety. The full moon cast lurid shadows over the plains. We all knew we were living through a night we would never forget. Gerhardt was trying to explain Schopenhauer's concept of the will (more or less to himself) when the boys returned with a differential gear in their hands. They looked like they had been to the underworld, to the realm of Pluto and old night, among the shades of Agamemnon and Ajax and swift-footed godlike Achilleus. Their clothes were a wreck, their faces were scratched and begrimed, and they were grinning like tardy school boys. They had already prepared heroically-exaggerated accounts of their adventure, and Ed soon had us roaring again with unquenchable laughter.

Jim climbed down into the pit and replaced the gear. It fit. He replaced the differential cover and fired up the car. The Buick was as good as new—though none of *us* would ever be quite the same. Gerhardt asked him how much he owed him. Jim hemmed and hawed and aw-shucked and kicked the dirt for a while and finally settled on $25. I made Gerhardt write the check for $200. Patti blurted out that there was no point driving up repair prices in that way, but I could see that she was pleased. Not only had Jim Martin done my friend Gerhardt a tremendous favor, but he really needed the money.

A lot of guys would have gone to bed now. It was almost 2 a.m. But Patti said, "Hell, let's go open up Merts and rustle us up some steak and eggs."

So we done it.

VI

ONCE I TOOK A GROUP OF UNIVERSITY PROFESSORS to Marmarth for a retreat. We were trying to create an experimental college within the university and we wanted it to have a special attachment to the landscape of North Dakota. I had made the mistake of believing that the new recruits would be as spirited, adventure-some, and open-minded as my core of friends from the university. What I had failed to consider was that Gerhardt Ludwig, Pat Sanborn, and Timothy Billings were highly unusual people, and that the others were, of course, academics. I have great respect for academics and have been one, quondam, for most of my adult life, but as my former wife used to say, "there is a reason they are

at the academy; these are people who could not live on the outside."
There was some insight among the deep sarcasm.

We checked into the bunkhouse and spread out, and the
newcomers found fault with everything from the quality of their
mattresses to the cleanliness of the group bathrooms. They worked
themselves into a patronizing detachment as assiduously as if they
were training for a decathlon. They made it clear to us—and
indeed to my friends in Marmarth—that they did not like
"slumming it" among the provincials of western North Dakota. I
spent much of my time apologizing for them to the citizens of
Marmarth, whose only crime was to have extended genuine
hospitality to a group of strangers I had—idiotically—vouched
for before the fact.

The next afternoon I drove our seminar group out to the base
of Pretty Butte. The idea was to climb the butte (strenuous but
by no means an ordeal), find a grassy hollow, rest a bit, and then
conduct a brainstorming session about our utopian college scheme
with a freshness and open-mindedness that emanated from the
landscape itself. It was a spirit of place experiment. It was one of
those cool summer days not uncommon in North Dakota, the
temperature approaching chilly, and as we scrambled up the butte
over rough cattle trails, it rained a little. By the time we got to the
top, most of our group was unhappy, uncomfortable, and—
frankly—pissed off. Several recruits urged an immediate descent,
a return to town, showers, and a second attempt at discussion
after everyone was warm and freshly clothed. Great-souled
Gerhardt Ludwig vetoed this idea, partly because he liked the
improbability of our butte-top seminar, partly because he did not
want to thwart my vision of revolutionary institution building.
We found a grass hollow more or less sheltered from the wind—
which was considerable—and not too damp from the rain.
Gerhardt asked me to say a few preliminary words. I pulled out

of my daypack a scruffy looking copy of Thoreau's works (that edition is sacred to me because it has been up all the best buttes of the Great Plains), and read a passage that I hoped would inspire us to create the most interesting experimental college in American history:

> Most of the luxuries, and many of the so-called comforts of life, are not only not indispensable, but positive hindrances to the elevation of mankind. With respect to luxuries and comforts, the wisest have ever lived a more simple and meager life than the poor. The ancient philosophers, Chinese, Hindoo, Persian, and Greek, were a class than which none has been poorer in outward riches, none so rich in inward. We know not much about them. It is remarkable that we know so much of them as we do. The same is true of the more modern reformers and benefactors of their race. None can be an impartial or wise observer of human life but from the vantage ground of what we should call voluntary poverty. Of a life of luxury the fruit is luxury, whether in agriculture, or commerce, or literature, or art. There are nowadays professors of philosophy, but not philosophers. Yet it is admirable to profess because it was once admirable to live. To be a philosopher is not merely to have subtle thoughts, nor even to found a school, but so to love wisdom as to live according to its dictates, a life of simplicity, independence, magnanimity, and trust. It is to solve some of the problems of life, not only theoretically, but practically. . . . The philosopher is in advance of his age even in the outward form of his life. He is not fed, sheltered, clothed, warmed, like his contemporaries. How can a man be a philosopher and not maintain his vital heat by better methods than other men?[†]

When I finished reading these words—among the most inspiring words in the English language—I looked up in satisfaction. I said, "I have been waiting many years for this moment." But not everyone seemed fully engaged in the moment. I began to say, "Well, let's begin by each of us envisioning our program and . . . ."

[†] *Walden*, "Economy."

The least adventuresome of the newcomers interrupted me. He had been a troublemaker ever since he had volunteered for the Integrated Studies program. It turns out that he was shopping around to find a new niche in the university outside of his department, where he was not particularly well liked. Now he forced his pathetic soul into the center of things.

He spoke in the whiniest voice I ever heard, at least in an adult. "I'm tired, I'm cold, and I'm unhappy, and I want to go down." He was the most obnoxious member of our troupe, but his sentiment, it was clear, was shared by everyone but the veterans.

So we threw up our hands and scurried down the butte side as quickly as possible. That was, for me, the beginning of the end of my enthusiasm for our experimental college within the university. The last thing I needed in my life at that juncture was graceless resistance, business as usual, root bind, soullessness. How were we going to take on the university bureaucracy and change the world if we weren't willing to take on the bourgeois boundaries in our little lives? If a gray day and a few drops of rain were enough to derail us, just wait till we butt up against a few reified deans and vice presidents. For the rest of the retreat I said very little. I listened to a series of discussions that would have been precisely the same if they had been held in the Holiday Inn of Grand Forks, or in an antechamber of the student union, or a department seminar room. I spent the rest of my time working on a Lakota beaded medallion for a white buckskin shirt I was making. Not only was this no longer the sort of retreat everyone had specifically agreed to undertake (we had made an explicit social compact), but now the combination of institutional duties and sour group dynamics had made it impossible for me to enjoy Marmarth and the Little Missouri River valley in their own splendid terms. It was an embittering experience.

We repaired to the Pastime.

The most mealy-mouthed of the professors spent the evening telling anyone who would listen of his ordeal, sounding very much like a survivor of the Donner Party or the Titanic. The folk of Marmarth are perfectly happy to hear exaggerated tales of woe so long as you don't actually mean them, but they have lived too close to the bone, suffered too much, and had too much truck with the law to be impressed by anything but serious trouble. Even then they tend to greet it with a knowing shrug of the shoulders. Professor Gloom's monologues were merely reinforcing the derision and contempt Marmarth felt for university pointy-heads.

As he descended into self-pitying drunkenness, the correct translation of slightly raised eyebrows around the bar seemed to be, "OK. Let's review. You drove out here in the big state-owned luxury van, which my taxes, which I cannot afford to pay, pay for, and we showered you with a potluck supper and hospitality and all the drinks you can pour into your pouty little mouth, while you have shown us nothing but condescension and contempt. You felt a little chilly this afternoon and you got a few drops of rain that we all desperately need and upon which our marginal ranch economy absolutely depends on your L.L. Bean shirt, and you climbed a nearby butte on your own legs, the first physical exertion of your pointless pudgy sorry life, while my sister over there at the bar is wearing the bruises of her old man who gets drunk every payday and lays into her with his fists and occasionally a broom handle, a brute who is currently between his stints in the pen, and she's now so messed up that she drinks away her welfare check every time it comes in, and I'm raising her autistic son on goat milk Patti Perry saves for me, and you are asking me to commiserate with your suffering? Is that about the size of it?"

Close reader of texts though he was, Professor Gloom was no great interpreter of eyebrows, and he continued to tell his story like Coleridge's Ancient Mariner.

Patti Perry walked in. She ordered up a rum and coke and sat down across from the hapless professor and made the mistake of asking him how the retreat was going. She downed one drink and started in on another, shouted something ribald at the barmaid, and smoked three cigarettes while he bemoaned his hard day. Apparently he intimated that I had bullied the group up the butte or something of that sort (eyewitness accounts vary widely). At any rate, Patti took a stiff swig of her drink, leaned across the table, extended her arm and grabbed a fistful of the professor's L.L. Bean shirt, lifted him about four inches from his chair, brought his face close enough to hers so that he could smell the rum and the cigarettes. And she said,

"Why, you're nothing but a cry baby pissy pants."

And got up and left the bar.

And so I say to Patti Perry: "may the gods give you everything that your heart longs for." If ever anyone deserved such a gift, you are she.

I feel, under my feet, the long
Grass and the short grass as of old prairie. . .
The dizzying musk of a summer noon: the olfactory rasp
Of sunflower and sage and the satiny scent of the wild rose.
And I hear the insects now: threading the heavy air
With their brilliant needles of colored sound while the birds of the day —
Field sparrow, meadowlark, robin, and all their friends and neighbors —
Are filling the dome of noon with the honey and crystal of song. . .

And perhaps there's another singing I hear — but I'm drunk and fainting—
In this gold rain of sound and scent — (For I drink the air:
Nectar of middle summer in the High Plains. . .).

My senses

Are being invented again!

Thomas McGrath
Letter to an Imaginary Friend, Part Four

Camping Out with Fuglie and the Boys

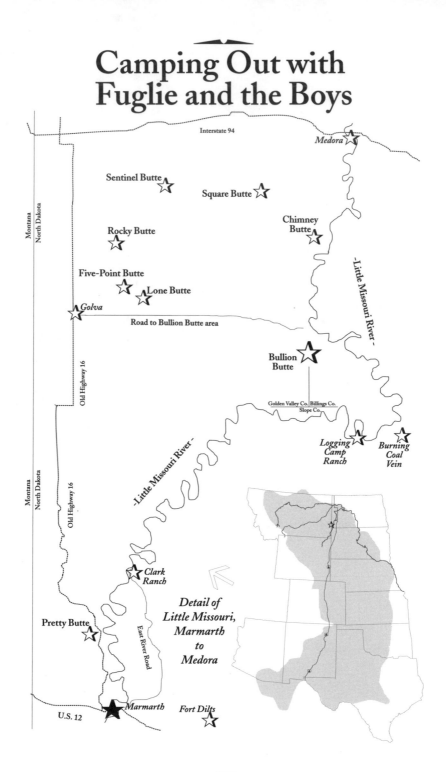

Interstate 94

Medora

Montana
North Dakota

Sentinel Butte

Square Butte

Chimney Butte

Rocky Butte

Five-Point Butte

Lone Butte

Golva

Road to Bullion Butte area

Bullion
Butte

- Little Missouri River -

Golden Valley Co. Billings Co.
Slope Co.

Logging
Camp
Ranch

Burning
Coal
Vein

Old Highway 16

Montana
North Dakota

Old Highway 16

- Little Missouri River -

Clark
Ranch

Pretty Butte

East River Road

Detail of
Little Missouri,
Marmarth
to
Medora

Marmarth

Fort Dilts

U.S. 12

Camping Out with Fuglie and the Boys

The Island of the Sun

YOU NEED TO DO THE WILDERNESS ALONE. Maybe one other person can come, but you cannot be sleeping with her or him, and if there's going to be a lot to talk about Christmas plans and presidential peccadilloes, or rehearsals of frivolous ego-triumphs ("So I said to her . . ," "Can you imagine?!"), what's the point of leaving home? I've only known one person I really want to be with in the wilderness, and now he lives in North Carolina, where somewhere in every camping trip you look over your shoulder and wonder if you are about to meet your *Deliverance.* Douglas, "Come home, come home, it's suppertime," as Garrison Keillor puts it.

I have known some great minds in the course of my life, and even two geniuses. I routinely spend my time with men and women who have mastered this or that field of knowledge. Every day I meet people who take their own intellectual superiority for granted, and make sure that everyone around them is aware of it. Most such men and women are essentially head delivery systems, minds attached to bodies because there is no more convenient way to get them around. They have soft hands. Most of them disdain physical labor. They assume that a superior IQ exempts them from the tawdriness and the scutwork of life. Two of my equalitarian college professors used to bait such rarified beings.

David Noble used to ask (rhetorically, I believe), "Does your shit stink?" And English professor Dick Barnes used to ask the most precocious of his students, "You wouldn't be an English major, would you?" There is, on the whole, nothing more pathetic than an intellectually gifted man.

I'd trade them all for Jim Fuglie. He's no intellectual, if by intellectual we mean someone who consistently reads and discourses about hard books. But he is as intelligent as anyone could ever need to be and he is the perfect North Dakotan, a man for all seasons on the Great Plains. In a jam—from a vehicle breakdown in the middle of nowhere, to a compound fracture, to an angry property-owner at the end of a shotgun—I'd rather have Jim Fuglie standing in front of me than anyone I have ever met.

It had been many years since I really spent time with my great mentor Mike Jacobs, who was as gifted as ever, but now infinitely more successful. He was the editor of one of the premier daily newspapers in North Dakota. He went on remarkable fact-finding trips around the world. He was a student of languages: German, Dutch, Afrikaans, and a smattering of others. He was almost certainly North Dakota's greatest reader. His literary tastes were catholic. He read widely, deeply, voraciously. He was a player in one of the principal newspaper chains in the country. He was prosperous. And he was, although none of us could know it at the time, about to win the Pulitzer Prize in 1998. He won it for heroic flood coverage,[†] but I see it rather as a lifetime achievement award earned in mid-life. If you were sending a delegation of fifty Americans to Mars, you would have no choice but to send Mike Jacobs as the North Dakotan.

[†] Mike is the first to point out that it was actually the *Grand Forks Herald* that won the Pulitzer Prize, but if ever there was a person ready when the moment came, it was Jacobs.

Mike and I had tried to work up a correspondence from time to time, without much sustained success. Each of us felt somewhere deep in his soul that our lives would never be quite right unless we renewed our ancient friendship, which, without ever being sexualized, was unquestionably the deepest intimacy of my life and, I'm guessing, his. We also each felt that it was not going to happen. Our roads had diverged in the yellow wood long since. But neither of us seemed quite satisfied walking his path without the other at his side.

So when Mike called me out of the blue and invited me to join his camping group for a canoe trip on the Little Missouri River, I decided I had no choice but to accept. There would be six of us. I knew two of the men: Ken Rogers, a gentle, thoughtful, bearded journalist, and Jim Fuglie, with whom I had worked at a newspaper twenty years ago. The others were government functionaries in Bismarck and Mandan, straddling the Missouri River in the center of North Dakota. Somehow my wife persuaded me to make the trip. Like Levin's Kitty in *Anna Karenina*, she usually knew better what was good for my soul than I did.

On the face of it, I cannot imagine anything I would less rather do than go on a four-day camping trip with five other men. It sounds like death on a stick to me. I'm not a man's man: no bowling leagues, softball tournaments, ski trips, Tuesday evenings at the Elks, golf holidays, hunting parties, poker matches, or forays out to the Mustang Ranch. I prefer the sensibilities of women. When delicacy, subtlety, irony, humility, emotional maturity, gentleness, and listening skills were handed out at the dawn of time, men were off belching at a wrestling match somewhere.

For many weeks I dreaded the adventure and worried that I would not fit in, that I would be perceived as Mike's old pal, too bookish, out of touch with North Dakota, an excrescence, a guest. But on the appointed day I flew to North Dakota, on a big jet to

Denver and then on a delightful propjet to Bismarck. I annoyed my fellow passengers with my antic attempts to see every feature of the landscape from the tiny windows on both sides of the aisle of the plane. We were cruising at well under 20,000 feet. Through the scratched Plexiglas I could peer down at the landscape of home. I traced the rivers and ID'd the hills from the sky. I could virtually hear the meadowlarks. I looked like a cadet returning home to see his mother and his girlfriend after the first great ordeal of military life. I rented a car. I made my way to Dickinson, where my parents live, and waited for Mike to pick me up.

How many times over the years had I sat in our den waiting for him to arrive, speaking nonchalantly to my parents about our probable itinerary, secretly knowing that my life would almost certainly be taken to a new level by the adventure he was about to lead? How many times had he driven up to our house to collect me for an excursion, speaking briefly and politely to my tolerant but skeptical parents, then hustling me away to improbable places for endless conversation and hiking? As I waited, half in a conversation with my frail, elegant father, who believed that any camping trip is a failure of basic good sense, I thought at one moment, "You can go home again," and then, "You can't go home again."

Mike rolled up in an expensive pickup, a company car. In the golden years of the 1970s he had driven first a Chevy Vega, then a Chevrolet Love pickup. He looked the same as when I knew him twenty years before, except that his hair was shorter and grayer. We shook hands. My father looked up from his *New Yorker* and said a few pleasantries. We were stiff and tentative around each other even after we drove away from my boyhood home. It was not one of those friendships that can be resumed in mid-sentence after years of separation. We no longer knew each other. Each of us felt that the other was responsible for the shutdown of our friendship, and each of us felt that he himself was probably responsible for the shutdown of the friendship. There was in each of us a plasma of black energy that we did not wish to stir up. Nor did we want to slide into nostalgia. Nothing would be more likely to kill off any chance of renewal. Each of us thought, "Ah, hell, how could it be worth it even to try this?" and each of us thought, "How could we ever have let ourselves drift apart?"

The inevitable drift. The friendship that once meant absolutely everything had somehow decayed into a few fierce shards of love and memory and resentment. How do you explain why you went silent when there was never an adequate reason to go silent? It's embarrassing. It's one of the greatest mysteries of life.

We bought supplies and in doing so carefully tested each other's politics. We noticed things by the side of the road. We talked about mutual friends, and particularly Mike's intelligent, curious, and uproariously funny wife Suezette. We described our professional activities.

Sometimes two people want things to go right with all their hearts, and all the elements of success are in place, and the circumstances are right, and there is nothing lacking, nothing amiss, and yet they cannot find resonance no matter what they do, not if they strain for it and not if they merely relax into the occasion. I could tell that each of us wanted there to be some kind of grand reconciliation that would redeem all the silence, all the hurt, all the tension, all the lost opportunities, a sudden glorious renewal of our friendship that would become the great event of our middle lives. But almost from the beginning we each realized it was not to be—not yet. There is something tragic in this. In the course of our four days together we rarely moved farther than a dozen steps out of each other's physical space, but the gulf between our souls was wide and deep and clouded, and neither of us, for all that we had mastered in life, knew how to probe the chasm. Mike withdrew into himself. He was unusually moody and detached. I talked in acre feet about everything I knew to any member of our party who would listen, like a probationary student at a Buddhist monastery.

You don't need to be Heraclitus to realize that there are analogies between life and rivers. A river is a virtually infinite series of tiny erosional acts, cause and effect, cause and effect, cause and domino effect. If you put a stone the size of a flattened egg near the edge of the current of the Little Missouri River at Marmarth, North Dakota, you will in time change the course of the Mississippi as it flows past Baton Rouge. The tiniest shift in the river's flow at an obscure, unnamed oxbow at 46° 18' north latitude and 103° 54' west longitude will ever so slightly change the course of the river all the way down, oxbow by s-curve by bluff by badland. In the short term New Orleans is unthreatened by my puny hydrological manipulations in southwestern North Dakota, but if I could return in a hundred thousand years, I might find New Orleans washed into the Gulf of Mexico, or the Little Missouri dumping its sluggish load into Hudson's Bay rather than into the Missouri proper—all thanks to one unconscious and seemingly insignificant gesture. Think of the power of the distracted visitor squatting at river's edge tracing rivulets with a driftwood stick. She is unconsciously playing with the levers of global geomorphology—at least from the perspective of geological time.

If a clod be thrown into the Little Missouri at Marmarth, a different Missouri River flows past Omaha, Nebraska, as well as if a cement slab were tossed into the river, as well as if the Barber Auditorium were. Who casts not up his eye on a bulldozer scraping a new cattle pond out of a plains draw, but who can take off his eye from the industrial gigantism of a U.S. Army Corps of Engineers dam project? Any man's deed impacts the universe, for we are all involved in a breathtakingly interconnected web of energies and forces and structures. And therefore, never send to know if you are alone in the universe. You are the universe.[†]

Mike Jacobs and I had flowed side by side in the same channel for so long in the upstream years that we expected to drift through our whole lives together. We could not know then that the river of our lives was hopelessly braided like the Platte, that we would lose sight of each other for extended periods of time, that each of us would attempt to negotiate alone what proved to be false channels, channels full of embarrassments, and that sometimes when we drifted back together after a long frightful separation, the surprise and the shock of recognition would leave us dumbstruck. We could not anticipate that each us would come to suspect that the other was dallying in some other channel of the river for no good reason, to keep away, or to seek some unseemly port. We could not know that we would often simultaneously drift down opposite sides of the same sandbar or an island, within shouting distance of each other, within whispering distance, but wholly unaware of each other's course or presence, like Evangeline and Gabriel on the upper Mississippi in Longfellow's great poem.

I am trying to force the tragedy of our friendship through the mill of geomorphological inevitability.

II

WE CAUGHT UP WITH THE REST OF THE PARTY at a pre-arranged rendezvous site, shook hands all the way around and engaged in the necessary small talk, then jumped in Jim Fuglie's rig and headed for the only oasis in the district, Marmarth. Jim drove far too fast over badly-engineered gravel roads in a vehicle full of boisterous men. He drove flawlessly. We threw our bags on the broken-down beds of the bunkhouse, what passes in Marmarth

[†]With apologies to John Donne.

for a bed and breakfast or a hunting lodge. We joined my friends Patti and Gary Perry for delicious beefsteaks at the Pastime. Patti was in her usual rare form, and we all fell in love with her, some for the first time. Then we drank and laughed and played pool and talked deep into the night. In Marmarth, if you buy one round just for your own table, you will, by a magic I have never understood, find drinks lined up in front of you for the rest of the night. It's the easiest place in the world to get drunk in. I was the last to stagger off to bed. So we began the adventure hung over. I could see that no one was as enamored of the Marmarth mystique as I was.

The next morning we coffeed up and drove out to Merle Clark's ranch. It was on the way to our river entry point, sort of, and Jim and I wanted everyone to get a chance to meet Merle. If there were an official cultural "voice of the Little Missouri badlands," Merle Clark would be it. Without ever having been elected spokesman for his tribe, but without ever having been resisted, he speaks for the entire district. He has the intelligence and sentimentality and folksiness of Paul Harvey. He may not be the Voice of America, but he is surely the Voice of Slope County. We called ahead. Long-suffering Linda Clark was waiting for us at the kitchen window. She is a serious woman, committed to community and Christ, a quilter with a national reputation, a lonely figure in a lonely place, at times almost a character out of an O.E. Rolvaag novel. She could not have been more hospitable, but my guess is that the hot spots in her soul lay somewhere other than Marmarth.

She ran out to the window of Jim's rig before we could skid to a stop in her driveway. Jim rolled down the window. Linda said, in a tone of command and some desperation, "Whatever you do, don't mention dinosaurs and don't mention old cars. I'm asking you this as a personal favor. Oh, hi everyone. Come on in and have some lemonade." So we piled out and went through the door into the Clark's modest living room. Linda bustled around like the hospitality god Hephaestus getting drinks and cookies into everyone's hands. After a few minutes, Merle sauntered in wearing a white pearl-buttoned shirt and a cowboy hat. He was tall, spare, erect, with a half-goofy expression on his face. "Why, what do we have hereabouts?" he asked in his stentorian voice. "Looks like a convention of the state's finest public officials and newspapermen." He shook hands all around in a courtly way.

Jim said, "Merle, think you could fire up one of the old Model T's and drive us out to look at one of your dinosaur bone piles?"

Merle was off and running. Linda was genuinely angry. We had to pry ourselves away with crowbars two hours later. We left Merle and Linda to their fate.

We drove up to our entry point on the southeast side of Bullion Butte. The road was bad. The road was extremely bad. "If it rains while we're here, we'll never get out," Mike said. I would not have ventured over some of the draws and crevices that we crossed to get to the site. But the boys had all been there before, and they knew what they were doing. Jim got his rig through first, then got out to direct the others, who were not as seasoned in this countryside as he was. It took about an hour to get to the place we wanted to be. We all leaned on something and drank a beer before we began to pack our gear in towards the river.

I pulled out my backpack and shouldered up. That's my idea of camping.

I soon realized that I had no idea what this group meant by a four-day camping trip. The boys pulled at least half a dozen giant coolers out of their rigs and carried them in teams over to the base camp. I had never seen so many coolers in one place in all of my life. My heart sank. It became instantly clear to me that this was going to be a low-mobility adventure, even if we floated down river in the three canoes lashed to the tops of our rigs.

We established a base camp that might have been a recreation display at K-Mart. The accumulated coolers looked like a caricature of covered wagons encircled to anticipate an Indian attack. Everyone scurried about looking for the best tent sites. Jim cleared a place for our fire pit. We drank beers. We all walked down to the river. One of the veterans took one look at the Little Missouri and said, "There's not enough water in it to float to Medora. This year's high water mark must have been a week or two ago. There's no way I'm going to drag or portage my canoe every couple of miles between here and Medora. I say we just stay here, and do a series of day hikes this year."

And that was that. There was a brief but unconvincing debate. Then everyone shrugged his shoulders and turned his attention to hedonism. The canoes stayed strapped to the vehicles. For the next four days nobody ever strayed more than three miles from camp. The decision was made so perfunctorily and with so little protest that for years afterward I have wondered if the boys ever had any intention of floating the Little Missouri.

We spent our four days drinking and eating, eating and drinking, and smoking. One of the traditions of the group was that each member cooked at least one gourmet meal for all of the others. They took this rite very seriously. I had never had an elegant meal in the wilderness—or wanted one for that matter. My idea of camping comes straight from the cynic philosopher Diogenes of Sinope.[†] Eat only to banish hunger. Sleep only to banish fatigue. I never take alcohol into nature. Why go out of your way to simplify things, to reduce life to lowest terms, to return to the primitive rituals of the species, to wake up to life again, while forcing a range of toxins down your throat? It was all very perplexing to me, and indeed objectionable to my code of the

[†]Diogenes (BCE, ca. 412-323) is the most famous representative of the Greek cynics, who subscribed to a philosophy of pursuing virtue for its own sake and living with a minimum of material possessions.

West. And yet, with Fuglie and the boys, I did my share of eating and drinking. Sometimes I was first in line. I enjoyed their cuisine immensely. They were all impressive men. I wanted to get along. It was their camping group, not mine. I knew the hospitality codes of the Homeric world—and of ours. But my disorientation was complete.

It began to rain the minute we established base camp, and it did not stop raining until we left. It's hard to say just how much it rained. My sense is that at least one inch fell over four days, and perhaps as many as two. We were wet all the time, and—on the whole—miserable, and it never ceased raining long enough for things to dry out. If there were such a thing as the rainchill factor, it would have clocked in at about ten inches. My code of the wilderness is that unless you are prepared to take what nature dishes out, you don't belong there—period. The rain dampened everyone's spirits and that was unpleasant enough, but the real issue soon became the fleet of vehicles. Everyone except Jim worried those SUVs like a loose tooth. How (or when) would we ever get our vehicles through the gumbo and the draws to good gravel or pavement? Even in advanced states of intoxication, members of the troupe took turns fretting over the problem of our eventual egress. Nobody wanted to cut the umbilical and float away into space. We all had to get back.

We huddled around the fire. We ate world-class meals, the product of dutch ovens, sustained marinations, secret spices and sauces, and the kind of *amour propre* you'd expect in a four star restaurant. And we drank. We drank prodigious quantities of alcohol in a number of its more popular forms. We drank designer gin, but it was—in the end—just gin. There was a great deal of good talk. And some bad.

There is something about men in groups. Every member of our company was a highly-intelligent, highly-accomplished, thoughtful and generous gentleman. With any of them I would gladly have walked the mountain spine to Tierra del Fuego. I would have taken any one of them to high tea at Windsor Palace. Each one was a reader of books, a thinker of thoughts, a doer of remarkable deeds. They were good family men, all, and leaders in their communities. They were, all of them, Thomas Jefferson's "natural aristocrats." I would trust any one of them with my daughter for sustained periods of absence—when she was six or when she was sixteen. But when we all came together without any women to cut our testosterone, without any women to monitor our inputs, without any women to raise the discourse—or at least nudge it in a different direction—we descended at times into something ugly and—to me—troubling. There was too much competitiveness. There was too much drunkenness. There was too much aggression. There was too much coarseness. There was, indeed, too much objectification of women. And there was some misogyny.

I was neither better nor worse than my camp mates. Without thinking about it, I simply zipped my "enlightened" self into one of the side compartments of my backpack for the duration. *Mea culpa, mea culpa, mea maxima culpa.*

I do not think that men should spend this much time alone together. Or perhaps we should spend a great deal more time alone together. There was something appalling at the core of our group dynamics. It seemed to me not male bonding but male bondage. The hearts of men are fractured. The experience gave me new respect for my father, who could not have been induced at the end of a gun to say something vulgar or ugly towards women. Out in the soggy Little Missouri country, in the presence of four of the most accomplished men of modern Dakota history, I looked into the mirror of my gender, and I did not like what I saw. Perhaps we were just blowing off steam.

Souls are born into the world rich with possibility and, as Wordsworth puts it, trailing clouds of glory. Some are born female, some male. I cannot speak for women, but I know from my own experience, boy and man, and from decades of careful observation, that western civilization, and particularly American civilization, narrows the souls of males until they are a mere sliver of what they might be, and indeed only a blockish fragment of what they were at birth. The gender coding of this culture is a severe funnel which confines all the potential of maleness into a narrow, frenetic, and ugly channel. This is nowhere more pronounced, unfortunately, than in the rural West. By the time a boy reaches puberty, almost all the poetry, the artistry, the emotionality, the sensitivity, the sweetness, and the open-endedness has been sliced off of him. What remains is aggression, ambition, sexual recklessness, and a cultural taste that seldom reaches beyond tractor pull and the softball league. The young man who perseveres in his soul's unfolding against such odds is taking a great risk and virtually insuring his marginality in his community. In a landscape where a desire to read Flaubert earns one the label "fag," and where attentiveness to one's spouse is seen as being "pussywhipped," most boys are going to acquiesce without much of a struggle. Those who refuse to succumb are often severely persecuted.[†]

I remember touring a ranch once, in the badlands of North Dakota, with a forty-something rancher and his wife in the cab, and four of us in the bed of the pickup, including his 13-year-old son, who was ostentatiously riding on the lip of the lowered gate at the back end of the truck. It was rough rough country. The rancher hit a prairie dog hole and the pickup bounced. With Archimedean precision his son pitched about 18 inches into the air, and came down on the gate hard on his tailbone. We all looked

---

[†]Mike Jacobs proves that it can be done.

at him with real concern. He started to cry. He looked up at us. And then he fought back the tears and looked away off the end of the truck, his face tight as a snare drum from the energy he was expending not to announce to strangers—and his universe— that he was hurt and frightened. In this country, his masculine stoicism is seen as character, as virtue. He would have been shamed for having a perfectly natural human response to his mishap. Out here, pretending not to feel pain is seen as a form of manliness.

The pioneer period of American history is over. It does not seem to me that we need any longer cling to a set of hypermasculine codes that were probably unnecessary in the first place, but which are positively stunting our development at the end of the twentieth century. We need to let men flourish as souls. We need to encourage them to express their beings in a wide variety of ways. We need to crack open American civilization and let the poetry out.

Fuglie and the boys lived on the enlightened end of the spectrum of American maleness. Even so, by the time we reached the halfway point of our encampment, we were a sorry lot.

III

EVERYONE WAS IN LOW SPIRITS. Most of our gear was seriously wet by now, and a kind of spiritual sogginess had crept through everything. The novelty of a boys encampment had begun to wear off. The heavy consumption of alcohol had begun to tell on our faces and spirits. Though we would not admit it, all of us were beginning to miss wives, girlfriends, and diurnal habits. We'd been out three days now, and our quarrel with civilization suddenly seemed petty in the face of industrial culture's ability to provide hot showers, clean clothes, and impervious roofs. We all felt deflated that we had been unable to put our canoes into the river, that what had been intended to be a strenuous, even heroic expedition—anticipated for a whole year—had turned out to look a great deal like bourgeois car camping. We were all secretly marking time until the trip was over. We were sleeping late as a counterpoise to boredom and alcohol.

I woke up in a little pool of water on the last full day of the trip, peed in the bushes, and exchanged wet clothes for merely damp trousers and a work shirt. Nobody else was awake, or rather willing to admit it, except Jim Fuglie, who had emerged effortlessly as the most resourceful and least whining member of the troupe. He was unendingly cheerful in the face of all of our adversity. Instead of succumbing to the carping, foul-mouthed funk that had become our group dynamics, Jim made things happen. He gathered wood. He started fires. He solved small camp problems. He kept the conversations from spiraling into rancor.

I had discovered in the course of our adventure that Jim Fuglie knew at least as much about the outdoor world of North Dakota as did Mike, infinitely more than I, and in practical resourcefulness he was probably more talented than the rest of us put together. He wore his mastery gracefully, with understatement, and he made sure never to trump any member of the troupe. He took himself much less seriously than did Mike, who was a great but essentially unteasable man. Jim was Sancho Panza to Mike's Don Quixote. He even had a pot belly to prove it. His belly, which was slightly ridiculous in appearance, contrasted sharply with his vitality and virility. I had decided early on in the expedition that if I had to survive an Andes plane crash—or in our case, the internecine struggle of a Donner party—with any of my colleagues, I would want it to be Jim, who seemed more at home with whatever circumstance threw up than anyone I had ever known. He was as hungry for intoxication as any of us, but he had a Hemingwayesque ability to function under the weight of prodigious amounts of toxicity and shake off the poisons whenever it was necessary.

At least three of us, egotists all, felt that we owned the place. I, because I had a special relationship with the ranch community, with the Little Missouri River, which I had hiked in its entirety a few years back. And because I was the adoptive son of the railroad ghost town Marmarth, where we had spent our first night. Jim, because he had traveled all the roads of the region in official and unofficial capacity, first as the best-ever director of North Dakota's tourism department, then as the director of the Medora (Theodore Roosevelt Memorial) Foundation. Jim knew everyone in the district, and he seemed to have wandered along every trail in the state. And Mike, because North Dakota belonged to him alone. I was a mere expatriate, all romance and longing. Mike had studied the state like a rune all his life and he, if anyone, had come to embody the idea of North Dakota. Mike was a genuine thinker. Jim just brought all of his presence to his experience, as he would surely have done in Minnesota or Madagascar.

Jim and I built a little fire and brewed coffee. While we waited for the others to stir we talked in a laconic way. We were perhaps a little wary of each other. We hadn't seen each other for a very long time. It is even possible that we slightly mistrusted each other, partly because there had been some work tension between us long long ago in another life, when we two constituted the entire sports department of the *Dickinson Press*, and partly because each of us could make some claim to be closest to Mike. I did not entirely approve of the way Jim had promoted the history and tourism of North Dakota, and he perhaps did not entirely approve of the way I had drifted off to the academy. Or maybe we were just shy because Mike usually brokered our relations.

The others drifted in to expose themselves to the fire, sipping sharp black fireside coffee, nuzzling their limbs towards the flames until their besotted denim jeans began to give off steam. Several began to lace their coffee with whiskey. Bad sign. It was not yet

yet 8 a.m. Morale was low this morning. Nobody could think of anything worth doing. The rain had diminished to a mere drizzle. There was an immense cloud cover close to the ground, so close that it was impossible to see the top of the butte or even the low hills to the east. It was not fog exactly. Everything at ground level was visible, indeed luminescent in the gray white dewy light of early morning. There was a kind of sound studio quality to the bird notes, the drip of water from the trees, even our muted conversations. The bottom surface of the cloud bank was surprisingly firm, a couple of hundred feet or so above our heads. It felt as if we existed in a razor-thin biosphere between the earth and the dense lenticular clouds above.

Mike appeared. He was in a black mood. He made it clear that there was nothing he cared to do, not even engage in dialogue and anecdotage through the morning. Nobody, anyway, seemed in the mood to engage. In the absence of peer pressure, each of us would already have gone home. It was going to be a very long day.

With a kind of instinctual surety I turned to Jim and said, "Let's go climb that butte." Jim said, "Good plan. Let's do it." This in itself was one of the most satisfying moments of my life. My dream of life is that we learn not to resist each other's impulses to adventure and exploration. Jim is the kind of man who does not need to be asked twice to eat the marrow. We were making a kind of statement of gumption—together—that said, we can mope or we can act, and we two prefer to act. We bustled about the camp for a few minutes taking care of preliminary tasks, while the others lined up their reasons not to make the hike. Mike, who was unwilling to stir, but not altogether pleased that we would think of stirring without him, drifted back to bed.

We set out. The groundcover of sage and juniper was thick and storm-saturated so that it was impossible to walk more than a few yards without becoming soaked and chilled to the bone. But the quality of light was exquisite and the air was all caress and we both wanted to see what was above those clouds. Besides, we hadn't managed to exert ourselves even once during the trip. Jim is a genuine outdoorsman. In the fall he often goes off alone in a camper for weeks at a time on the Grand River grasslands south of Hettinger, North Dakota. He's from there. Ostensibly he goes to hunt birds. Mostly he reads and reflects and walks on the grasses of Dakota in the cool of the evening.

It was a long slow hike through a landscape eerily silent and calm. Gentle too. We walked a couple of miles through the grass and shrubbery towards the base of the butte. Neither of us had much to say. We were trying to determine whether the discomfort level was too great to proceed, and we were flexing our limbs like winter-stale horses. I looked back from time to time hoping we would see Mike striding after us in his confident way, but the grass was motionless back to where the camp must be. We began to feel a bit superior. And wonderfully alive.

After about an hour we stopped for a drink of water. Jim lit up a cigarette. Now we talked for the first time. We caught up on each other's lives a little, asking each other questions that we would not have ventured in front of the group, except in swashbuckling terms—for such are the souls of men. Since I last had seen Jim, he had ceased to be a journalist, had become an important functionary in the North Dakota Democratic Party. He had singlehandedly taken the ancient stodginess out of the state tourism bureaucracy and he was, by now, one of the best known North Dakotans. For all of this accomplishment, there was something ad hoc about his professional life, something unsatisfied, certainly unpensioned, and he had recently taken a kind of sinecure for North Dakota's celebrated rich man, Harold Schafer, the entrepreneur who had developed the tourist village adjacent to Theodore Roosevelt National Park. Among other things, Jim had engaged North Dakota's finest writer Larry Woiwode to write the biography of its greatest philanthropist.[†] I did not know the first thing about Jim's domestic situation, but I could tell that he was not happy then. He has since remarried, changed jobs, survived a serious bout of illness, lost much of his belly, and taken a river home on the Missouri north of Bismarck. He still seems professionally somehow at loose ends. I was in the last years of a dying marriage then, too, but I confined my expressions of discontentment to my homesickness for North Dakota. We did not know each other well enough to ask the really personal questions.

We resumed our hike.

For most of an hour we walked side by side and said very little. We had by now reached the base of the butte. There is a rhythm in a long walk that becomes almost trancelike, in which the presence of another person is enormously comforting without being even slightly intrusive. Each of us relaxed into the meditation of the walk. It was clear that conversation was permissible but not required. You can measure any friendship by the quantity of silence it can stand. This was a friendship with potential. In the old times, Mike and I used to spend whole days in silence together.

The rest of our hike would be up hill. The grass was slippery and the bentonite mud was balling up on the bottoms of our boots. It was hard work ascending Bullion Butte on such a day. I could tell that Jim was getting winded. Cigarettes will do that. I slowed down a little, not wanting him to see that I had slowed down a little. Soon he was stopping every thirty or forty seconds and bending over with his hands on his knees to catch his breath.

[†] *Aristocrat of the West: A Biography of Harold Schafer*. Fargo: Institute for Regional Studies, 2000.

I said, "Let's take a break."

"I don't think I'm going to be able to do this today, Clay. I'm feeling pretty whipped. Why don't you go on ahead."

I said, "No, let's not worry about getting to the top. We're in no hurry and we have no goal. I'm just glad to be out here with you. I've been to the top a couple of dozen times before."

So we stopped for a long long time about two thirds of the way up the butte. We drank water. We talked in a quiet and desultory way, neither one of us exhibiting any perceptible ego. We were both fascinated by the life of Theodore Roosevelt. So we talked much of the time about Roosevelt's four-year sojourn in western Dakota Territory. Jim was now professionally interested in Roosevelt. For years I'd read everything I could about the Roughrider, if only to lift him out of the sad marketing caricature he'd become in North Dakota mythology.

IV

ROOSEVELT CAME TO THE LITTLE MISSOURI COUNTRY IN 1883, just seven years after the debacle of the Little Big Horn. Had there been no railroad he would not have made the journey. The transcontinental railroad did more to finish off Indian resistance than all the Custers who ever lived. Roosevelt came to Dakota Territory for the wrong reason—to bag one of the last of the buffalo—and he stayed for the wrong reason—to make money as a mostly-absent cattle rancher on the open range of the Great Plains. He was an exploiter to the core of his being. One could chart his strenuous life by the list of quadrupeds he boasted of bagging throughout the planet. But he was, for all of that, a great-souled man, whose vitality and love of adventure were irresistible. Dakota improved Roosevelt; Roosevelt improved Dakota. He pursued three boat thieves down the Little Missouri

River because he believed in the sanctity of private property and the rule of law, and then he marched them overland to Dickinson—an immense journey—more or less for the fun of it. He had to wait because the river was jammed with ice. So he read *Anna Karenina* through the night. He was, thus, the first person in North Dakota history to read Tolstoy. Roosevelt, the New Yorker, read the greatest of novels in the badlands of Dakota. I, the North Dakotan, first read *Anna Karenina* in a Spartan bedsitter in Oxford, England. Like Roosevelt I read through the night. It was the only book I have ever read that I literally could not put down. I read it in five days, sleeping only enough to refresh myself enough to read on.

It's easy to caricature Theodore Roosevelt (when you've heard the words "bully," "old four eyes," "Teddy," and "talk softly and carry a bit stick," you've pretty much got the profile), but he was an enormously gifted man, arguably the most intellectually gifted president of the twentieth century, almost certainly the writingest president, and that includes the prodigious John Adams and Thomas Jefferson. TR became the most serious establishment reformer in American history. And the greatest designator of wilderness America has ever seen.

It is quite possible that Theodore Roosevelt remains to this day the most remarkable white man who ever stepped foot in North Dakota. I'm giving Meriwether Lewis "runner up." Years later, Roosevelt paid the highest possible tribute to the badlands of Dakota. "Here," he said, "the romance of my life began." Most people, especially most men, don't make their lives a romance. But Roosevelt had the character of a pugilist and the soul of a poet. Deep virility leavened with genuine culture—learning, wit, vocabulary, curiosity, an aesthetic sense, a grounding in history, a susceptibility to the romance of things—that's the elusive ideal, that's what we ought to aspire to nurture in ourselves and our sons.

Roosevelt bagged his buffalo. In fact, he killed it not so far from Bullion Butte. He and his guide hacked the head off the great beast, and Roosevelt hauled it back to New York to display on the wall of his study.

He left the Dakotas in 1888 but the Dakotas never left him. He went on to do more to preserve the public lands of the American West than any president in American history. He was tough enough to embrace African-Americans and get away with it. He was bully enough about capitalism to challenge some of its excesses and survive. He was virile enough to wear his emotions on his sleeve.

The more you know Theodore Roosevelt, the more you must admire him.

Jim and I talked about tracing his hunting trail to the Bighorn Mountains in Montana. If we shot one roll of film for every beast he killed on that excursion, we'd be impoverished men, except in our photo albums.

V

JIM AND I PAUSED FROM TIME TO TIME to look around. It was a strange and even eerie day. We were just below the base of the massive cloud bank that stretched to the horizon in every direction. The cloud was full of moisture, which precipitated onto our foreheads and forearms like dew, like manna. The cloud base was luminous and white, not black like a storm cloud. We were so close to the base of the clouds that we felt we could stand upright and disappear into another world. The sky cast a bizarre, almost florescent light on the valley of the Little Missouri River. I don't think I ever saw that country more green than it was that day. We felt like balloonists descending into Emerald City. The quality of the light was magnificent. The green of the country was not a dark sensuous summer green, nor quite the sagebrush washed green of arid country. It was a luminescent and even enchanted green, brilliant with a hundred billion perfectly spherical water droplets distributed over its foliage, and it rolled endlessly in every direction to the end of the world. The clouds, the moisture, and the sudden greening of the countryside made the features of the landscape stand out in relief as I had never seen them before. It was as if we were in the most sophisticated virtual reality theater of all time, looking down at a computer-generated relief map of the Great Plains. We could see every knoll, every draw, every ridge in the landscape. Every subtlety stood out and demanded attention. I would have given anything to have had Thomas Jefferson here to appreciate this moment.

You can almost experience geological time in a place like that, can almost feel the history of the good earth plate-shift by plate-shift, epoch by era by age, like the slow flow of the batter of the thickest fruitcake ever made by the stoutest German farm woman in Minnesota. It was as if we were seeing for one brief shining moment with the eye of God herself. It was one of those five or six timeless, unmediated moments one gets in a lifetime, and we were both fully aware of it. On this occasion, North Dakota looked like a land of embrace, the new Garden of Eden that had been promised so cynically in the pioneer literature to attract dreamers and idiots to venture beyond the grid. The whole earth was flux—albeit a flux in exceedingly slow motion—and we were standing together in one marvelous instant of its unfolding. We were learning to see our home landscape with new eyes—together. Somehow the Big Bang seemed close at hand.

Eventually I asked Jim to tell me how he saw life. He provided some hints and fragments in his sure and humble way. He asked me how I saw life. I, likewise, teased the edges of the vast abyss. We were in perfect harmony in that moment, a harmony that was an act of grace—unearned, un-looked for, un-sustainable, un-repeatable—and we both knew it. We knew that any second the sun would burst through the clouds, or one of our colleagues would "hullowwwwww!" from the middle distance, or we would snap back into our character armor. And we knew we were going to have to face Mike when we came down the butte-side and that he would know what he had missed, and that he would either make an issue of it or not, but he would know. For nothing escapes Mike's brilliant eye. He was as sensitive a man as I ever met.

If I could freeze my life at any single moment and live there forever, it would be that moment standing next to Jim Fuglie on the squat shoulder of Bullion Butte. As we stood there in that numb sweet mystic trance that comes from being with the right person in the right place at the right time in the right mood with the doors of perception open, in the words of Robert Frost, "we said some of the best things we ever said." It was an interlude of total harmony. It could not have occurred had the whole group been assembled near the summit of Bullion Butte. It could not have occurred on a sunny day. It could not have occurred had we been steady friends of twenty or even two years. Probably it could not have occurred without the setup of the rain and the alcohol and the group dynamics. Grace is capricious. John Calvin was right on that score.

Suddenly Jim was ready to finish the ascent. We scrambled up the last couple of hundred feet of the butte.

We reached the summit.

We stood on the rim of the butte looking around to the rim of the world. We wanted Mike there with us. And the Roughrider.

It is not *my* past that I mourn — *that* I can never lose —
(Nor my future, which is assured, and in which I sing more cold
And passionate still as the passing years swing over my deadheading
Mortal part
                    heart at home on the wind
                                        bourne
In the blood of strangers. . .
                              carried
                                    forward forever
                                                this song. . .)
— No, but the past of this place and the place itself and what
Was: the Possible; that is: the future that never arrived. . .

Thomas McGrath
Letter to an Imaginary Friend, Part Two: V

The Message on the Wind

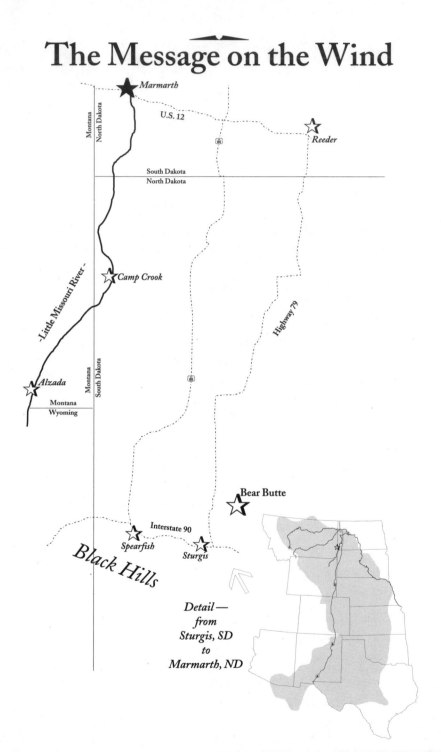

Marmarth

U.S. 12

Reeder

Montana
North Dakota

South Dakota
North Dakota

Camp Crook

-Little Missouri River-

Highway 79

Montana
South Dakota

Alzada

Montana
Wyoming

Bear Butte

Interstate 90

Spearfish

Sturgis

Black Hills

Detail—
from
Sturgis, SD
to
Marmarth, ND

The Message on the Wind

Circe

BLASPHEMY IS A GREEK WORD. Literally it means, "to speak evil of." At one time it was one of the core words of Christian civilization. Now it is lives in an obsolete backwater of the great river of western culture. In its purest sense, to blaspheme is to make impious utterances about God or sacred things. Over the course of time the word has been metaphorized so that it is possible to blaspheme without uttering a word. Examples: Pamela Anderson Lee's surgically altered body blasphemes female beauty, not to mention the Hippocratic nobility of medicine. *Hogan's Heroes* is a blasphemy of the holocaust. When a sportscaster says, "In today's NFL action, the Dallas Cowboys massacred the Washington Redskins," there are several varieties of blasphemy at work. If he can use "massacre" of a football game, what's left for Sand Creek, Wounded Knee, and Mi Lai?

We forget that language is a moral enterprise. In the course of time, the collective throat of humanity has, with geological ponderousness, pressed out the words it needs to signify its ideas. To use them precisely is to clarify existence. To use them sloppily is like golfing with a soccer ball. Although it is always useful to be as careful with language as possible, when the subject is sacred, precision is not merely a desideratum of good English, but a moral imperative. When the commandment says, "Thou shalt not make wrongful use of the name of the lord your God" [Exodus 20:7], the focus is not so much on "goddamning" as on careless invocations of things divine. My father had a knot-headed friend named Virgil, a repo man with a heart of gold, whose response to almost any proposition was, "I'll be goddamned." "Virgil, we're going on vacation this year to Yellowstone Park." "I'll be goddamned." "Virgil, I just got engaged." "I'll be goddamned." Any God worthy of his omnipotence can only smile at this. If Virgil goes to hell, it will surely not be for "being goddamned." This is not the sin of the commandment. The *paterfamilias* of a British family I lived with for a summer nervously foreshortened any serious conversation by saying, "Right, well," and then suggesting tea or sherry. His was, I believe, a more serious crime than the repo man's, though perhaps somewhat more elegantly articulated. These are mere verbal stratagems. God surely is not a stickler for insignificant lapses.

We break the commandment and damn God when we commingle the sacred and the profane. My friend the Very Reverend William Chrystal was conducting a funeral recently at a Reno, Nevada, funeral home. Deputies of the Washoe County Sheriff's Department interrupted the funeral to arrest the son of the deceased in front of his family and one hundred family friends. His crime: child support, parking tickets. The Reverend Chrystal wrote a letter of protest to the Sheriff. His response: it was a lawful arrest. This was blasphemy. I do not doubt the man was guilty of heinous offenses against the social order, but timing is everything, and all great cultures delineate sacred times and places.

To say, "God, if you love me, let me win this bridge hand," is blasphemy. When the Super Bowl car ad uses the *Ave, Maria* to sell a Jeep, that's blasphemy. The sacred is not to be used to merchandise the profane. The profane is not to be used to make the case for God. This is why Protestant children's sermons invoking Barney and Tweetie Bird are so odious. So, for that matter, are adult sermons laced with "you know you're getting old," quips and patter drawn off the Internet. The sacred has its own precincts and we are bound to respect them.

It is true that some of the world's greatest art negotiates the border between sacrament and blasphemy. John Donne's *Holy Sonnet* XIV, "Batter My Heart, Three Person'd God," invites God to possess a sinner's soul by way of divine rape, for example.[†] *The Ecstasy of St. Theresa*[‡] by the baroque sculptor Bernini explores the dynamic between spiritual ecstasy and orgasm. The pop-star Madonna in our time has unsubtly exploited the blasphemy-sacrament axis to line her pockets and, apparently, her many beds.

II

I GO TO SACRED PLACES TO *CONFESS* in St. Augustine's sense of the term: both to confess my sins and to praise and pray to my god. I'm not quite sure who my god is, but I have a hunch that he does not answer to Jehovah or Adonai, unless these are just two of his many names, and not particularly his best foot forward. Perhaps the tetragrammaton is fundamentally imprecise. But St. Augustine said if God is God he must understand us in whatever pitiful way we attempt to address him. When I was in college I affected paganism, and I spent a couple of days tracking down Horace Walpole's letter describing the brothers Serendip [††] so that

---

[†]"Divorce me, untie, or break that knot again,
Take me to you, imprison me, for I,
Except you enthrall me, never shall be free,
Nor ever chaste, except you ravish me."

[‡]Gianlorenzo Bernini (1598-1680) captured in marble St. Theresa's experience of being pierced through the heart by a flaming gold arrow cast by an angel. Theresa had written, "The pain was so great that I screamed aloud; but at the same time I felt such infinite sweetness that I wished the pain to last forever. It was not physical but psychic pain, although it affected the body as well to some degree. It was the sweetest caressing of the soul by God." The famous statue can be seen in the Cornaro Chapel of the church of Santa Maria della Vittoria in Rome.

[††]to Horace Mann, 28 January 1754.

I could pray to the Great God Serendip, who seemed—then—to be hovering over my shoulders. The truth is that Serendip is virtually the only god who has ever answered my prayers. Even though my rational being recoils at the idea of a serious divinity whose basis is an eighteenth century man of letters' pseudo-Asiatic gag, delivery on prayers ought to amount to something, especially since the establishment gods have, without a single exception, stiffed me with breathtaking indifference or inexistence.

At some point in my education I came under the fatal spell of John Neihardt's *Black Elk Speaks*, after which nothing can ever be quite the same. Black Elk was a Lakota medicine man whose life spanned the transition between Sioux horse culture hegemony on the northern Great Plains to the massacre at Wounded Knee and the collapse of Native American resistance to European-American encroachment. Black Elk began his life at the high water mark of Sioux horse culture (1863), and ended it, in 1950, when the Sioux had been reduced to utter dependence and peonage. *Black Elk Speaks* is a tragedy. At the end of his extraordinary life, Black Elk had come to believe that his people lost the "good red road" because his medicine (meaning the discipline he had brought to his divine work) had not been strong enough. When his interviews with John Neihardt were ending, Black Elk pointed to Harney Peak,[†] the highest point in the Black Hills, and said, "I wish I could stand up there in the flesh before I die, for there is something I want to say to the Six Grandfathers." Neihardt immediately arranged it. A few days later, on Harney Peak, in the heart of the Black Hills, Black Elk confessed failure:

> With tears running, O great Spirit, Great Spirit, my Grandfather—with running tears I must say now that the tree has never bloomed. A pitiful old man, you see me here, and I have fallen away and have done nothing. Here at the center of the world, where you took me when I was young and taught me; here, old, I stand, and the tree is withered, Grandfather, my Grandfather!

[†]Named for William Selby Harney (1800-1889), an Indian fighter.

Since my first close encounter with *Black Elk Speaks*, in my most earnest moments, and especially in nature, it has been the Great Spirit, *Wakan*, or the *Manitou* that I have implored in my devotions. Keeping in mind that I would not survive ten days in a Cheyenne or Mandan Indian village, and that I seem to lose all productivity when I go more than two days without a shower, I still make myself believe in such moments that I am essentially a white Indian and that Crazy Horse would want to high-five me if we met on a pine ridge somewhere. The human capacity for delusion is infinite.

The Lakota term for White Man is Wasichu. The meaning and origin of the word are unclear. Black Elk believed that it meant something like "big-talkers" or "fat-takers" and that it could be used of unusually large herds of buffalo, as well as of white men. In his recent biography of Crazy Horse,[†] Larry McMurtry argues, without evidence, that it means, "they just won't go away." That is certainly the sense of the word in recent decades. According to Raymond Demallie, in older Lakota culture the term *wasicu* referred to "certain kinds of spirits." I use it out of respect to the Sioux and also because in the mouths of the Lakota it sounds slightly contemptuous. Naming is an act of enormous power. "Wasichu" puts white man in his place.

I visit a place called Bear Butte every chance I get. Bear Butte is a lonely volcanic spur about twenty miles northeast of the Black Hills of South Dakota. There are no presidential—or Indian—faces carved on its slopes. What makes Bear Butte so remarkable is that it has not been ruined by civilization—not quite at least. It is just far enough away from the Black Hills to be left alone, like a moderately attractive woman in the company of a stunning one. Wasichu's response to the beauty and the sacredness of the Black Hills proper has been to erect wax museums there, to create

---

[†] *Crazy Horse* (1999).

concentration camps for reptiles and bears, to find out the sublime places—the caves, the canyons, the granite needles, the waterfalls—and then bombard them with crackling patriotic music and garish floodlights in red, green, and yellow, and of course to carve up the mountains so they conform to the Lilliputian dimensions of the human imagination. That a million white people per year make the pilgrimage to Mount Rushmore, and get teary-eyed by contemplating highly-imperfect (if that's Jefferson, Kahil Gibran is Chaucer!), but impressive-because-gargantuan likenesses of dead presidents, while shrugging their shoulders at the magnificent crags and gorges that Nature's God carved over eons all around them, is a sufficient measure of our breathtaking alienation from creation.

Which "western" president do you prefer? Thomas Jefferson, who loved Indians and treated them rather shabbily, or Theodore Roosevelt, who hated Indians and treated them rather well? As one of my mentors, the great David Noble of the University of Minnesota puts it, Mount Rushmore is a shrine to the saints of our secular religion. George Washington as God the Father. Abraham Lincoln as God the Son. Jefferson as the Holy Spirit. And I suppose Theodore Roosevelt as Peck's Bad Boy or Huck Finn. Meanwhile, across the way a much larger mountain is being reduced to rubble to represent the Oglala warrior Crazy Horse, who, if he had access to all the dynamite that has been wasted to commemorate his ghost (his body we assassinated in 1877), would, I feel certain, not detonate it in the Black Hills. The Crazy Horse Monument, should it ever be finished, will be the largest sculpture in the world, dedicated to a man who did not call attention to himself, who did not want his image "captured" by friend or foe alike, and who did not want white people degrading the Black Hills with their industrial tools. Thus the Crazy Horse Monument could not be more profoundly misguided if it tried. Do white people really honor his spirit? Crazy Horse loathed us, our values, our habits, our purposes, and the way we pursue them.

In short, what we have done to the Black Hills is the very definition of blasphemy. We've stripped the hills of trees, fouled the rivers, exterminated the wildlife, extracted the minerals, paved everything that is close to being level, and then thrown up the worst, most shallow, most soul-numbing recreational institutions that human vulgarity can devise. Elk have been supplanted by neon effigies celebrating elkiness. The Black Hills support thousands of souvenir shops, reenactments, gravity deprivation sites, trout ponds, hurdy-gurdies, miniature golf courses, water slides, video arcades, patriotic pageants, pageant plays, and caramel apple shops. (I have two questions about taffy and caramel apple shops: a) why does everyone who goes on vacation want to eat a caramel apple? and b) what do we gain by watching stout teenagers make our taffy right before our eyes?) The psychology of the tourist trap is baffling. We have, in essence, used every form of human alchemical technique to transform the Black Hills into cold cash.

Although you can buy fake (and some real) Indian souvenirs on every corner, most of the "culture" of the Black Hills celebrates the conquest era of American history: Custer, Calamity Jane, Wyatt Earp, claim jumpers, steam railroads, and the usual panoply of white hucksters, prostitutes, gamblers, etc. You can go into the fake frontier storefront (tie your sport utility vehicle to the rail) and put on fake Victorian clothing and have your fake sepia photograph taken with you pretending to be a gunslinger and your girlfriend a drab. Everywhere you go, it's Custer this and Custer that, thus making one of the most loathsome genocidal nitwits in human history the patron saint of the place. Western South Dakota's celebration of the triumphalist energies of American history is roughly as sensitive as Stalin's creating a gulag theme park. That we find such travesty quaint and harmless is a sign of how desperately we are still clinging to our national monocultural mythology. At Al's Oasis at the other end of the South Dakota badlands, you can buy a Crazy Horse Burger—blasphemy. If it were a Jesus burger, we might not find it so taste-tempting.

In short, the Black Hills make Wall Drug look like an Enlightenment salon. Wall Drug,[†] the world's most pointless general store, billboarded in fifty states, is essentially an "authentic period" soda shop plopped down in a Quonset the size of the Astrodome. At Wall Drug, as at Minnesota's pathetic Mall of America, and to a certain extent at Disney World, merchandise has become a destination resort. With King Lear I ask, "Is man no more than this?"

And yet, Keystone, South Dakota, is not essentially different from West Yellowstone, Montana, or Gillette, Wyoming, or indeed the strip mall in Fort Meyers, Florida. There is no place in American where you cannot buy a shot glass that says "Keep on Truckin!" There is no scenic wonder in the land where you are not bombarded with requests to turn your attention from the sublime to ephemeral artifice instead. We're not a people who are comfortable with nature. When Custer rolled through to "discover" gold in 1874, he concluded that the Indians did not deserve the Black Hills because they weren't extracting anything from them. "It is a mistaken idea," he wrote, "that the Indian occupies any portion of the Black Hills. They neither occupy nor make use of the Black Hills, nor are they willing that others should. . . . If the Black Hills were thrown open to settlement, as they ought to be, or if simply occupied by the military, as they must be at an early date . . . a barrier would be imposed between the hostile camps and the agencies, and the well-disposed Indians of the latter would be separated from the evil influences and war-like tendencies of the hostiles." One wonders at what point a

---

[†]Wall Drug is fifty miles east of Rapid City, South Dakota, on Interstate 90.

not very well educated army officer[†] became a profound social philosopher. Not only is Custer either ignorant (likely) or dishonest (likelier) about Sioux and Cheyenne use and occupancy traditions, but it is clear that his idea of responsible "use" could not be more purely Eurocentric if he had tried. I extract, therefore I am. If permanent settlement and a permanent campaign of tree-felling are the proper markers of occupancy, virtually the entire continent was unsettled in 1876.

Given the appalling vulgarity of Wasichu's "development" of the Black Hills, it is not just ironic, but indeed blasphemous that every time the sensible (not to mention just) proposal to return some of the region to the Sioux and Cheyenne Indians is mentioned, the response of the conquistadors and their heirs is, "Yeah, and what will they do with them? They'll just run 'em down." To degrade the Black Hills from their current state of "settlement" would seem to require imagination and resources that Native Americans simply do not command. But remove the vestiges of zoning laws in the Black Hills and just watch what white capitalists still can do.

One such cornpone philosopher, no doubt, is the man who lives in a little house tucked into an alcove off U.S. 385 in the heart of the Black Hills. His yard looks like the town dump except that there are no spent diapers among the sewing machines, barrels, gas cans, crates, shells of cars, rusted engines, lamp shades, bald tires, old suitcases, piles of glass, wire, lumber, tools, barrels, boxes, clothes, and sticks, and washing machines, all strewn as if by hurricane across his sacred private property. For twenty years, every time I have driven up U.S. 385, I have stopped on the shoulder of the highway to take pictures of this commonwealth man's home sweet homestead, and each time he has burst out of the house

---

†George Armstrong Custer graduated from West Point in June 1861. He ranked at the bottom of his class of 34.

cursing and shaking his fist at me for invading his privacy. As if such a man can be said to have a sense of privacy! Or deserves property! In many—perhaps most—of its manifestations, private property is blasphemy against Gaea and a providential universe. It is hard to quarrel with Rousseau: "The first man who, having fenced in a piece of land, said, 'This is mine', and found people naïve enough to believe him, that man was the true founder of civil society."[†]

Lovely lonely Bear Butte is more blessed. The butte is "owned" (if a butte can be said to be owned) by the state of South Dakota. In some mad stray moment of good sense and sensitivity the state set the butte aside as an ecumenical prayer site for Native American peoples. To call such an action astonishing is not to do justice to the genius of South Dakota, a state not known for its sensitivity to anything—William Janklow, after all, has four times been elected its governor, in spite of the fact that he went after the rebels of the second standoff at Wounded Knee (February-May, 1973) with an obsessiveness that would have been considered comic had it not been so dangerous and so abusive of public power. According to Peter Mattheissen, Janklow is said to have said, "The only way to deal with the Indian problem in South Dakota is to put a gun to the AIM leaders' heads and pull the trigger."[‡] I saw Governor Janklow interviewed once on ABC's *Nightline*. The camera frame could not contain his manic gesticulations. Viewers kept losing sight of the governor as he jabbed at America like the caricature of a pugilist. A state truly interested in healing the rift between whites and Indians would not place the baton of authority in the hands of a man so sure of his own tribe's superiority.

Bear Butte is a volcanic laccolith (translation: a volcanic pimple that never popped) that stands 1,253 feet above the surrounding

---

[†]*Discours sur l'Origine et le Fondement de l'Inegalite parmi les Hommes*, 1754.
[‡]*In the Spirit of Crazy Horse*, 107.

plain of South Dakota at 44° 5'north latitude, 103° 4' west longitude. From the proper angle it resembles a recumbent bear, a creature once common throughout the Great Plains, but made rare (in the case of grizzlies, nearly extinct) thanks to the gunpowder, railroads, steel traps, pesticides, and the land lust of the conquistadors. The elevation of Bear Butte is 4,422 feet, which makes it almost a thousand feet higher than the highest summit in North Dakota (White Butte: 3,506 feet). Aside from the Black Hills (Harney Peak: 7,242 feet) and Devils Tower (5,117 feet), Bear Butte is one of the tallest features of the upper plains landscape.

Wasichu is incapable of leaving nature to itself, of course, and Bear Butte is no exception. On the top of the butte there is a state-funded "observation deck"—created apparently to allow one to see slightly better the utter desolation of the Great Plains in every direction—and the observation deck stands a few feet higher than the butte itself. This is Wasichu's way of saying to Bear Butte:

> We chose not to bulldoze you. We are choosing to let you be. But lest you grow proud, we are building this deck to overtop your summit, thus fixing your height by human rather than God's will. For man is the measure of all things. We can top God and nature. Should we need your minerals—or your location—we would not be afraid to level you to serve our will. We are happy for you to be a sacred place so long as you are—in our terms—valueless real estate. Still, we cannot leave you untouched and be what we are.

I do not mean to be sarcastic here. I believe that I have, just now, accurately articulated the mission statement of white American civilization. I have, in fact, articulated the philosophy I tacitly hold—no matter what my rhetoric—23 hours per day, 345 days per year. All nature is on probation to mankind. In the heart of the heart of the deepest outback, a jet airplane breaks the spell and perforates the sublime with industrial potential. Occasionally a rancher or an environmentalist, weary of intrusion, saunters out and snaps a few rifle shots at a 747 or military jet flying overhead, banging away at the plane, the "conspiracy," and the Industrial Revolution at the same time. Then we jail him as an unbalanced nut. When I was camping once with my friend Pat Sanborn in the Little Missouri River Valley and our wordless twilight conversation was interrupted by a passing commercial airliner, she said, "That's my definition of evil." And yet either one of us might have been on that plane, hurtling off to a conference on the future of the wilderness in America.

III

I HIKE UP BEAR BUTTE TO PRAY. I always pray for the same thing: integration with the energies of the cosmos, integration with the earth, integration with the Great Plains, integration with the hot spots in my soul. I invariably pray to Crazy Horse, the Oglala warrior and spiritualist, even though after years of reading I now know he was more warrior than spiritualist. Sometimes I ask for a sign: thunder, lightning, a thunderbird (whatever that is), something seismic. "Show me, Great Spirit, that you hear my pitiful cry!" Alas, the sign has never come. I'd settle for the drizzle and clap of weak thunder Black Elk experienced on his last visit to Harney Peak. But the fact is, whatever I read in the wilderness, I read into the wilderness. If Crazy Horse can be said any longer to exist in any dimension, it seems unlikely that he loses much time shedding providence on me. Which raises an important question about God.

After years of reading, thinking, meditating, and writing about it, I conclude that there is only one legitimate prayer: "Thy will be done." Everything else is a demand for advantage—against the odds, against the rival, against the spread, against the ex. Prayer is mysterious. If "Thy will be done" is the only legitimate prayer, and there is only affirmation and no beseeching in it, it would appear to be neither useful nor necessary. What is the point of saying, "Thank you, God, for ordering the cosmos in a way that I cannot control or understand, and do not seek to"? What possible reply can one expect from such affirmation? From on high, an Elvis-like, "Thank you, thank you very much"? God needs no encouragement from me to do her will, and if I am only in fact praying to align myself with a destiny that is beyond my manipulation, there would seem to be no good reason to address my soliloquy to God. Even the enlightened tend to play a Pascalian wager with prayer: "Thy will be done, of course, but if for some reason you wish to know my position on this. . . ." Prayer is thus a paradox.

But of course we are weak beings, sinners all, and we pray to get loved or laid, and pray to evade punishment, and pray to get rich, pray to get even, blaspheming any notion of a providential universe every time we kneel beneath the mountain of our troubles and beg God to save our miserable souls. Mark Twain explored this paradox in his dark "War Prayer," in which each side assumes that the same God favors its cause and should be willing to smite the enemy. "O Lord our God, help us to tear their soldiers to bloody shreds with our shells . . . blast their hopes, blight their lives, protract their bitter pilgrimage, make heavy their steps, water their way with their tears, stain the white snow with the blood of their wounded feet. . . ."

About the same time Abraham Lincoln wondered—without Twain's savage indignation—how both North and South could pray to the same God and yet tear out the bowels of the American republic. Finding the exact balance between humility and judgment, Lincoln wrote, "It may seem strange that any men should dare to ask a just God's assistance in wringing their bread from the sweat of other men's faces; but let us judge not, that we be not judged. The prayers of both could not be answered—that of neither has been answered fully." This is, I believe, the finest sentence ever uttered by a president of the United States.

My certainty that Crazy Horse is the one to pray to comes from two facts. First, I know he spent a great deal of time at Bear Butte, and in particular that he came here, as a young man, with his father, for the great pan-Indian council of 1857, and was apparently made to swear here never to make an accommodation with the white world. He never did. Or rather, when he finally did, he was almost immediately cut down by the United States government, which was the willing agent of the materialist, propertyist, industrialist world order. Second, one evening when I camped at a (to me) sacred place on the Little Missouri River north of Camp Crook, South Dakota, and watched the sun set after a very long day of hiking through some of the most barren country on the earth, I stood up to stretch as the sun slipped over the disk of the earth, and miraculously cast a giant Anasazi-shaped shadow a hundred yards, at least, to the east.

A whole range of things became clear to me at that moment— from this distance I can articulate almost none of them—that is how the sacred protects itself from scribblers—and I found myself saying, unplanned, and as amazing to my consciousness as if I were being possessed by a demon, as I stretched my arms up to the vault of the heavens, "Crazy Horse, I am here," and then a long spontaneous, simple and eloquent prayer that no white boy of my rhetorical training could ever have uttered.

It was perhaps the most shocking moment of my life. Somehow I had found his spot, or one of them. Through the course of the night that followed I had glimpses of a divine dimension that I did not know existed. By morning my whole body was an erect, raw nerve. I have since explored the historical literature to "prove" that I was right that September evening, that I had pitched camp where Crazy Horse had spent time. But the literature is inconclusive, and I am left with a much higher standard of spiritual truth—the certain resonance of my soul to a not-unlikely fact. My conviction is absolute. I have more doubt that my father sired me than that Crazy Horse stood where I blundered to a halt.

From that moment, Crazy Horse ceased to be merely my fantasy of the aboriginal absolutist, and became for me a kind of Lakota *daimon*. I did not, and do not, claim his regard. I know enough of the historical Crazy Horse to know that he ate white bread like me for breakfast. But I know what my soul honors. It does not much honor the wily, accommodationist Red Cloud, and certainly not the plains triumvirate George Crook, George Armstrong Custer, and Nelson Miles. If Crazy Horse had not vowed his absolutist, isolationist vow there, Bear Butte would not mean half so much to me. Had he uttered such a vow and then spent his after-years performing scalp dance tableaus in Buffalo Bill's Wild West Show in New York and London, he would be—with most of the rest—mere humbug. Like Socrates and Jesus and Gandhi, he lived his vision. And like them he was cut down early by those who cannot stomach purity.

In fact Crazy Horse was born not far from Bear Butte, on the Belle Fourche River (Lakota name: forks of the *Wakpala waste*, the Good River) around 1841 in white man's time frame. Crazy Horse was the son of a shaman also named Crazy Horse and as a boy he was known as Curly. Indian names, as well as Indian family boundaries, are much more fluid than Wasichus like. A Lakota child was frequently named first by a respected relative (sometimes an honorary relative), and then renamed later when her or his identity or character had been revealed by experience. But there were also conventional family names: thus Old Man Afraid of His Horses was named descriptively, but his son Young Man Afraid of His Horses was a mere junior. Once I worked for a summer with a Lakota storyteller and hoop dancer. His wife had given birth a few months before we began our lecture tour. I asked what they had named their daughter. He said, "Born on the Day when the First Breeze of Spring Appeared and a Meadowlark Sang in the Grass." The Lakota term for all of this was somehow short enough to fit on an American Express card. I had a sudden consciousness of the poverty of my own cultural traditions. "Great," I thought, "my name is Bob!"

Crazy Horse is considered a great hero to his people, the Oglala, perhaps their greatest hero. He whipped George (Gray Fox) Crook on the Rosebud (June 17, 1876) and played some sort of central role at the Little Bighorn (June 25, 1876), and at the time of his "surrender" in May 1877 he had never been defeated by a Wasichu army. Unlike his uncle Spotted Tail and the sly perennial Red Cloud, he refused to come to terms with the military and technological superiority of the United States, and unlike Sitting Bull, he never allowed himself to become a traveling cultural artifact posing for photographs for a silver dollar a pop. In other words, the core of his reputation comes from his unyielding resistance, his unwillingness to be photographed, liquored, chieftainized, be-scouted, or trotted off to Washington, D.C., to gape and be gaped at. His acquaintances among white men were very late and very few, not to mention very wary.

But he is also a hero to the Lakota because he was, by their own description, a strange man. He was light-skinned. Thanks to an early dream experience, he eschewed power, wealth, ceremony, fancy dress, and all forms of ostentation. Here is Thoreau's voluntary poverty. He wore plain clothes, a single hair feather, and a stone amulet behind his ear whose medicine was said to be so great that horses who carried Crazy Horse on their backs did not last long. He was a loner. He said he was happy to live in caves and crevices. He frequently hunted and raided alone. There were several women in his life, two of which he loved fiercely.

Unfortunately, the love of his life, Black Buffalo Woman, was married to another man named No Water (a Freudian slip of a man), and Crazy Horse's undying commitment to her came at an enormous cost. When he "eloped" with her after she had been married to No Water for some time and borne him three children, No Water shot him at close range in the jaw with a pistol (fortunately there was not much powder in the gun), and the tribal elders stripped Crazy Horse of his status as one of the four honorary Shirt-Wearers of his band. He had a daughter named They Are Afraid of Her. When she died in infancy of cholera, Crazy Horse was inconsolable.

His great dream had warned him to keep nothing for himself, and to give whatever he had to the elderly and the poor, especially old widows. This he did all of his life. In fact, his famous surrender in 1877 had more to do with the 900 or so refugees who depended on him than with his own inclinations. Without clan and clients he might well have lived out his life on isolated ridges with the coyotes.

He had a kind of moral purity that is virtually Christ-like, and it doesn't hurt that he was assassinated, partly by Rome and partly by his fellow Jews, at about the age of 33. Larry McMurtry has written that what little we actually know of Crazy Horse comes almost exclusively from the last months of his life, and that the variorum accounts that we possess of those months have the feel of the gospels. When he was assassinated—mortally wounded in a bayonet scuffle—at Fort Robinson on September 6, 1877, Crazy Horse had himself laid on the floor rather than on a cot. After he had received his mortal wound, he said, with Biblical economy, "Let me go, my friend—you have hurt me plenty bad." In his last hours he said, "All we wanted was peace and to be left alone. Soldiers were sent out in the winter [1876], who destroyed our villages. Then 'Long Hair' [Custer] came in the same way. They say we massacred him but he would have done the same to us had we not defended ourselves and fought to the last.[†] Our first impulse was to escape with our squaws and papooses [there's the humanitarian streak], but we were so hemmed in we had to fight."

With Shakespearean adroitness, John Neihardt has turned this into one of the great passages in American literature:

I had my village and my pony herds
On Powder where the land was all my own.
I only wanted to be let alone.
I did not want to fight. The Gray Fox sent
His soldiers. We were poorer when they went;
Our babies died, for many lodges burned
And it was cold. We hoped again and turned
Our faces westward. It was just the same
Out yonder on the Rosebud. Gray Fox came.
The dust his soldiers made was high and long.
I fought him and I whipped him. Was it wrong
To drive him back? That country was my own.
I only wanted to be let alone.
I did not want to see my people die.
They say I murdered Long Hair and they lie.
His soldiers came to kill us and they died.[‡]

"And when at last the lyric voice was dumb / And Crazy Horse was nothing but a name," his friend Touch the Clouds (descriptively named for his seven-foot height) threw a blanket over him and said, "This is the lodge of Crazy Horse. This is good. He sought death and now he has found it."

There are those who will find any comparison with Jesus to be blasphemous, but nobody can doubt that Crazy Horse was one of the greatest absolutists in American history, and that he came to symbolize the higher law of American Indian resistance to the white conquest of America.

[†]Hard to argue with this.
[‡]*The Twilight of the Sioux.* Lincoln/London: The University of Nebraska Press, 1971.

He was buried secretly somewhere on the edge of the badlands of South Dakota. Endless efforts have been made to locate his grave, and false prophets have risen, especially recently, to intone its GPS (global positioning) coordinates, but so far the unconquerable Lakota warrior and visionary has eluded grave violators as assiduously as he did photographers. As usual John Neihardt gets it exactly right:

Who knows the crumbling summit where he lies
Alone among the badlands? Kiotes prowl
About it, and the voices of the owl
Assume the day-long sorrow of the crows.
These many grasses and these many snows.

IV

THE NATIVE AMERICAN PIPE CEREMONY IS MANY THINGS. It essentially opens the doors of perception by making the breath of the Great Spirit visual, and thus inspires the ritual participant to envision the godhead. There is a eucharistic comingling about it—ingesting through the hand-carved pipe stem the breath of god, mingling the soul of the universe with one's own life-breath, one's own prana, then breathing a tendril of commingled medicine back at the vault of the sky. For me, since I do not smoke cigarettes, there is also a strange form of intoxication that takes me out of myself. Eventually it leaves me slightly sick to my stomach, but there is a brief corridor of eerie (and spiritually useful) intoxication between inhalation and nausea. I love to watch the beautiful elongated wisps of smoke as they come out of the pipe's mouth: it's the same experience a child has watching motes of dust when the sun suddenly sends its shafts into a murky room. I try to breathe out the poetry of smoke through my pipe, signing a little song of love to the cosmos through a stem shaped like an eagle claw holding the egg of the world.

Thanks to the pipe, we become conscious of the materiality of air. As the smoke tendrils seek the apex of the heavens (a spiritual reply to gravity), there is a sudden reaffirmation of the Platonic distinction between carnality and airy spirituality. My soul is braided into the nexus of smoke striving, searching, spiraling upward to its home. The body is not to be despised but it is not the best of us. Ritualized smoking reminds us of that.

Black Elk tells the story of how the sacred pipe first came to his people.

A very long time ago, they say, two scouts were out looking for bison; and when they came to the top of a high hill and looked north, they saw something coming a long way off, and when it came closer they cried out, "it is a woman!" and it was. Then one of the scouts, being foolish, had bad thoughts and spoke them; but the other said, "That is a sacred woman; throw all bad thoughts away." When she came still closer, they saw that she wore a fine white buckskin dress, that her hair was very long and that she was young and very beautiful. And she knew their thoughts and said in a voice that was like singing: "You do not know me, but if you want to do as you think, you may come." And the foolish one went; but just as he stood before her, there was a white cloud that came and covered them. And the beautiful young woman came out of the cloud, and when it blew away the foolish man was a skeleton covered with worms.

Then the woman spoke to the one who was not foolish: "You shall go home and tell your people that I am coming and that a big tepee shall be built for me in the center of the nation." And the man, who was very much afraid, went quickly, and told the people, who did at once as they were told. . . .

This is one of the most profound of all parables, equally interesting for its insight into gender relations and sexual security among the Sioux, as for what it reveals about the claims of the sacred. It makes the story of Lot's wife seem like a dull etiological myth. To mistake the sacred for the carnal is blasphemy, and the libidinous scout pays a heavy price for his sin. Avoid vermiculate thoughts. I first read this story when I was a boy of eighteen in an introduction to Native American studies course at the University of Minnesota. It is a story that I have never been able to forget. Each time I reread *Black Elk Speaks* I experience this parable in a different way, but the lesson is as unmistakable as it is virtually impossible for a man (a male) to accept. I have believed for more than twenty years that to realize (that is, fully internalize) the lesson of the White Buffalo Calf Woman is to learn how to be a spirit being, or—to put it in secular terms—to become a fully integrated man. It is a lesson that is almost impossible to learn even when we wish to, and most men (I among them) actually make themselves believe they can live their lives in systematic violation of this law. Virtually all of my suffering in adult life has come from closing my ears to the commands of White Buffalo Calf Woman.

V

THE YEAR MY DAUGHTER WAS BORN I SOJOURNED TO BEAR BUTTE, a few weeks before she made her appearance in this sublunary world, and prayed and prayed and prayed. Wasichu is not supposed to leave the trail, but I have always felt, as Joe Fontaine, the Ojibway man who initiated me into the world of the sweat lodge, puts it, that anything anyone does with purity of intention is its own justification. I always slip off the trail to an isolate place as unobtrusively as possible, and I make it a point never to interrupt any Native American activity—anywhere.

As I sat on the southwest slope of the butte, next to naked, breathing yogically, high by my pipe, stretching my limbs to the sky the way a love-aching woman does to her lover ("ravish my heart three personed God"), feeling sun on nooks and crevices of my body that never breath the free air, ashamed of my loose flesh, trying not to wave away the mosquitoes and the horseflies, listening closely to the universe for the first time in a long long time, I could hear the low sobbing incantation of Cheyenne and Lakota prayers, now here, now there, across the face of the mountain, men and women with much more to pray about near the surfaces of things, but almost certainly much less to pray for at their souls' cores. Heartbreaking. I comprehended my own deep shallowness and ached to have a soul to fight for. What is America but a Mephistophelean trade of the potential of soul for pneumatic tennis shoes, instant meals, and designer deodorants? Vapid, soulless, bland, dis-connected, dis-turbed, dis-heartened, dis-spirited, Disneyfied, dis-eased dys-topians. Amerika. And the merest bonehead Indian who is unemployed and unemployable, functioning on one cylinder, all the others blown by fetal and then adolescent and then adult alcohol syndromes, broken down by battery and bewilderment—busted in every conceivable way—is connected to the soul of the universe and the *omphalos* of the earth, in a way that no white superachiever can ever be with or without the cash of Kevin Costner or the new age golden girls Whoppie Goldberg and Goldie Hawn. Here is a paradox. Indians are connected to the root of things. We are not.

It reminded me of a time when I was a student at the University of Minnesota, living off Franklin Avenue, which was an Indian ghetto, the fruit of the failed relocation movement of the 50s and 60s, which merely transferred the impossible conditions of the reservation to the most dilapidated corridors of major American cities, without carrying with it clan, family, and the spirit of place which are the reservation's only true resources. I used to study on winter afternoons at the old Carnegie public library on Franklin Avenue. It was one of those architecturally-gorgeous but neglected (because in the ghetto) urban brick Carnegie libraries. Inside the books consisted of best-selling fiction and outdated second rate tomes on gardening, sports heroes, and popular biography. The encyclopedias were greasy from heavy use and some numbers were altogether missing. Inside there was very little activity and almost no sound, except for the far-off whirr of the copying machine, chugging dimes from libertarians and IRS-obsessives. I loved to study there. There was just enough activity to keep me from getting bored, not enough to distract me from my reading. The quality of light was exquisite—a mix of fluorescence and the blue-white snowcast of Minnesota winter.

Hardly a day went by when I didn't encounter Indian beggars on Franklin avenue, their faces stinking of cheap alcohol, their skin bloated and blotted, full of recent and ancient scars. Sometimes I gave them a few dollars even though it seemed clear that I was contributing to a suicide in doing so, and sometimes I questioned them like a righteous college student, and once in a while I offered to take one of them (they were always men) to a restaurant to get some food. This they declined. So in the same year of my young manhood I learned to love Indianness and despair over Indians. I never blamed them. Indeed I spent a fair amount of my time spinning out arguments for their victimhood, and silently raging at the price of the American dream.

One day I was reading Shakespeare quietly at a polished but scratched oak table, dipping to the footnotes to find out what "miscreant," "zounds," "go to," and "quintessence" mean, scratching out elaborate notes in my narrow-lined University of Minnesota notebook as if life were eternal, when I heard the low rhythm of an Indian man singing a traditional song, as if far off. It had that characteristically thin Indian timbre that one hears at powwows and on Indian FM radio. The voice slowly gained confidence and volume, as if some nearly-spent batteries were putting forth their last flare of potency. At first I was annoyed that the sacred silence of the library was being violated. I tried in vain to stay focused on my reading, but even the language of Shakespeare could not compete with the frail intonations of a broken-down Sioux poet. I dropped my pen and listened. The sound was haunting, full of infinite lament, but pure like the sound of a reed pipe. It seemed to me to be a song of lost love, of a girl who had let a strong, horse-skirmishing young man court her, had even thrown her shawl over his head when he came to stand downcast in line before her father's lodge, but something had gone terribly wrong, and she had in the end married an important man she did not love.

I sat immobile for ten minutes perhaps, not daring to move because the man's voice was not very strong and I had to strain to hear him. Then he stopped singing. He seemed to choke off the song. There was a period of silence. Now I looked around the room. Along one of the short walls there was a stairwell down to a sunken doorway that had been reduced to an emergency exit, with one of those red metal flags covered with dire warnings about the consequences of non-urgent egress. Sitting on the old mottled linoleum was an Indian man, elderly in appearance if not perhaps in actual age, in an old and cheap green zip parka with a fake fur collar. He was a mess. He was drunk. He appeared to be close to passing out, though most of the seriously drunk Indians I saw on the streets of Minneapolis seemed to be able to hang on in that state indefinitely. His eyes were red and sunken and yellow as his teeth. His face was bristly and covered with dirt and what might be dried blood. His legs were splayed out in front of him. It was clear that he was not going to get on his feet without help. But he was in no mood to go anywhere. He began another song— hauntingly beautiful, surely the story of how the horse, the "elk dog," came to the plains and made life good for everyone.

And then the cops came and hauled him away—roughly. Apparently they dance to a different drum. I was so shocked and angry that I meditated a hundred remedies and revenges. The Indian man's vagrancy was more interesting and more beautiful than a hundred crisp housewives checking out Danielle Steele between the cleaners and picking up the kids. From the pool of his bottomless sorrow and pukey breath, this man was offering a spontaneous concert that no amount of money could buy for the stage at the university's Northrup Auditorium. His art was pure because entirely uncommerical and because he had stupidly squandered all of the resources that a professional would bring to a public performance. He was reinvigorating Song at the public library, free, no advance tickets required, and his lament was as pure and unpremeditated as the song of the meadowlark. They plucked him off the floor and threw him into drunk tank for the night.

It was one of those moments in a young person's development when you pierce through the mythologies that have been ladled over you all your life like fat gravy on a meatball, and see the world for what it is, all power and propriety and huff and puff, and in an instant you collapse four or five levels into cynicism and disgust. And, for all of your Congregational pieties, you realize there is a reason why some folks call them pigs.

Such people as the broken bard of Franklin Avenue visit Bear Butte, if they can cadge a ride.

VI

WHEN AT LAST I STOOD UP and began returning to my clothes, on the Bear Butte prayer quest of 1994, it came to me that the highest tribute I could pay to the spirit of the place would be to burn my clothes and leave the sacred precinct as naked as a newborn child. Since this seemed unlikely to be generously understood by other visitors to Bear Butte, particularly the park rangers whose duty it is to supervise human activity there (as if the sacred required clothes!), I decided to walk down the butte barefoot, so that at least the part of me in direct contact with the earth would be naked and unprotected. I tied my hiking boots together and slung them over my shoulder, and began to piece my way down the face of the butte.

It is a hike of several miles along a well-marked path with periodic observation posts. The trail is covered with small rocks and debris, and on a couple of occasions near the top it crosses serious scree piles. It is rough enough to twist the ankles even of boot-wearers, and as I walked on my soft, civilized feet, which slip the surly bands of shoes no more than three or four waking hours per year, I was the very definition of the tenderfoot. I tiptoed and limped over the sharp objects, trying not to focus on the interface of foot and nature's edge, and trying not to grimace when I blundered onto a pebble or a woodchip. To any rational being I must have seemed simply idiotic, with perfectly good hiking boots strung over my shoulders, wince-footing it slowly down a rugged trail, wearing a sweat-stained cloth fringed Indian shirt. A boy of ten looked up at me in a guileless way and said, "Mister, why don't you put on your boots?" I ignored him. He asked his parents the same question as I rounded the next bend in the trail. They shushed him.

I met dozens of hikers on their way up the mountain, avoiding eye contact and thus casual challenges put forward by people whose business I was not about. About two-thirds of the way down, I rounded a bend in the trail, and saw in the middle distance three young women. At least two of them were completely white, Anglos, but all of them were dressed like extras from the movie *Dances with Wolves*. They wore leggings, and shawls, and fur pieces, and elaborate beaded belts and medallions. They were standing by the side of the trail, looking off towards the southeast, two of them leaning on expensive hiking staffs. The third woman, clearly the leader of the pack, looked like an Indian woman. She was pointing to something along the horizon, and the other two were hearkening like acolytes of the Dalai Lama.

My erotic antennae perked.

Tana Blackwood was beautiful. She was lean and Indian, provocatively if fully dressed and Indian, aglow with the energy of spiritual integration and Indian, delicate and beautiful in her facial structure and . . . did I mention Indian? Just by existing at that moment at Bear Butte she was ringing all the bells of my deepest fantasies: the nerd who comes to possess the Land-o-Lakes lady, Meriwether Lewis and Sacagawea alone in the Bitterroots, the Canadian Mountie singing "When I'm calling you" to the Algonquian princess, Custer taking solace on the Washita with Mo-nah-se-tah, Kevin Costner taking a break from dancing with wolves to roll in fleecy buffalo robes with Mary McDonnell.

I know of very few white men who don't cherish a fantasy of having sexual relations with an Indian woman. In the mind's eye, she is always Miss Indian America, in an unstained deerskin dress, her hair parted in perfect jet-black braids, her features chiseled and delicate at the same time, her eyes black as a sloe's. In this fantasy utopia, she undoubtedly uses feminine hygiene products, and she smells more like an Irish spring than a smudge fire. One of the greatest of my college professors, at the University of Minnesota in the 1970s, David Noble, an Americanist, used to ask us rhetorically, from time to time, whether we reckoned that Dorothy of Oz and Becky Thatcher menstruated. The white man's fantasy Indian woman turns out not to be Indian at all. She is a slightly exotic but thoroughly scrubbed white girl with somewhat darker than normal skin tone. Like the black women that white men love to love, Halle Berry, Whitney Houston, and Shari Bellafonte, she is a mixed blood, with a dash of the Negroid to spice her otherwise White genes and facial features. She is Sally Hemings, biologically white, legally black, with a hint of dark passion to make her alluring. She lives along the racial boundary and she is, therefore, willing to cross boundaries that a mere white woman is bound to respect. Ask a thousand men (and probably most women) to close their eyes and picture Lewis and Clark's Sacagawea, and virtually all to them will imagine a beaded, buckskinned waif from a fashion runway, or the icon of a butter package, rather than a scrappy (sometimes battered) woman who spent two and a half years camping with an infant and forty-some sex-starved infantile men, the Jeffersonian equivalent of a squad of oil field workers or longshoremen.

And even though I know better, I confess to being not a whit liberated from this testosteronic—and not a little racist— mythology. And here was Sacagawea standing before me at Bear Butte, like the opening stanza of an erotic medieval romance, poised to blow the doors off of my sad, left-brained life.

I did not wish to intrude upon the activity of the three women before me, whatever it was, so I moved purposefully and as unobtrusively as possible down the trail past them. At some point they all turned to watch me as I hobbled over the debris. Each of them adopted a look of puzzlement and real concern. When we were separated by only a few paces, one of the women said, "Excuse me, but may I ask you why you are doing this to yourself?"

Tana Blackwood turned on her companion with some asperity. "Let him be!" She walked over to where I was standing on the trail. She put her hand on my arm just below my shoulder. She looked me directly and deeply in the eye. "What you are doing is very brave—and very loving."

I managed only to nod in gratitude, said nothing, and moved on as rapidly as the pain in my feet would permit.

By the time I reached the trailhead (and Kentucky bluegrass) my feet were pretty beat up. They were bruised and even a little bloody. But along with my pain I felt the smugness of the man in the hair shirt.

I limped over to the spring. It's an artesian. Crazy Horse and his father drank out of it more than one hundred years ago. It has been capped and transformed into a drinking fountain by state health codes. Towards the bottom of the fountain there is a spring-loaded faucet, which you can turn on to fill your canteen but not leave on to sog up the picnic area.

Thomas Jefferson was wrong. People do not govern themselves. They are not naturally enlightened. Put a standard suburban house faucet on that well, and hark what discord follows. Bear Butte would be gullied and eroded by sheer feckless stupidity. Ask any rancher who has been generous with hunting access how often his gates have been left open. Jefferson trusted the people to govern themselves, but he insisted that they be educated liberally at public expense to make them capable of self-government. The fatal error of American history has been to cling to the idea of Jeffersonian self-government without ever having gotten serious about public education. We don't teach civics. We don't teach ethics. We don't teach art. We don't teach the humanities. And we expect a 24-year-old who grew up on *Three's Company* to show thoughtfulness, respect, and self-restraint?

As I sat on the grass and studied my dirty, bloody feet, I felt like a character from ancient Palestine slaking his thirst and washing his feet at the well of an irascible sheep man with a comely daughter. If, as Percy Bysshe Shelley says, poetry reinvigorates language, wilderness teaches us to love macrobiotic simplicities again: a flap between me and the rain, a salty cracker at the end of the day, cool water. I decided to rest a few minutes before ministering to my cut feet.

The women who run with wolves came round the corner—at last—looking serene and righteous. They unlocked their gleaming Suburban and dug for kerchiefs with which to mop their dazzled upper middle class brows. They looked a bit like the tourists who queue up at national park kiosks to get their system passports stamped. Yosemite, check. King's Canyon, done. This year Bear Butte. Next year Canyon d'Chelly. Don't get me wrong. I admire the spirit quests of these women, and the fact is that mine is not fundamentally different. It is better to embrace Bear Medicine Cards and dream catchers (both, in my view, pan-Indian manqué frauds) than Deuteronomic dietary codes or British Israelism, or to form a committee to get *Catcher in the Rye* banned from the public school curriculum. Any life-affirming act deserves respect, even if it veers from one's own formula for taste or decorum. Women in their forties and fifties, as often as not divorced, their children off to college or nearly so, feminized with respect to work issues, but not otherwise enamored of the movement, embittered by the patriarchal institutions they endured until their marriages broke down, unwilling to let their spiritual urges flow through the traditional church, hungry for erotic connection but weary of men . . . these are the raw recruits of the New Age movement. They are legion. Who has a right to deride them? Their quest is soulful in ways that a stint on the local library board and the Republican National Committee is not. And the fact is that these women have had to overcome a great deal more than I ever have to be in this place trying on forms of romanticism that—through history—have been overwhelmingly the province of men. Let *them* be.

Tana Blackwood glided up to me as I sat in that numb state that follows a painful hike. "I just want to tell you that I admire what you were doing back there," she said. She had changed into moccasins. She was wearing a long thin deerskin dress. Her hair was semi-braided, just disheveled enough to be completely alluring. She had some kind of claw necklace around her neck. And of course blue beads. As I looked up at her, standing tall between me and the sun, I noticed, in the microsecond that her approach gave me, that she had black eyes, an attractive but not beautiful face, a lean neck. I could see the swell of modest breasts behind the unsmooth brown surface of her dress.

"It took a lot of courage for you to do that. If I hadn't been leading those two women from Milwaukee, I'd have joined you."

I said, "Well, your feet and your friends can both appreciate your choices."

"Did you hurt yourself much?"

"Not much. A nick here, a cut there, and some serious bruising. I'm trying to make my feet match my soul."

She laughed.

There was a pause. It felt like the pause of erotic potential, the pause at an art reception when you meet someone you are powerfully attracted to, and your knees buckle, and you are both poised on the brink of a sexual odyssey, but you probably won't plunge in the end, and each of you is trying to pay attention to the ostensible line of conversation while simultaneously calculating risk and reeling from the sexual chemistry. Or the pause when you are getting drunk with someone you are already intoxicated by, and you have lost control of control, and you make that last fatal eye contact, and you both realize, in the same instant of time, "I think I'm going to go to bed with this person tonight."

It was the pause from which somebody usually flees.

I broke the silence. "My name is Clay. I come here sometimes to pray. I am going to make an odd request. I hope you will take it in the innocent spirit with which I offer it. I've never done anything like this before.† Would you permit me to wash your feet in this spring?"

Tana Blackwood said, "That is so strange! I was just going to say I wanted to wash *your* feet."

---

†I was telling the truth.

Now we blushed together. The urge to flee was almost overwhelming. It's an old Groucho Marx paradox. I wouldn't want to wash the feet of any woman who would be willing to let me wash her feet this side of major persuasion. Probably I had half-spoiled the effect for her, too, though each of us invoked the language of synchronicity—she was, on top of everything else, well read too! Did I mention Indian?

Tana Blackwood sat down a little way away from me so that our feet occupied the same circle that pivoted on the spring. She had lean muscular legs, freshly shaved (Sacagawea shaved every day, didn't she?) She was prettier than I had thought. I sat up, and kneeled before her. I placed my hands near her right foot. I said,

"May I?"

"Yes."

I untied the lace of her moccasin, and (like a shoe salesman on his first day) carefully removed it from her foot. Then the other. I pulled back so that I could work the spigot and she scooted forward so that her feet were directly below it. We avoided eye contact. I lifted one of her feet with my left hand and turned the spigot with my right. The water burst out of the pipe and splashed the top of her foot where it met her slender ankle before I could get the volume right. The dust on her feet turned to dark, alluring rivulets of mud. When there was water enough I took her right foot in both of my hands and gently washed it. I continued with slow and deliberate motions until both of her feet were clean and gleaming. Homeric feet. I tried to use enough pressure with my hands so that she would recognize that I might like to massage her feet, but not enough to cross the boundary from the washing we had agreed to. I had never washed anyone's feet before. I wanted myrrh or succulent oil in a clay jar to lave over her ankles. I wanted long hair to let down onto her feet to dry them in the New

Testament way. I wanted her to look up and say, "I have to spend the rest of my life with a man who is as sensuous as you are." I wanted. When she was clean I placed her feet side by side on my knees to dry. I made sure my ministrations advanced no farther than two inches above her tight ankles, and I rested her feet so far from my pelvis that there could be no mistaking my innocence.

Then she got up on her knees and washed my feet. She rubbed away the blood with healing hands. She was as gentle as female attention can ever be, and as innocent, and yet I could hardly breathe as she let her delicate fingers trace their way down between the cleavage of my toes, and pinched my ankles between her thumbs. At the base of Bear Butte, time ceased to be, and yet I felt the way you do when you are getting a therapeutic massage and you realize that it is well over half-finished, and that it will have to end—too soon, too soon. She dried my feet in her lap, in the splendid concavity of her deerskin dress.

It was heaven on earth.

We could not have exchanged more intimacy if we had kissed at the base of the butte, if we had groped each other, if we had interpenetrated in the bushes. Our gifts to each other could not have been more complete if we had spent the rest of our lives together.

There was a pause. Each of us knew enough to let it be.

I said, "I have something for you in the car." I walked over and fetched out of the rubble of my peripatetic existence a copy of *The Sixth Grandfather* by Raymond J. Demallie. It is a study of the undigested interviews of John Neihardt—and his remarkable daughters Enid and Hilda—with the Lakota Medicine man Black Elk. It was one of my favorite books. More to the point, I had carried that dog-eared, travel-worn, and much-studied paperback all over the sacred corridor for many years, until it was imbued with the smell of sagebrush and prickly pear, until it bore the stains of my sweat and peeled oranges, spilled coffee, and the warpings of the plains wind. Wild prairie flowers were pressed between its pages. To have given her a gleaming new copy of the same book would have been to have given her a trifle compared to this. I placed it carefully in her hands. "Perhaps you know it." I said. "It is a book that changed my life, and I want you to carry it with you."

"I have heard of it," she said, "but I have never read it. I'm a bit new to the literature of my people. Like you, like everyone, I'm having to learn to be an Indian." I admit that I found this statement a bit off-putting. Spare me, I thought, the Pocahontas trope.

Then she untied from her left wrist a simple bracelet made of hemp and a few small translucent red beads. It was the kind of friendship bracelet that one might buy in a convenience store or a souvenir shop. It might cost up to $3.50. But as it slipped off of her delicate, and encircled my thicker, wrist, it became priceless. I felt like a creature out of Arthurian romance.

I am well aware that, from a skeptic's perspective, I had, like Homer's Glaukos, traded gold for bronze.[†] But the skeptics have always misprized Glaukos' great soul. To find a guest friend in the nightmare of war, and to be swept up in a moment of extravagant generosity to redeem blood and havoc, is a pearl of price that no assaying scale can ever measure. I cannot speak for Tana Blackwood, but I had just received a gift that I can never forget.

It was one of the most erotic experiences of my life. I knew that I would never see her again. I understood for the first time that

---

[†] In *Iliad* VI, Glaukos the Trojan and Diomedes the Greek are about to engage in single combat when they discover that they have family ties of friendship. There can be no combat now. In his enthusiasm Glaukos suggests that the warriors exchange their armor as a token of good will. Homer writes: "But Zeus had stolen Glaukos' wits away—the young man gave up golden gear for bronze, took nine bulls' worth for armor worth a hundred."

possibilities unrealized are often more satisfying than consumption and possession. Without putting my shoes back onto my feet, I got into my car and drove away. I left the radio off that whole endless day, and the next. . . . Was Tana Blackwood White Buffalo Calf Woman?

VII

BUT OF COURSE THE LESSON OF BEAR BUTTE and Tana Blackwood did not take. That moment was pure, but I was far from purified. Once I was down off the mountain, the Old Adam reasserted himself, and I reverted to all the seductive, objectifying, superficial habits of my sex. I returned to patriarchy like a diver with the bends. A couple of years later I pissed away a marriage by way of nickels and dimes, without even having the good sense to engage in a towering inferno of a love affair.

And there followed the prolonged aloneness that comes when a corrupt man finally looks into the mirror for the first time. My celibacy stretched out like the Black Rock Desert in Nevada — endless, without a stick of life in any direction, from the right angle beautiful in its starkness.

VIII

THIS LAST CHRISTMAS I DECIDED TO DRIVE HOME from exile to see my mother and sister. It's a journey of about 1,500 miles no matter which route you take and aside from Salt Lake City you can dash through the scattered snow without encountering much of a population center. I was counting on Rapid City to complete—that is, conduct start to finish—my Christmas shopping. Ten weeks earlier I had made the same drive with new camping equipment and heroic, post-divorce plans to sleep under the stars and pray to the gods of the West. But Serendip turned her back on me. The West threw a freak October blizzard in my path, and I bivouacked at Motel 6 and Fairfield Inns instead.

This time (thanks to winter) I had no expectations of camping, but I did hope to do some hiking and praying in Crazy Horse country, if possible. By the time I got to Bear Butte a few days before Christmas it was blisteringly cold, but the air was clear and the snow pack was light. I woke up road-stunned and bleary-eyed in a Super 8 in Spearfish, South Dakota, checked the weather channel, looked out into the crystalline plains air, found that my new Honda barely turned over, filled up with gas, dropped in a bottle of HEET, bought a pair of $9 gas station gloves, drank a cup of bitter quickstop coffee, and then paused by the side of the highway. To wimp out or not to wimp out? As a moral dodge, I decided to drive up to the entrance gates at Bear Butte—wondering if the monument would be open in midwinter and on such a brutal day, secretly hoping that it would be all locked up and that I would not only be able to wimp out but express disappointment too.

It was a dangerously and appallingly cold day. No rational being should be outside on such a day. It was far below zero and the wind was blowing pandemonically straight off Hudson's Bay.

The gate was open. The road was clear. The visitor center was closed for the winter, but the butte trail was unobstructed. The mountain was deserted. I drove up to the upper parking lot and stopped the car, then realized that I should park facing the south and away from the fierce wind to prevent my Honda from freezing solid while I was on the butte. It was that cold. Precaution cold.

I stripped off my blue work shirt. I pulled my Ghost Dance shirt out of my kitbag. It is a simple muslin fringed shirt, made at a campground under Devils Tower a few years ago, just before my daughter Catherine was born, cut out of a pattern purchased at a Tandy leather store, sewn by hand on a gorgeous summer's evening. I had attached blades of fringe under the arms and along the sides, which, by now, had frayed until the shirt was even more wild looking than it had been meant to be. Originally I had planned to paint Ghost Dance symbols on it: crescent moons, stars, the sun, a rainbow. But I had always worried that this would gunk up the shirt somehow, make it look like a church bizarre craft item, so in the end I had merely left it alone. I've worn it a dozen times in all, mostly in the summer, almost always on prayer hikes, and I have never washed it, so the shirt is stained with sweat lines, some grime, and even some blood. It is one of my prime possessions, partly because I made it to prepare for and celebrate the birth of my daughter, my redeemer, partly because I have, thanks to the seriousness with which I worship in it, been more present in that shirt than in anything I have ever worn, and partly because it cost a total of perhaps $1.50 in materials.

The Ghost Dance was an apocalyptic pan-Indian despair and renewal ritual that began in western Nevada in 1888 and ended on December 29, 1890 at Wounded Knee creek on the Pine Ridge of South Dakota. It was the invention—or revelation—of a Nevada Paiute man named Wavoka, who was known at some points in his life as Jack Wilson. Inspired by a vision, Wavoka declared that if the Indians of America would purify their hearts and dance incessantly in a certain way, white people would be swallowed up by the earth, and all the dead Indians would be resurrected, along with the buffalo and elk and unlimited pastures of grass. Black Elk describes it thus:

> . . . his name was Wavoka. He told them that there was another world coming, just like a cloud. It would come in a whirlwind out of the west and would crush out everything on this world, which was old and dying. In that other world there was plenty of meat, just like old times; and in that world all the dead Indians were alive, and all the bison that had ever been killed were roaming around again. . . . The people must put paint on their faces and they must dance a ghost dance.

Eventually a range of tribes sent representatives to Nevada to learn what they could of the new medicine dance, including the

Lakota, who listened to Wavoka with respect, but went home and made some adjustments in the direction of militancy. Among other things, the Lakota invented Ghost Shirts, made sometimes of leather, more often of muslin, which they believed were impervious to Wasichu's bullets. They could not have been more wrong.

The massacre at Wounded Knee was one of the most shameful moments in American history. In simplest terms, the U.S. military indulged in genocidal overreaction to the Ghost Dance craze on the Pine Ridge Indian Reservation. Confusing despair with rebellion, a craven, incompetent Indian agent named D.F. Royer, whom the Lakota derisively nicknamed "Young-man-afraid-of-the-Sioux," demanded military intervention. He got it in the form of the Seventh Cavalry, still drunk with bloodlust and dreams of revenge from the whipping it had received at the Battle of the Little Big Horn in 1876. Under the command of Colonel James W. Forsyth[†] the fabled Seventh Cavalry was attempting to disarm the Miniconjou Sioux at Wounded Knee Creek when a melee erupted. The U.S. Army trained its Hotchkiss guns on the defenseless Indians. At least 146 men, women, and children died in the slaughter which followed.

Black Elk, who witnessed the massacre as a teenage boy, provided the epitaph of the Lakota nation:

And so it was all over.

I did not know then how much was ended. When I look back now from this high hill of my old age, I can still see the butchered women and children lying heaped and scattered all along the crooked gulch as plain as when I saw them with eyes still young. And I can see that something else died there in the bloody mud, and was buried in the blizzard. A people's dream died there. It was a beautiful dream.

And I, to whom so great a vision was given in my youth,—you see me now a pitiful old man who has done nothing, for the nation's hoop is broken and scattered. There is no center any longer, and the sacred tree is dead.

[†]Forsyth, Montana, is named for him: talk about blasphemy.

The United States government's blasphemous insistence on reading rebellion into what was nothing more than the *dans macabre* of the Sioux, is one of the few American stories that always make me literally sick to my stomach. The government also managed to use the Ghost Dance phenomenon as the rationale for assassinating Sitting Bull on December 15, 1890, even though he was skeptical of Wavoka's messianic prophesies, even though he was minding his own business in his cabin on the Grand River in northern South Dakota. In fact, the great Hunkpapa leader was fast asleep in philosophic tranquility when agent John McLaughlin's goons cut him down at dawn on the Ides of December. Now Crazy Horse *and* Sitting Bull were dead.

I made and wear a Ghost Shirt because as a citizen of the United States, as a scholar, as a plains historian, as a North Dakotan, as a lover of justice, as a humanist, as a believer in the verities of Thomas Jefferson's charter of human rights, I conclude that the orgiastic dancers of Wounded Knee were merely exercising their first amendment rights when they were massacred by Wasichus who were unwilling to share this vast continent with the fewscore thousand people whose continent it was. I wear my Ghost Shirt also because if by purifying my heart and dancing incessantly, I could help to bring back the Great Plains of March 4, 1801 (the day Jefferson was inaugurated Third President of the United States), I would not hesitate to dance until my heart fell to the ground for the last time. I would want a word or two with the Third President before my exit.

IX

I SAT IN MY FRAYED MUSLIN SHIRT for a few minutes on that bitterly cold December morning in the winter of my discontent, and tried to formulate what it was I was seeking from the mountain. Integrity—renewal—a new sense of wonder—rootedness—an opening of the doors of perception—above all the flourishing of my daughter. Nothing more specific than that. The usual. Thy will be done.

In the car, I changed into hiking boots, and put on a sweater, a sweatshirt, and a high-tech yellow and purple wilderness coat made of a miracle fabric unknown to Crazy Horse or Custer, or Kennedy for that matter. The coat had cost me a small fortune, and it had the look and feel of a counter-culturalist's exemplum of appropriate technology, but in fact it was the tiny apex of an immense industrial pyramid, supported by strip mines, oil refineries, dead rivers, Third World labor pools, industrial-interventionist medical delivery systems, hegemonic monetarism, and government big enough to swallow, like Polyphemus, all the Jeffersonians who ever lived. But it was warm and indeed stylish and I had slapped down a card to buy it.

I forced the car door open against the mighty wind, squeezed out, and lumbered up the trail. It took most of an hour to reach the top. There was a three-inch mantle of fresh snow on the butte. After a quarter of a mile, I saw no more boot tracks on the trail. I was alone on the mountain. That had never happened to me before. In all of my previous visits, I was just one of a hundred or more people scrambling across the face of the butte. It felt immensely good—and a little eerie—to be there alone. I mumbled, "So I get the gods to myself today." But this was as arrogant as it was stupid.

On almost every shrub or tree within a dozen yards of the trail, I saw Indian prayer strings: pieces of bright cotton cloth tied to lengths of string, usually containing marble-sized bundles of tobacco. I stopped to inspect some of them—a string of fifteen red bundles, a cluster of five black ones, a shard of yellow cloth simply tied to a bare limb, shredded cotton strips as thin as old

American flags. They were astonishingly moving, these prayer strings, for each one signified a prayer pilgrimage taken by an American Indian. It was impossible to know what they sought, these ravaged pilgrims, most of whom were so poor that the purchase of a handkerchief, a pouch of tobacco, and a small ball of string is a true sacrifice. What do they pray for here? What does anyone pray for?

Love and release.

If I closed my eyes, I could see them (as I *have* seen them in other seasons) struggling up the trail, dangerously overweight, toxic from cigarettes and cheap drink, their faces pockmarked from the disaster of Washicu's processed diet, huffing and puffing as they settled beside a promising tree or bush, or perhaps the tree nearest to where their body-strength wore out. For all of the collapse of Indian culture and the wreck of most Indians' lives, there is a dignity and a connectedness and a beauty in their lives that make the rest of us—coiffed, tucked, treadmilled, and root-canalled America, with saline balloons bulging in our chests—seem ugly and frivolous. The spirituality that brings Indians of all tribes to this place, against such colossal odds, cannot be anything but pure.

When I finally reached the top of Bear Butte I stood for a minute on the observation deck and surveyed the Great Plains. The view from the mountain is as stark as anything can ever be. Think of not-quite-flat, not-quite-gently-rolling country stretching like fruitcake batter to the far horizon in every direction, world without end, Amen. At the vanishing point to the east, the north, the west, faraway lone buttes standing barely visible through the haze, swallowed by the sky. They all have names. They are all massive in their parishes. Each one is the loneliest place in the world. There is always a ranchstead on the northeast corner of the butte. To the southwest the Black Hills, Paha Sapa, reduced by the tricks of distance to a kind of gray-green mushroom head resting on the infinite swell of the plains. Below me that major north-south U.S. highway, 85, a pitiful thread of asphalt hugging the base of the butte before needling it to Canada. A semi-truck the size of a matchbox toy droning its cattle to slaughter in Nebraska. A nuclear family in a Chrysler K car on its way to Grandma's house for Christmas, not laughing all the way, the teenagers in the back seat eating sunflower seeds and reading *Mad* magazine and *Glamour*, pushing their bare feet against the seatbacks, infinitely annoying their *paterfamilias*, and bitching the desolation; even the *paterfamilias* thinking, to himself, "Jesus, what if we had a flat tire out here?" (My father did once, before I was old enough to help, and it unstrung him.) A UPS truck. On the 21st of December so much depends on a box-brown UPS truck fanning out from Rapid City to Belle Fourche and Buffalo, Bowman and Bucyrus, Rhame and Reeder, farmstead and ranch house, bearing gleaming gifts for the purpose of completing the great homogenization of America.

I scrambled down into a niche of the mountain that was protected from the wind, forced my back up against the trunk of a ponderosa pine. I pulled my hands out of my gloves long enough to fumble for my pipe, my pipe stem, my pouch of tobacco, a pocket knife, and a lighter. Every twenty seconds I had to drop whatever I was holding and beat my hands against my thighs like a bad actor auditioning for a part in a Jack London novel. It was very cold, dangerously cold. Maybe 20 below. Everything went numb in seconds. Eventually I managed to light the pipe, and felt again the satisfaction of Fire, and worked my way through a truncated version of the Lakota pipe ceremony. I invoked the four quarters of the world: the East first, always the East first, the quarter from which the sun appears each day to relume the world; then the South, the land of fine horses, whence returns the summer and the grass and the world's fecundity; then the

West, land of the thunder beings, which bring the life of the spirit and the storm clouds that nurture the winged ones, the two-leggeds, the four-leggeds, and the things that crawl the land; and finally the North, the source of the winter wind and the snow that scours the impurities off of creation (it was a day of the North); then the earth itself, the kindly mother of all the fruits of existence; and finally the place of the Grandfather Spirits, the endless firmament of crackling blue sky. Invoking the quarters in itself restores me to my center of gravity. Ritual slows us down long enough to open our souls.

I prayed and meditated and smoked and blew smoke rings and visualized God for a long long time. Three bowlsful of tobacco and kinnikinnick, audible prayers, and even some wisps of chanting. Perhaps an hour passed. Perhaps eighty minutes. My legs were splayed out in front of me. I was numb. I was intoxicated from the tobacco. It was not clear whether I would be able to stand up. When at last I struggled to my feet and stomped around on my numb stump legs, I felt high from the smoke and at the same time perfectly calm. I felt that if I simply gave up the pointless struggle (think of humans contributing to their 401K accounts in the face of the Cosmos, or as Thoreau puts it, "Think, also, of the ladies of the land weaving toilet cushions against the last day, not to betray to green an interest in their fates!") this day on the slope of Bear Butte, it would, as the fatalist Lakota used to say, be a good day to die. Better to be gnawed by the coyotes of Bear Butte than die sedated in utter sterility with a tube up your nose. Or worse.

But I chose to live, to finish capping my teeth, to read 2,500 more books, to give a thousand more lectures, and above all to go home for Christmas with my mother.

As I walked down the trail placing my feet as nearly as possible in the tracks I had made on the way up, taking breaths so deep that I felt stinging in my lungs, I began to pray for the people who matter in my life: my child first—always my child first, my beloved daughter Catherine Missouri, They Are Afraid of Her, who will come to this place with her pa one day, and drink from the artesian well of Crazy Horse, and make heroic vows and keep them too, and change the world, and—later—bring her son here and say, "Your grandfather wanted to be buried here, but in his seventh term Governor Janklow. . . ." Then I prayed for my mother, my sister, and my outstanding former wife. Then Douglas the gentle physicist of Oxenford, whom I wear in "my heart's core, ay in my heart of hearts." Then my half-dozen friends, scattered across the rootless surface of America. In each case I prayed aloud and explicitly for whatever would make each person whole, and not for what she or he might bring to me. It was my first brush with *agape* and it was the gift of Bear Butte. I had never done anything like this before. It certainly beat a subscription to *Sports Illustrated* as a Christmas gift.

Eventually I got to the fifth circle with no *magister Vergil* to serve as my guide, and I began to pray for the women who live out on the periphery of my Eros, women who have turned their magnets towards me in some low-level but promising way, and all the women I have tried to lure into my lonely orbit. Many of them are married and off-limits, some of them are single, and off-limits. They are the coterie of a life of travel, of public performance, of ego, of accumulation. Without premeditation and unconscious of any higher purpose, I invoked one after another by name and sang songs of praise to them, out loud, and thanked them for their many gifts to me, and blessed their existence, and then—finally—gently but firmly cast them back into far-off nebulae where I would not be able to find them if I changed my mind. It was a process of cleansing and regret, a long long overdue housekeeping of my heart. We do not lose anything, says the Stoic philosopher Epictetus. We merely return it to the part of the universe where it belongs. I had come to the butte to renew not renounce, but the Wakan had another path in mind and I did not feel free to resist it. I knew my life was changing forever on the slope of Bear Butte and there could be no return to the old bad habits now (not at 43) without a kind of suicide of the soul. As I stood there shivering in the wind, alien words suddenly burbled out of me, "I will not tug erotically, I will not tug erotically." Again and again. These words were unplanned, certainly uncharacteristic. The word "tug," for example, is not a part of my active vocabulary. I had not come to Bear Butte with the intention of shedding the scales of my erotic integument. Like everyone else, I have integuments in every direction, every category. But now that is precisely what was happening and it would, I realized, be blasphemous not to let the mountain teach me my way.

It wasn't just about mating and sexual relations, of course. It was the wisdom St. Augustine achieved in mid-life, through a different avenue of grace, in a different desert, in a different era: always to seek the Creator through the creation, not to lose sight of the Creator and *get stuck* on the Creature, to see the Creator *in* the Creature. In other words, when we think we are in love with the creature, we are in fact seeking God in an understandable but highly imprecise way. Wisdom is the realization that it is the Creator we want, not the earthly manifestation of his work. If we could always remember that in loving a woman (or a man, or a child, or a pet) we are loving God-in-woman, that every erotic encounter—rightly understood—is an encounter with the divine, we might avoid some common and highly destabilizing mistakes. Amazing that puritan patriarchal St. Augustine of Hippo and the White Buffalo Calf Woman could be on the same page, but I realized now that they were.

Our souls are more of a piece than we care to admit. Somehow, at some point, a hectic restlessness crept into western civilization. The result is Marco Polo and Columbus and Amerigo Vespucci and Lewis & Clark and Buzz Aldrin and Amelia Earhart. But the result is also the extinction of species, the extinction of other cultures, and the extinction of the enchanted world. The triumph of the west embraces the smallpox vaccine *and* biological warfare, cruise control *and* the cruise missile, the Internet *and* cyberporn, Bach *and* Buchenwald.

For me, on this occasion, at this crossroad of my life, in the particular social milieu in which I found myself at that moment, given my biorhythms and habits and predilections, the message on the wind involved my relations with others, chiefly with women. On another day it might have been my relations with books, or gadgets, or meat, or the state, or the great globe itself.

After all, the question (the entreaty of all worthy prayer) is, how can I integrate my life?

And the wind said: *agape*. Always *agape* in all things.

We need to learn to let the world *be* a little more than we do, to celebrate the fruits of life without always consuming and classifying and commodifying them too. We need to learn to practice a certain detachment from the things of this world. We need to overcome the urge to objectify the universe and fence in a piece of it for our exclusive enjoyment. This is the great Jeffersonian desideratum in the world of ideas and politics. It is the great desideratum in our quest to live more lightly (and with dignity) on the planet. It is the great desideratum for the future of the American male, who (like me) tends to see in women the potential for satisfactions rather than the sovereignty of their souls.

To love without possessiveness. To love without reservation. To love without expectation. To live on the earth without—in Francis Bacon's darkly revealing words—fretting it into a kind of artificial fecundity.

If we men can just learn to stop fretting women, to see them first as sacred beings, White Buffalo Calf Women, second as souls, third as female souls, fourth as beings who should be free freely to choose their partnerships, fifth as creatures for whom the dance of sex and mating represents a minor chord in the concertos of their existence, if we can do that, the greatest bloodless revolution in human history will have taken place. And it will have implications in every direction, from mining policy to militarism to medical delivery systems.

The parable about White Buffalo Calf Woman is not just about men's attitudes toward women. It is more profoundly about human responses to the fruits of the earth.

My relations with women have constituted one of my primary lenses on the universe, but by no means my only or most important lens. If I had not been praying for wisdom in this arena on my way down the butte, it undoubtedly would have been the same process through a different vocabulary. For what are words but the tokens by which we do the stupendous work of the soul?

Each time I set another woman adrift, not by way of heroic rocketry, but rather as a satellite is eased into orbit from the bay of the Shuttle, I felt lighter and more whole, more me. I knew I was giving each of these remarkable women the greatest gift of love in my possession, because in my heart of hearts I did not want them and they did not in their hearts of hearts want me— we were just filling voids in ourselves with the moral equivalent of the plastic peanuts that accompany UPS-delivered toys, and then cling to the drapes—and our flirtatious play was a dangerous diversion from their true relationships and a criminal distraction of our souls.

I came to the end of the list. But as my soul prepared to take a modest little Kitty Hawk flight, freed from the millstones that I had piled on it to protect myself from life, I faltered, like Lucifer on the brink of Milton's "vast abyss." I had in the course of these unlooked-for meditations become oblivious of my surroundings, partly because I was so focused on my self-scouring, and partly because I was walking along a protected face of the mountain and the wind and cold had slipped below the threshold of my nervous system.

I had exempted just one woman from my ritual cleansing.

As I came upon her name at the end of this incantation of liberation, and even started the process of confessing and releasing her, I stopped in mid-sentence and carved out an exception clause for her. She is indeed a preternaturally remarkable being, who in look, in life, in mind, in humor, in style, in vision, in sensuality, in work, in sensibility, in creativity, and in drive pushes every one of my erotic buttons, until in her presence I am like Horace's loverboy, abashed, ah-shucks and "bedewed in liquid odors." She is, of course, married, the mother of splendid children. I said, "Well, perhaps if X is willing, we can make some sort of chaste romantic friendship this year that will preserve. . . ."

As those words found their way through my teeth's barrier, the Cosmos blew me down. A gigantic blast of wind burst out of the December sky and literally knocked me off my feet. Suddenly it was the coldest day in history again. I found myself lying flat-out and face down on the snow. I struggled to get up in my thick clothing like a just-born colt or a downed moonwalking astronaut. The gusts of wind battered me with hammer blows from several directions. My nose was running. There was a pounding in my ears. My legs were lead and my right hip hurt. I lay on the trail like a gut-shot buck for three or four minutes trying to take in what had happened. I wondered whether I was bleeding.

The message on the wind was also a call to thoroughness and integrity that had nothing to do with one's mating rites. It's no good to cleanse the soul and leave a lonely little turd of corruption behind. Whatever the soul's quest—responsible gender or environmental relations, the alchemy of soul transmutation from lead to gold, the search for the essence of coyoteness in the dark abyss of the night—our duty is to pursue that grail with a whole and a pure consciousness. There is no seeking macrobiotic integrity by night and Big Macs by day, no day-trading with Cargill and night-trading with Gaea, no sacramental commitment to eros *and* a subscription to *Playboy*.

My impurity had blown me down.

Finally I got to my feet and steadied myself. I smiled a wan ironic smile. "Well, perhaps I shall release you, too," I said, and for the first time in perhaps twenty-five years I stood alone in the universe with no one in the wings, no one in the roster of possibilities, no one peeking over the rim of my sovereignty, and my antennae fully retracted like the radio whip on a parked Cadillac.

"White Buffalo Calf Woman," I said in the way that one experiences the profoundest truths: simple utterance, actually voiced but not "out loud," with the sound columns radiating not out to the world but inward into the skull chamber and down the spine to the heart and the gut and the root.

I do not exaggerate. When I had corrected my mistake (St. Augustine once said, "Lord, let me be chaste, but not yet!"), the wind rushed away as quickly as it had burst upon my narcissistic being. The evangelist is right: "The spirit bloweth where it listeth, and thou hearest the sound thereof, but canst not tell whence it cometh or whither it goeth. So it is with all things of the spirit." I padded down the rest of the trail in the perfectly still December air. . . . I walked in complete silence. . . . I walked alone. . . . And in some way I was not the man any longer who had lurched up Bear Butte with his pipe and his sweat-stained Ghost Dance shirt clinging to the ghost of his patriarchal self.

I wanted now to find my way back to the reading room of the

Carnegie library on Franklin Avenue in Minneapolis, sit next to that broken Lakota bard, in the sacred way, if by sacred one means that he deserved to be visited thoughtfully, on foot, in hushed tones, and with all of one's sensitivities on special alert. He'd have drifted in off the heartless street in his cheap green parka and he'd start his song in low lost tones, the song about the young man who led the horse raid against the Crow in the year of the red moon, where things had gone disastrously wrong, and four of his comrades had been killed, and he was captured near where the driftwood gathered and given as a prize to Sleeps in the Creek, a harsh man, and things had been very difficult, but Sleeps in the Creek's daughter had smiled on him as he gathered water, and she brought him a morsel of pemmican on the day the blizzard came, and he knew then . . . . I'd sit next to him there on the grayed linoleum and frown off his persecutors, and when he was finished and spent, ask him if I could please wash his feet.

We can never guarantee that we will not relapse. We are, as Samuel Johnson paraphrased Shakespeare, "all men frail and capable of frailty." But I do not intend to turn back. I do not wish to turn back. I will not turn back.

Thy will be done.

And so you are now at last safe, with me, White Buffalo Calf Woman. Or rather, I am at last safe with you.

> With visible breath I am walking.
> A voice I am sending as I walk.
> In a sacred manner I am walking.
> With visible tracks I am walking.
> In a sacred manner I am walking.

I fired up my car and turned north towards Marmarth—and home in time for Christmas.

Afterward

IN THE END, DOES IT MATTER that I grew up in North Dakota and not Houston or San Bernardino? I wonder.

If this book is essentially about spirit of place, it is also about waking up to the meaningfulness of our experiences, breaking out of the paradigms into which we are born and reared. With the right mentor I might have awakened anywhere on earth. (Ah, yes, but he was the quintessential child of the plains). Without Mike Jacobs, Patti Perry, and great-souled Gerhardt Ludwig, I feel certain that the Great Plains might have as easily planted me in a Barcalounger as in the Bodleian or Franklin Avenue public library. The probabilities are overwhelmingly with the Barcalounger.

Thoreau believed that we can only wake up in a simplified landscape. Jefferson believed we are at our most civilized on a farm. I do believe our best chance is out where the grid begins to break down, where the wind blows and the horizons are endless in every direction, and I feel enormously fortunate to have come of age on the Great Plains, but I also feel certain that we can wake up anywhere, at any time. Waking up always seems to be about opportunity and discipline, but in fact it is only about choice. When we are ready to hear the answer, the teacher will come. I wish everyone who reads this book would move to North Dakota, or at least vacation in Marmarth, but I know too that the fruits of the soul are available on every street corner in the land. Do not wait for North Dakota.

An ancient Greek hero carried a small cask of his native earth wherever he went, lest he forget his humble roots. I carry North Dakota with me wherever I go. Literally: I carry a tiny medicine bag around my neck, filled with prairie earth and other shards of the sacred corridor. At night, I sometimes sprinkle a few drops of the water of the Little Missouri on my daughter's forehead as she sleeps. The twin legacy of having grown up on the northern plains is, for me, a militant populism and a love of the improbable and the absurd. Where the land reminds us of our littleness, the human persona gravitates to the outsized and the grandiose. Patti Perry can live in the village of Marmarth. Los Angeles is too tiny to contain her.

I know only this. I would not trade North Dakota for Berlin or Paris or San Francisco or the lake district of England. I would not trade my third-rate education on the Great Plains for all the Jesuitical mastery of all the urban Loyolas of the world. I would not trade the decent, leisure-suited citizens of Dakota for all the miniaturists, philosophers, or tone poets of St. Petersburg. I do not consider myself anything special. But all that is special in me is North Dakota to the core.

It makes my heart ache.

Clay Jenkinson
Written from exile
November 2001

My Dream for Marmarth

Ithaka

*I*F THIS BOOK HAS BEEN ANY GOOD, you have, after a fashion, fallen in love with the village of Marmarth, North Dakota. Not everyone fancies it as much as I do, but everyone who has been there agrees that there is something positively unforgettable about the place. I like to think of it as Lake Woebegon on LSD, or the Jungian shadow of Lake Woebegon.

I have three dreams, two of which seem reasonable enough. The last one may seem a bit improbable, but it is in fact not so wild a dream.

DREAM ONE: Go there. You'll find it tucked away in extreme southwestern North Dakota. You can fly to Rapid City or Billings or Bismarck (sometimes even Dickinson) and rent a car. There are no motels in Marmarth, but you can stay in Bowman, 30 miles away, and commute to your adventures. The restaurant at the Pastime Bar is actually a very fine one. It would be worth frequenting in Minneapolis or Denver if your tastes run to beef or transportable seafood. Seek out Patti Perry. Just ask anyone how to find her. Don't be put off by the fact that the exterior of her house, across from the town's lone elementary school, has needed paint for decades. She'll greet you warmly, inform you that I'm a damned fool, and then tell you how to enjoy what Marmarth has to offer. If you love dinosaurs she'll call Merle Clark. Merle, like the Sistine Chapel, cannot be done in less than half a day, but he's one of the great characters in rural America and you cannot help being charmed by his stories, his knowledge, and his self-delight. If you spend two days in Marmarth and spend money like a sailor, you will be hard pressed to part with a hundred dollars, but you'll have made an important contribution to the local economy. I'm serious. That's capitalism.

DREAM TWO: Send a contribution to the Marmarth Historical Society. The money will be exceedingly well spent on worthy projects: keeping the vaudevillian (Mystic) theater open, repairing the bunkhouse and, possibly, the Barber Auditorium, keeping some of the dinosaur bones in Slope County, where they are being unearthed, bringing humanities programs to Marmarth. To give to Marmarth is the most remarkable of all charities: fully 100% of your gift will be used for good works and never a penny on administration. Your modest contribution will be a godsend for the Marmarth Historical Society. Checks should go to

Marmarth Historical Society
c/o Patti Perry
Marmarth, ND 58643.

That's philanthropy.

DREAM THREE: My dream for many years has been to create something called the **Marmarth Institute**, an improbable think tank, retreat center, and publishing house in the old Barber Auditorium on main street. The shell of the building is intact, but the roof has collapsed. Restoration of the building—to include meeting rooms, an auditorium, a media studio, a library, offices, and some sleeping rooms—will cost as much as $300,000. Then there are the bunkhouse and the old Milwaukee Road depot. The whole complex could become a retreat center for artists, thinkers, dreamers, wilderness lovers, dinosaur seekers, railroad buffs, malcontents, and others. The lovely marginalia of American industrial capitalism. The idea is to create a space for people to

come have life-changing retreats, but with the amenities that will make it a bonafide, though unusual, rural conference center. It would emphasize Great Plains studies, ranching, farming, wilderness, sustainability, and related themes, but it would be useful for a range of artistic and intellectual purposes. I'm dedicating a significant percentage of the profits from this little book to that cause, and my dream is that others will want to help. Such a center would not only be a lifeline for Marmarth; it would be a new source of energy and financial stability for all of southwestern North Dakota. You could write a fat check for $25,000 or $1 million and send it to:
Marmarth Institute Fund, MHS
c/o Patti Perry
Marmarth, ND 58643.

You'll get a plaque and I'll teach you how to speak coyote. I'll be there, still listening for the message on the wind, custodian of the Marmarth Institute. That's renaissance.

You'll understand all this once you come to see Marmarth for yourself. Be sure to spend part of a day along the banks of the Little Missouri River. That's the reason Marmarth exists. If it's summer of fall, sit in the river. You won't want to, but you'll be glad you did. Don't worry. There are no minnows in the Little Mo.

Clay Jenkinson
Custodian
The Marmarth Institute

A Key to the Odyssey *Subtitles in* Message on the Wind

Invocation: Every epic begins with an invocation to the Muses. The bards of the ancient world believed that they were merely mouthpieces for poetic energies that were divinely inspired. The most famous of all invocations, in Homer's *Iliad*, begins,

> "Sing, goddess, the anger of Peleus' son Achilleus
> and its devastation, which put pains thousandfold upon the
> Achaians, hurled in their multitudes to the house of Hades
> strong souls of heroes, but gave their bodies to be the delicate feasting
> of dogs, of all birds, and the will of Zeus was accomplished
> since that time when first there stood in division of conflict
> Atreus' son the lord of men and brilliant Achilleus.
> What god was it then set them together in bitter collision?"

Even in our secular, skeptical, scientific, and disenchanted age, it seems clear to me that a book is not written solely by its author. However we wish to explain it, in Socratic or postmodernist terms, there is a Muse in the mix somewhere.

Scylla and Charybdis. (*Grailing in the Sacred Corridor*). In order to get home, Odysseus must sail between these two deadly perils. He will lose either way. Scylla is a female monster with six heads who devours passing sailors. Charybdis a vortex that swallows boats that veer too close. Odysseus chooses to try Scylla. She snatches up and devours six of his men. Odysseus asks Circe: "Come then, goddess, answer me truthfully this: is there some way for me to escape away from deadly Charybdis, but yet fight the other one off, when she attacks my companions?" Answer: no. Life is loss. *Odyssey XII.*

Athene/Mentor. (*Growing Up on the Edge of the River*). Athene is the guardian god of Odysseus. She also superintends his son Telemachos' awakening into young manhood. She appears to the boy disguised as an old family friend Mentor, and offers him advice about how to learn more about his absent father's whereabouts and about how to deal with the suitors who are eating him out of house and home. Our word *mentor* comes from this episode in Homer. "So spoke the goddess gray-eyed Athene (Mentor), and there she departed like a bird soaring high in the air, but she left in his spirit determination and courage, and he remembered his father even more than he had before, and he guessed the meaning, and his heart was full of wonder, for he thought it was a divinity." *Odyssey I.*

The Lotus Eaters. (*Rampal, Opus 47, in Marmarth*). The Lotus Eaters are a North African tribe who subsist on the lotus, which inspires forgetfulness and happy indolence. When Odysseus and his men land among the Lotus Eaters, some of them lose interest in going home. Odysseus has to drag his men back to the ships kicking and screaming. By now they have come to prefer sweet lassitude and intoxication to their long-delayed homecoming. Odysseus says, "I myself took these men back weeping, by force, to where the ships were, and put them aboard under the rowing benches and tied them fast, then gave the order to the rest of my eager companions to embark on the ships in haste, for fear that someone else might taste of the lotus and forget the way home." *Odyssey IX*.

Cyclops. (*Barcalounger*). The Cyclops Polyphemos is a one-eyed monster who lives at the edge of the civilized world. The ever-curious Odysseus decides to visit Cyclops' cave in hopes of receiving hospitality and hospitality gifts. The Cyclops devours a number of Odysseus' men. "He sprang up and reached for my companions, caught up two together and slapped them, like killing puppies, against the ground. Then he cut them up limb by limb and got supper ready, and like a lion reared in the hills, without leaving anything, ate them, entrails, flesh and the marrowy bones alike." Eventually, Odysseus gets him drunk and pokes his eye out, and escapes from the giant's cave by clinging to the underbelly of Cyclops' favorite ram. The Cyclops encounter is the most famous episode of the *Odyssey*. Survival is humiliation. *Odyssey IX*.

Penelope & Telamachos. (*Let Them Be Rock Stars and Scholars and Such*). Faithful, long-suffering Penelope is doing the best she can to hold her household together with her husband absent and scores of suitors pressing her from every side. Suddenly her son begins to assert himself in his first brushes with adulthood. When he had been outspoken for the first time, "Penelope went back inside the house, in amazement, for she laid the serious words of her son deep away in her spirit, and she went back to the upper story with her attendant women, and wept for Odysseus, her beloved husband, until gray-eyed Athene cast sweet slumber over her eyelids." *Odyssey I*.

Telemachos. (*Learning to Hunt with the Wally Brothers*). If ever there was a perfect young man—virile, intelligent, sensitive, loyal, and innocent—it is Telemachos, the son of Odysseus. "Now when the young Dawn showed again with her rosy fingers, the dear son of Odysseus stirred from where he was sleeping, and put on his clothes, and slung a sharp sword over his shoulder. Underneath his shining feet he bound the fair sandals and went on his way from the chamber, like a god in presence. He gave the word now to his clear-voiced heralds to summon by proclamation to assembly the flowing-haired Achaians, and the heralds made their cry, and the men were assembled swiftly. Now when they were all assembled in one place together, he went on his way to assembly, in his hands holding a bronze spear, not all alone, but a pair of light-footed dogs went with him." *The Odyssey* is both about Odysseus' journey home and Telemachos' journey into manhood. *Odyssey II*.

Nausicaa. (*Nausicaa*). This magnificent nymph, the daughter of royal parents, bold, resourceful, witty, and passionate, is the last—and greatest—temptation of Odysseus. To Odysseus, Nausicaa says, "My friend, since you seem not like a thoughtless man, not a mean one, it is Zeus himself, the Olympian, who gives people good fortune, to each single man, to the good and the bad, just as he wishes; and since he must have given you yours, you must even endure it. But now, since it is our land and our city that you have come to, you shall not lack for clothing nor anything else, of those gifts which should befall the unhappy suppliant on his arrival." *Odyssey VI.*

The Island of the Sun. (*Camping Out with Fuglie and the Boys*). Odysseus is told that the one thing he must not do, if he wishes to get home, is eat the sacred cattle of the sun god, Helios, no matter how hungry he gets. His starving men succumb to the temptation to eat the cattle. This brings them headlong destruction. Odysseus says, "But when I came back again to the ship and the seashore, they all stood about and blamed each other, but we were not able to find any remedy, for the oxen were already dead. The next thing was that the gods began to show forth portents before us. The skins [of the dead cattle] crawled, and the meat that was stuck on the spits bellowed, both roast and raw, and the nose was like the lowing of cattle." The challenge of life is to help self-mastery triumph over appetite, no matter how great the temptation. *Odyssey XII.*

Circe. (*The Message on the Wind*). Circe is a minor goddess, a witch who has the power to turn men into animals. Curiously, they are all metamorphosed into the animals whose characteristics they exhibit as men. Odysseus manages to avoid a descent into bestiality thanks to a sacred herb called Moly. He does make sweet love with Circe and in the end—pressed by the gods of Olympus—she helps Odysseus go home. "But when the water had come to a boil in the shining bronze, then she sat me down in the bathtub and washed me from the great caldron, mixing hot and cold just as I wanted, and pouring it over shoulders and head, to take the heart-wasting weariness from my limbs. When she had bathed me and anointed me with olive oil, she put a splendid mantle and a tunic upon me, and made me sit down in a chair that was wrought elaborately and splendid with silver nails, and under my feet was a footstool." Every man aches for these lustrations. *Odyssey X.*

Ithaka. (*My Dream for Marmarth*). No matter what happens to him, no matter how glorious the temptation, Odysseus never forgets that his one true desire is to go home. Athene says, "Come, I will show you settled Ithaka, so you will believe me. There is the harbor of the Old Man of the Sea, Phorkys, and her at the head of the harbor is the olive tree with spreading leaves, and nearby is the cave that is shaded, and pleasant, and sacred to the nymphs who are called the Nymphs of the Wellsprings, Naiads. That is the wide over-arching cave, where often you used to accomplish for the nymphs their complete hecatombs; and there is the mountain, Neritos, all covered with forest. So speaking the goddess scattered the mist, and the land was visible. Long-suffering great Odysseus was gladdened then, rejoicing in the sight of his country, and kissed the grain-giving ground, then raised his hands in the air and spoke to the nymphs." Amen. *Odyssey XIII.*

How to Learn More
about Chautauqua

THE GREAT PLAINS CHAUTAUQUA is the brainchild of another of my mentors, a genius, Everett C. Albers of the North Dakota Humanities Council. Ev is one of the most gifted humanities executives in the United States. In 1976 he envisioned a traveling summer tent show that would feature humanities lectures, debates, dialogues, and readings. So, with the help of the National Endowment for the Humanities (the most Jeffersonian thing in America), he bought a tent, hired a crew, and recruited historians, philosophers, writers, literature professors, and legal scholars to venture out from their academic lives into the villages of North Dakota, there to share their insights, as Wordsworth puts it, in a "language really used by men," with the citizenry of the Great Plains. I was one of the early roustabouts.

It was a wild dream. At first everyone was skeptical, including my frail, elegant father. I signed on early and I have never looked back.

In 1981 Ev Albers decided that we ought to take inspiration from Hal Holbrook's *Mark Twain Tonight* and Steve Allen's *Meeting of the Minds*, and invite our humanities scholars to assume—on the Chautauqua tent stage—the costumes and the characters of historical figures.

After infinite fine-tuning by trial and colossal error, Chautauqua became one of the most respected humanities programs in the

United States. We began to share it with other western states in the early 1980s. Now the Great Plains Chautauqua is the flagship of a significant national Chautauqua movement that has flourished in more than twenty-five states. The Great Plains Chautauqua visits six, eight, or ten communities each year, from Oklahoma to North Dakota, residing a week in each community, and offering a variety of lectures, breakfasts, discussions, children's programs, and, of course, a half-dozen scholar-characters performing on the stage in the evening. These Chautauquas are organized around a central theme: "Writers of the West," "American Visionaries," "Great Men and Women of the Early Twentieth Century."

You have to see it to believe it. Come spend a week in the shadow of the big blue and white tent. Mike Waldera (the greatest of the Wallys) has gone on to other enterprises and the sweet tug of marriage, and tentmaster Ed Sahlstrom keeps alive the sacred fire of Toby Shows, circus, Lyceum, and Chautauqua closer to home these days, but we'll still lure you into the Stockmans or the Pastime, and you'll see some of the finest public humanities programming in the United States.

For more information contact:

Everett C. Albers
Great Plains Chautauqua Society, Inc.
Box 2191
Bismarck, North Dakota   58502
1-800-338-6543

Reading the Great Plains: An Annotated Bibliography

Stephen Ambrose. *Crazy Horse and Custer: The Parallel Lives of Two American Warriors.* 1975. To my mind, this is Stephen Ambrose's greatest book, written before either Crazy Horse or Stephen Ambrose was cool.

Black Elk. *Black Elk Speaks: Being the Life Story of a Holy Man of the Ogalala Sioux as Told to John G. Neihardt.* 1932. If my little book inspires you to read only one other, let this be the one. Thoreau says, "How many a man has dated a new era in his life from the reading of a book!"

Willa Cather. *My Antonia.* 1918. Almost certainly the best piece of art the Great Plains has produced. Arguably the greatest American novel.

Dayton Duncan. *Miles from Nowhere: Tales from America's Contemporary Frontier.* 1993. A poignant commentary about life in the empty quarter, or rather the emptying quarter. Duncan, one of the talented writers in the Ken Burns circle, studied the 132 least populated counties in the American West to create this book.

Ian Frazier. *Great Plains.* 1989. On the whole I'm skeptical of easterner carpetbaggers trying to make sense of our land. But there are great things in this book, especially Frazier's phrases. Besides, it led to an even better book, *On the Rez.*

Ian Frazier. *On the Rez.* 2000. If you want to make sense of life in Indian America at the beginning of the twenty-first century, you must read this book. The story of SuAnne Big Crow is one of the greatest of Great Plains stories. The resilience of the Indians of the plains is staggering. Frazier's book has been heavily criticized by some as a biased, insensitive, and simply inaccurate portrait of reservation life today. Among his critics, novelist Sherman Alexie, who has impeccable credentials.

Ken Haruf. *Plainsong.* 1999. Some critics say the plot is contrived, the characters caricatured. All I know is that I *lived* in Holt, Colorado, and there are no exaggerations or distortions in this novel.

Lois Philip Hudson. *Bones of Plenty*. 1962. North Dakota farmers gut it out through the Depression.

Thomas McGrath. *Letter to an Imaginary Friend*. 1962. North Dakota's supreme poet. North Dakota's greatest poem. Pieces of *Letter to an Imaginary Friend* grace pages between some of the essays in this book.

Richard Manning. *Grassland: The History, Biology, Politics and Promise of the American Prairie*. 1995. Most of what we think of as native grasses are actually imports from the steppes of Asia.

Kathleen Norris. *Dakota: A Spiritual Geography*. 1993. There is much insight about the plains social structures here. If you want to know why Jell-O matters in rural America, the answer is in this book.

Jonathan Raban. *Bad Land: An American Romance*. 1996. Raban too writes about Marmarth, the Pastime Bar, and the Milwaukee Road. For the future of Great Plains economic initiatives, see the sad funny chapter on the dreams of Joe, Montana.

O. E. Rolvaag. *Giants in the Earth*. 1927. Wind, locusts, prairie fire, madness, killer blizzards, poverty, economic exploitation: one of the greatest novels ever written about the Great Plains and a compendium of the mythology of the oppressiveness of the place. All that wind can drive you insane.

Ron Schultheis. *The Hidden West: Journeys in the American Outback*. 1980. The essay on the Great Plains is powerful and evocative, if perhaps too pessimistic.

Wallace Stegner. *Wolf Willow*. 1962. Spirit of place issues on the Canadian plains. Everything Wallace Stegner writes is deep in insight. While you're at it, don't miss his biography of John Wesley Powell, *Beyond the Hundredth Meridian*.

James Welch. *Fools Crow*. 1986. Possibly the best novel ever written about American Indians. It will lead you to attend to your dreams.

Larry Woiwode. *Beyond the Bedroom Wall*. 1975. The best North Dakota novel by North Dakota's best writer.

About Clay Jenkinson

AFTER GROWING UP ON THE PLAINS OF NORTH DAKOTA, Clay
Jenkinson studied first at the University of Minnesota, and then
at Oxford University where he was a Rhodes and Danforth
Scholar. All of his degrees are in English Renaissance literature.
His poet is John Donne. He has taught at Pomona College, the
law school of the University of North Dakota, the University of
Colorado, and the University of Nevada. Co-founder of the
modern tent Chautauqua movement, he was for nine years the
director of the Great Plains Chautauqua. His first-person
historical interpretations of Thomas Jefferson and Meriwether
Lewis are nationally-acclaimed. In 1989 he won the National
Endowment for the Humanities' highest award, the Charles
Frankel Prize, and in 2000 he won the Nevada Humanities
Committee's scholar-of-the-year award.

In 1985 he walked the entire course of the Little Missouri River,
from Wyoming to central North Dakota, with a critical stop in
Marmarth, where Patti Perry patched him back together.

Aside from North Dakota, the center of his universe is his
daughter Catherine Missouri Walker Jenkinson (Little Mo). His
mother Mil Jenkinson, to whom this book is dedicated, still lives
in the house Clay grew up in in Dickinson, North Dakota.

Clay lives and teaches in Reno, Nevada. He is a senior fellow at
the Center for Digital Government in Sacramento, and a

humanities scholar in residence at Lewis and Clark College in Portland, Oregon.

His book, *The Character of Meriwether Lewis: "Completely Metamorphosed" in the American West* was published in December 2000. His next book, *The Paradox of Thomas Jefferson*, will appear early in the millennium.

About *Letter to an Imaginary Friend*
by Thomas Matthew McGrath

WRITTEN OVER THE COURSE OF THIRTY YEARS BY NORTH DAKOTA POET Thomas Matthew McGrath (1916-1990), the epic *Letter to an Imaginary Friend* was published in a definitive edition in 1997 by the poet's friend, Sam Hamill of Copper Canyon Press in Port Townsend, Washington. Among the thousands of lines in this poem are some that seem almost mysteriously appropriate for moments of pause and reflection between chapters of *Message on the Wind*. Author of more than a dozen collections of poetry and two children's books and a novel, Rhodes Scholar, documentary film script writer, teacher, labor organizer, blacklistee during the McCarthy era, recognized during his lifetime with the awards and fellowships from a Guggenheim Fellowship to a Shelly Memorial Award, Thomas Matthew McGrath wrote poetry to change the world.

McGrath Credit

Cover/Maps

The photograph on the cover is by the author, Clay Straus Jenkinson. His friend, Everett C. Albers of Otto Design in Bismarck, North Dakota, created the maps in this book and prepared the text for publication.

Colophon

This book is set in Abobe Caslon, designed by Carol Twombly after studying specimen pages printing by William Caslon, who released his first typefaces in 1722. Printer Benjamin Franklin hardly used any other typeface. Both the American Declaration of Independence and the U.S. Constitution were set in Caslon. The dingbats above titles and at the end of sections are from the Adobe Woodtype Ornaments font.